COLUMBIA UNIVERSITY GERMANIC STUDIES
EDITED BY ROBERT HERNDON FIFE
NEW SERIES

NUMBER TWO

MAX DAUTHENDEY
POET-PHILOSOPHER

Max Dauthendey

MAX DAUTHENDEY

POET-PHILOSOPHER

BY

H. G. WENDT

AMS PRESS, INC.
NEW YORK
1966

Copyright 1936, Columbia University Press,
New York

Reprinted with the permission of the
Original Publisher, 1966

AMS PRESS, INC.
New York, N.Y. 10003
1966

Manufactured in the United States of America

To

O.F.S. *and* M.C.S.

PREFACE

IN THE preparation of this volume I have been singularly fortunate in obtaining assistance from many sources. The collection of original material and other pertinent information was greatly facilitated by the gracious aid and interest of Mrs. Annie Dauthendey. To her I am also indebted for permission to print hitherto unpublished poems. I have freely availed myself of the mature counsel of my teachers, Professors F. W. J. Heuser, H. H. L. Schulze, and R. H. Fife. The completion of the work is due largely to Professor Fife's constant encouragement and invaluable guidance. For helpful suggestions I am indebted to Professors G. Prezzolini, G. L. van Roosbroeck, H. W. Puckett, E. E. Neff, and C. A. Manning. To Alice Howard Wendt I am greatly indebted for her untiring help in preparing the manuscript for the printer. Professor Heuser gave generously of his time to the arduous task of proofreading. I also gladly acknowledge the many courtesies enjoyed at the libraries of the Universities of Stockholm, Copenhagen, Berlin, Leipzig, Munich, Vienna, Princeton, and Columbia.

H. G. W.

New York, May 1936

CONTENTS

	Page
Preface	vii
Introduction	1
I. General Characteristics	10
II. Early Influences	18
III. Atomistic Basis	32
IV. *Verdensaltet*	41
V. Synaesthesia	59
VI. "Universal Language"	73
VII. "World-proximity" and "World-detachment"	78
VIII. "World-festivity"	84
IX. Dauthendey and the Orient	96
X. Love	106
XI. Dauthendey's Search for God	117
Conclusion	124
Appendix A. *Meine ersten Gehversuche auf der steilen Dichterlaufbahn*	127
Appendix B. Chronology of Max Dauthendey's Life	144
Appendix C. Chronological List of Works	147
Bibliography	153
Index	173

LIST OF ILLUSTRATIONS

Max Dauthendey .... frontispiece

Title page of Casparus Dauthendey's *Fundamentum Geographicum* with family coat-of-arms 7

Title page of *Josa Gerth* 19

Cover of *Bänkelsang vom Balzer auf der Balz* 29

Designs for embroidery by Max Dauthendey, Stilisierten Rosen, *Dekorative Kunst*, IV, 1899, p. 204 61

Title page of *Sun, Sehnsucht* 69

Cover of *Weltspuk* 75

Sumatra, 1914 .... opposite 90

Manuscript of "Qual", *Gesammelte Werke*, V, pp. 479, 480 (reduced) 93

Cover of *Die Ammenballade* 107

Page from Max Dauthendey's *Bible* (reduced) 121

INTRODUCTION

On the eve of the World War it was still possible to say that to the great mass of German readers Max Dauthendey was unknown. As late as May 8, 1914, the poet wrote to his wife: "Is it not strange? It will soon be more than twenty years that Elise[1] and I have been writing, and the Germans know nothing about it. Not until one is dead do they take down from their professors of literature who one was, where one was born, where one died, and the names of one's wife and sisters."[2] Those who did know of his existence believed him to be a fantastic modern, reveling in orgies of light and color and in bizarre art forms. Not until the poet's life came to an end in August 1918, far from his native land, did his name become known to a wider public. He who had always desired popular recognition was denied it during his life-time.

During the post-war indifference to literature Dauthendey was apparently forgotten by the public. Interest in him was rekindled, however, by several successive incidents. In 1925 the collected works were published. In 1927 the sixtieth anniversary of the poet's birth was celebrated. In 1928 the tenth anniversary of his death was remembered. And in 1930 his reinterment at Würzburg during the celebration of the seven hundredth anniversary of the death of Walther von der Vogelweide occasioned much comment.[3]

[1] Elisabeth Dauthendey, one of the poet's four stepsisters, author of the much discussed work *Vom neuen Weibe und seiner Liebe*, 1900; she also wrote *Im Lebensdrange*, 1898; *Hunger*, 1901; *Zweilebig*, 1901; *Im Schatten*, 1905; *Erotische Novellen*, 1919; *Die heiligen Haine*, 1920, etc.

[2] *Mich ruft dein Bild. Briefe an seine Frau.* Munich, 1930: Albert Langen Verlag, p. 224. *Cf.* also Albert Langen Verlag advertisement in *Börsenblatt für den Deutschen Buchhandel*, no. 283, December 6, 1926, p. 12394: "Wer ist denn Dohsendih?—so wird unser Reisender öfters von Sortimentern gefragt. . . ." The correct German pronunciation is, of course, 'Dau tən dai.

[3] In 1932 the total number of Dauthendey volumes which had been printed was more than 375,000, while as late as 1914 it had barely reached a modest 60,000. The following 1931 figures for the more important volumes were kindly furnished by the various publishers: *Der Venusinenreim:* 710. *Die Spielereien einer Kaiserin:* 5,000. *Lingam:* 13,000. *Die geflügelte Erde:* 5,000. *Maja:* 1,250. *Die acht Gesichter am Biwasee:* 36,000. *Raubmenschen:* 10,000, edition of Deutsche Buch-Gemeinschaft: 110,000. *Der Geist meines Vaters:* 6,000. *Die Heidin Geilane:* 1,000. *Gedankengut aus meinen Wanderjahren* (two volumes, 6,000 each): 12,000. *Geschichten aus den vier Winden:* 8,000. *Des großen Krieges Not:* 2,000. *Das Märchenbriefbuch der heiligen Nächte im Javanerlande:* 10,000, edition of Deutsche Buch-Gemeinschaft: 25,000. *Erlebnisse auf Java:* 6,000. *Letzte Reise:* 6,000. *Mich ruft dein Bild:* 5,000. *Ausgewählte Lieder aus neun Büchern:* 10,000. *Der Garten ohne Jahreszeiten:*

Critical opinion of Max Dauthendey's work has varied since he first appeared in print in the early nineties. He has been considered "the greatest German impressionist,"[4] and, more modestly, a "point on the golden mantle clasp which Germanic poetry wears near her heart."[5] Max Jungnickel compares his poetry to an "exuberant little flute,"[6] while Kasimir Edschmid admiringly calls him a "descendant of the Minnesänger."[7] Adolf Bartels' derogatory epithet "Farbenschwelg"[8] is in contrast to Peter Hamecher's characterization of Dauthendey as "Germany's greatest color poet."[9] While one critic calls his poetry empty and glaringly unintelligible,[10] another just as readily hails it as "great, well-matured art."[11] Although one author curtly dismisses Dauthendey's philosophy as "childishly primitive,"[12] another in a searching study[13] finds it representative of modern poetic "panpsychism," precursor in many ways of the philosophic tenets of the expressionists. A change of attitude in a fellow poet's evaluation of Dauthendey's poetry may be traced through the four editions of Hans Benzmann's *Moderne deutsche Lyrik*. Although sympathetic to Dauthendey's poetry at first,[14] Benzmann relegates it in the second

---

18,000. *Das Schönste von Max Dauthendey:* 25,000. *Den Nachtregen regnen hören in Karasaki:* 16,000. *Gesammelte Werke* (6 volumes of 5,000 each): 30,000. Comparative figures for 1914 and 1931 for a few very popular works are as follows: *Lingam:* 4,000 vs. 13,000; *Die acht Gesichter am Biwasee:* 5,000 vs. 36,000; *Raubmenschen:* 3,000 vs. 120,000.

[4] Edgar Steiger, "Gedanken um Max Dauthendey herum." *Zeit im Bild*, X, 48, November 19, 1912, p. 1,528.

[5] Walter von Molo, "Max Dauthendey," in *Das Schönste von Max Dauthendey*. Munich, 1919: Albert Langen, p. 7.

[6] "Max Dauthendey," in *Raubmenschen*. Berlin, 1927: Deutsche Buch-Gemeinschaft, volume 180, p. 8.

[7] "Nachfolger der Minnesänger," *Bohemia, Deutsche Zeitung*, Prague, XCV, 259, November 4, 1922, p. 3.

[8] *Die Deutsche Dichtung der Gegenwart*. "Die Alten und die Jungen." Leipzig 1910: Avenarius, p. 311.

[9] "Max Dauthendey." *Deutsche Allgemeine Zeitung*, Berlin, LXIV, 582, December 11, 1925, p. 2.

[10] Eduard Engel, *Geschichte der deutschen Literatur von den Anfängen bis in die Gegenwart*. Leipzig, 1907: G. Freytag, p. 105.

[11] Max Lederer in a review of *Lusamgärtlein*, *Die schöne Literatur*, XI, 1, January, 1910, column 11.

[12] Carl Mumm: *Max Dauthendey's Sprache und Stil*. Dissertation (typewritten manuscript). Frankfurt am Main, 1925 p. 3.

[13] Ferdinand Joseph Schneider: "Max Dauthendey und der moderne Panpsychismus." *Zeitschrift für Ästhetik und allgemeine Kunstwissenschaft*, XXIII, 4, October, 1929, pp. 326-347.

[14] First edition, Leipzig, 1903; Philipp Reclam, jun., p. 68.

edition to a minor position, holding that Dauthendey frequently showed a "complete misunderstanding of the means and the nature of art."[15] The third edition, however, limits unfavorable criticism to the early works and speaks of a noticeable improvement in the later ones,[16] while the fourth, the post-war edition, unreservedly praises Dauthendey's change toward a "real understanding of the nature of lyric art."[17] Eduard Engel's attitude is perhaps characteristic of the disdainful treatment of Max Dauthendey by some of his critics since the publication of the experimental *Ultra Violett* in 1893, a treatment which seemed to stamp him, as he tells us in *Gedankengut aus meinen Wanderjahren,*[18] with the indelible brand of the galley slave. "His very titles are unintelligible," says Engel in his *Geschichte der Deutschen Literatur*.[19] "One could change them about at liberty and say without harm 'Die brennende Hochzeit' and 'Der ewige Kalender.' "[20]

Although the poet is still practically ignored by a number of literary historians, one may note today a new and juster interpretation of his works as a whole, rather than an emphasis primarily on the peculiarities of his poetic youth. This is perhaps best exemplified by Hans Naumann[21] and Albert Sörgel.[22]

In certain academic circles researches dealing with a modern poet are frowned upon. The usual criticism has been ably answered by Professor Berendsohn in his illuminating study of Knut Hamsun: "Many scholars still consider it quite unscientific to study a living author and to write about him. But one ought not to forget that not only will the poet be dead some day, but also all those who knew him personally. Quite apart from what they can relate, they are the most vivid guides to trustworthy sources, which today are still within reach, but later are often lost and forgotten. I am thinking particularly of letters. In every trivial remark which one discovers by accident, there scintillates life; there is a crackling of witty flashes and sallies where the author

[15] Second edition, 1907, p. 68.
[16] Third edition, 1913, p. 66.
[17] Fourth edition, 1924, pp. 43, 44.
[18] *Gesammelte Werke*, I, p. 552.
[19] *Loc. cit.*
[20] Instead of "Die ewige Hochzeit" and "Der brennende Kalender."
[21] *Die deutsche Dichtung der Gegenwart*. Stuttgart, 1927: J. B. Metzlersche Verlagsbuchhandlung, pp. 314-318.
[22] *Dichtung und Dichter der Zeit*. 19th edition, Leipzig, 1928: R. Voigtländers Verlag, pp. 655-664.

becomes most personal. Mere references in the letters to dates and places furnish props for the biography, quite apart from their content. Here the scholar has a firm footing."[23]

The sources upon which the following work draws are both personal and literary. In my researches I was particularly fortunate in being able to consult a number of first-hand authorities among whom were: Frau Annie Dauthendey, the poet's widow; Axel Johanson, his brother-in-law; the late Gustaf Uddgren, Swedish author; Arnold Villinger, who initiated Dauthendey into the mysteries of his atomic philosophy; and Ernst Rowohlt and Korfiz Holm, who were associated with the poet as publishers of his works.

While gathering material in Europe in 1927, I suggested to Mrs. Dauthendey that she include letters to his friends in a volume originally intended to contain only letters to her while Dauthendey was on his world tour (1905, 1906). I was then able to assist her in the collection of letters from many sources. Late in 1927 and in 1929, I was permitted to read these letters, among which there were a great number to Willy Panzerbieter, Arnold Villinger, Siegfried Loewenthal, Annie and Korfiz Holm, S. Fischer, Consul Rademacher, and others. Through the kindness of Frau Ida Dehmel and the Staats- und Universitätsbibliothek in Hamburg (Dehmel-Archiv, Blankenese), the Dauthendey-Dehmel correspondence, so important for Dauthendey's Swedish period, was made available to me. For numerous other details I am indebted to Mrs. Dauthendey who allowed me to consult early diaries of her husband, as well as pertinent excerpts from her own valuable personal diaries. Otto Goetze, the well-known German painter, graciously copied unpublished Dauthendey letters from his files and sent me an unpublished essay on Max Dauthendey, informative for the Berlin and Munich periods. The Nachlaß was kindly opened to me for perusal by Franz Langguth, Traben (Mosel), in whose possession it was in 1929.

The critical literature on Max Dauthendey is impressive in its extent. The articles and references are, however, for the most part of small journalistic calibre and are filled with inaccurate statements. While the total harvest gleaned from them, as was perhaps to be expected, is small, they were, nevertheless, very useful for

[23] *Knut Hamsun. Das unbändige Ich und die menschliche Gemeinschaft.* Munich, 1929: Albert Langen, pp. 10, 11.

occasional striking comments and comparisons. Important biographical details were furnished in feuilletons and articles by Blei, Elisabeth Dauthendey, Gebhardt, Goetze, Holm, Kubin, Loerke, Marholm, Rademacher, Rostosky, Schmitz, Straub, Wadenklee and Wencker.[24]

Imaginative material has also been helpful. Pen pictures of Dauthendey appear in certain works where he has been taken as the prototype of a poetic hero. *E.g.*, the play *à clef*, *Hundstage*[25] by Korfiz Holm, pictures Max Dauthendey and his wife in the characters of Fritz Loos and Lilly, respectively. *Herz ist Trumpf*[26] by the same author, valuable as it is to the student of Dauthendey for the nature descriptions in the Koster-episode[27] and for occasional illuminating insights, as a whole appears to rest on slight factual basis. Its poet-hero Philipp Ladurner is obviously a caricature of Max Dauthendey.

When first gathering material in 1927, I visited Würzburg, the poet's native city. In 1929 during a second visit, after a fuller acquaintance with the poet's works, I realized very vividly the truth of Goethe's much quoted motto:

> Wer den Dichter will verstehen,
> Muß in Dichters Lande gehen.

It seems that strange, exotic surroundings were necessary in order that Dauthendey might realize the irresistible charm of his home. To Würzburg he always returned after his wanderings. Every nook and cranny of the old Franconian town is identified with the life and works of one of its greatest lovers. I was also fortunate enough to see the west coast of Sweden,—Göteborg, Fjellbacka,

---

[24] *Vide* bibliography, 12, *infra*.

[25] *Hundstage. Lustspiel.* Munich, 1911: Albert Langen.

[26] *Herz ist Trumpf. Der Roman eines starken Mannes.* 16th to 18th thousand. Munich, 1928: Albert Langen.

[27] Chapter: "Die Zauberinsel." In the summer of 1910 Korfiz Holm spent a few weeks on the island of Koster (off Strömstad) with Max and Annie Dauthendey. The latter are easily identified in this novel as Philipp Ladurner and his wife Brita. In spite of the many curious statements to be found scattered through this novel, Holm does admit, p. 42, that Ladurner was a poet to the manner born. In a recent book by Korfiz Holm, entitled: *ich-kleingeschrieben*, we have an account (pp. 179ff.) of his Würzburg visits to Max Dauthendey, which, being autobiographical, is a more accurate account than the two transparent imaginative works mentioned above. Their frequent quarrels are traced to Dauthendey's being continually impecunious. In another chapter entitled: "Mainberger Erinnerungen," the publisher's ironical treatment of the poet is again more evident (pp. 146-148).

Strömstad, Quille—which meant so much to Dauthendey's development in the early nineties. A personal knowledge of this country-side is indispensable to an understanding of his early poetic endeavors. Late in the summer of 1927 it was my good fortune to meet Mrs. Dauthendey in Paris, where she kindly identified for me the scenes in the French capital which are important for the student of Dauthendey.

As we shall have repeated occasion to notice, Dauthendey's works abound in autobiographic detail.[28] As a matter of fact, all the works may be considered a transcript in poetic form of some period of his life. The poet, probably realizing that his personality was shrouded by a fog of weird myths, felt the importance of leaving for posterity a literary monument fixing the main facts of his life. This he did in several strictly autobiographical works. His ancestry, particularly the life of his father, is chronicled in *Der Geist meines Vaters*, while the interesting decade from 1890 to 1900, formative as it was for the poetic character of Dauthendey, is described in *Gedankengut aus meinen Wanderjahren*.

[28] Very little, however, has been published elsewhere concerning the facts of Dauthendey's life. Literary handbooks and encyclopedias as a rule repeat familiar material and contain many mistakes.

Misstatements of easily ascertainable facts are apparently copied without checking. Thus the date of the poet's death, July 29, 1918, is generally given as September 4. Cf. *Der große Brockhaus*, 15th edition, 1929, IV, p. 438; *Meyers Lexikon*, 7th edition, 1925, p. 326 (the date of *Ultra Violett* is there given incorrectly as 1903); *Deutsches Literatur-Lexikon*, 1927 (editor: Wilhelm Kosch), p. 254; *Deutsches Biographisches Jahrbuch. Überleitungsband II*, 1917-1920, p. 684. M. Gebhardt, *Lebensläufe aus Franken*, III, p. 54, gives September 3. The date of birth is given as July 15, 1886, by Henri Guilbeaux, *Anthologie des lyriques allemands contemporains depuis Nietzsche*, Paris, 1913: E. Figuière et Cie, p. 75. According to *Mich ruft dein Bild, op. cit.*, p. 447, the poet died in *Tosari*. Schleichert makes him a *Russian* by birth, giving *Petersburg* as his native city, *Norddeutsche Nachrichten*, Altona-Blankenese, July 23, 1927, while according to Georg Hermann both Dauthendey and his father were born in *Norway*, *Die Brücke*, Monatsschrift zum Heidelberger Tageblatt, IV, 6, June, 1923. Julius Maria Becker, led astray perhaps by Dauthendey's mention of the Bombay Parsees, extends Dauthendey's globe-encircling tour to include Persia, *Bavaria, Wochenschrift für bayerische Kulturpolitik*, I, 8, May 17, 1930, p. 6. J. G. Robertson in his *History of German Literature*, 2nd ed., 1931, p. 622, associates Dauthendey with Otto zur Linde's journal *Charon*, although our poet had no relations with the group which it represented. Finally, Friedrich Wencker might be mentioned, who states that Dauthendey often entertained Japanese students in his Würzburg home, and that he conversed with them by preference in Japanese, a language of which he had a fluent command. The poet, however, had no knowledge of Chinese or Japanese at all, as he very frankly admitted, *Gedankengut aus meinen Wanderjahren, Gesammelte Werke*, I, pp. 325, 326. *Fränkischer Kurier*, October 15, 1924, p. 21.

Title Page of Casparus Dauthendey's *Fundamentum Geographicum* with Family Coat-of-Arms.

An account of his experiences in Paris is given in the humorous poetic confession, *Bänkelsang vom Balzer auf der Balz*. Here the author covers not only the same ground as in *Gedankengut aus meinen Wanderjahren* but also the "Mohrle" adventure, concerning which all other works are silent.

Very often the same episode is treated in different literary forms. Thus we find the Swedish interludes described in *Festliches Jahrbuch, Erster Gesang,* in *Bänkelsang vom Balzer auf der Balz,* and in a long prose description in *Gedankengut aus meinen Wanderjahren*. The trip to Greece in search of an idyllic home for his muse is likewise described fully in each of these works. The Mexican fiasco is treated both in *Bänkelsang vom Balzer auf der Balz* and in *Gedankengut aus meinen Wanderjahren,* and forms the subject matter of the long novel *Raubmenschen*. The scenes of *Josa Gerth* reflect the poet's early impressions of Würzburg, Leipzig, and Geneva.

After *Gedankengut aus meinen Wanderjahren* Dauthendey did not continue his explicitly autobiographic works until his seclusion on the island of Java during the World War. However, most of the imaginative works written between 1900 and 1914 have a personal basis and I have drawn upon these revelations wherever they are supported by other evidence. In particular, one may follow Dauthendey's wanderings in this period in the exotic background of his stories and sketches. While on the trip around the world, 1905, 1906, on a Cook's Tour, the poet found it impossible to do anything creative, but he wrote voluminous letters,[29] and kept a diary entitled, *Charakteristikum aller Städte der Reise*.[30] *Die geflügelte Erde,* however, is a careful account of the journey although not begun until a year after his return. Many of the Novellen take place in the cities visited during this tour. The Novelle "Den Abendschnee am Hirayama sehen," retraces the journey from Marseilles to Japan. Bombay, where the poet spent several days, inspired "Unter den Totentürmen," "Dalar rächt sich" and "Der Zauberer Walai." Jeypore, a town in central India which was visited on the way to Delhi, is the background for "Der Knabe auf dem Kopf des Elefanten." Darjeeling in the Himalaya Moun-

---

[29] Included in practically their entirety in *Mich ruft dein Bild, op. cit.* Unfortunately stylistic changes have been made there by the editors, *cf.* my review in *The Germanic Review,* VI, 3 (July, 1931), pp. 302-306.

[30] Among the Nachlaß, Traben.

tains relives in the somber "Himalayafinsternis" of *Geschichten aus den vier Winden*. The zoological garden of Calcutta furnished the material for "Eingeschlossene Tiere," while "Der Kuli Kimgun" was suggested by the pagodas of Rangoon, the capital of Burma. Colombo, the capital of Ceylon, and the mountain resort Nuwara Eliya are the scenes of "Der Garten ohne Jahreszeiten." The peculiar blue atmospheric light of Penang, which so deeply impressed the poet, illuminates the Novelle, "Im blauen Licht von Penang." The poet's experience in China produced "Der unbeerdigte Vater," with Canton as its background, and "Im Mandarinenklub," a Novelle suggested by his five hours' stay in Shanghai. "Die Auferstehung allen Fleisches" has Nagasaki for its setting, while the neighborhood of harp-shaped Lake Biva, with its far-famed eight scenic beauties, produced the delicate novelettes gathered under the title of *Die acht Gesichter am Biwasee*.

The island of Koster, Dauthendey's summer abode for two years, he lovingly described in "Das Giftfläschchen." Lake Garda, also a favorite goal of his restless poetic wanderings, appears in all its magnificence in "Das Iguanodon."

From the time of Dauthendey's departure for Java in 1914, until his death he gave an almost daily account of his activities in diaries and in numerous letters to his wife and friends. Most of these are now available in published form.[31] The diaries which he kept religiously during his long stay in war-time Java, are perhaps his most personal revelations. The seclusion for which he had so often longed, enabled him to clarify his ideas, and his almost daily notes have become an integral part of his poetic works. Unfortunately these diaries are not available in their entirety, portions of them having been destroyed.[32] However, even in their present decimated form they ably supplement the biographical materials available to the student of this relatively little-known poet.

---

[31] *Cf. Letzte Reise, Gesammelte Werke*, II; *Mich ruft dein Bild, op. cit.;* and *Ein Herz im Lärm der Welt*, Munich, 1933: Albert Langen/Georg Müller.

[32] I cannot subscribe to Willy Seidel's statement, *Die literarische Welt*, III, 29, July 22, 1927, p. 1, to the effect that Mrs. Dauthendey destroyed in bigoted fashion everything which did not constantly express the poet's love for her. The greater part of the Nachlaß came into the hands of outsiders and she destroyed other precious documents in an effort to prevent further unauthorized dissemination. In a reprint: "Gruß an Dauthendey," in *Die Himmel der Farbigen* (Munich, 1930: Georg Müller, pp. 7-10), this reference to Mrs. Dauthendey's supposed "bigotry" is fortunately deleted.

I
GENERAL CHARACTERISTICS

The advisability of reducing a poet's work to a philosophy, be it only a "Lebensanschauung," a philosophy of life, may in general be questioned. A too decided reliance on metaphysical analysis seems to be futile in an effort to recapture the essence of poetry, particularly that of the impressionists;[1] and a search for a "philosophy" in a poet's works too often forces into rigid categories and thus misinterprets random thoughts not consistently formulated. Even poets of a decidedly metaphysical attitude, such as Richard Dehmel, do not present rigid systems.[2] However, Professor Lowes in commenting on Coleridge's remark, "All other men's worlds are the poet's chaos,"[3] says, "Every great imaginative conception is a vortex into which everything under the sun may be swept.... The notion that the creative imagination, especially in its highest exercise, has little or nothing to do with facts is one of the *pseudodoxia epidemica* which die hard. For the imagination never operates in a vacuum. Its stuff is always fact of some order, somewhere experienced; its product is that fact transmuted."[4] Although it may be claimed that poetic creation is irrational and unconscious,[5] if varied experiences and ideas do necessarily enter into it, those of a philosophic nature need not be excluded. Certainly when the poet himself considers that his works are of a philosophic nature, we are justified in studying their philosophic content. And when appreciation of the poet's work increases as his philosophy is better understood, a study to discover and clarify that philosophy is not only justified but essential. This is particularly true in Dauthendey's case. Paradoxically, although not gifted with a trenchant mind, he constantly stressed the philosophic content of his literary

---

[1] Fritz Löffler: *Das epische Schaffen Eduard von Keyserlings*. Dissertation. Munich, 1928, p. 22.

[2] Harry Slochower: *Richard Dehmel. Der Mensch und der Denker*. Dresden: Carl Reißner, 1928, pp. 17, 288 (footnote 26).

[3] *Miscellanies*, p. 347, quoted by John Livingstone Lowes. *The Road to Xanadu. A Study in the Ways of the Imagination*. Boston and New York, 1927: Houghton Mifflin Company, p. 426.

[4] *Op. cit.*, pp. 426, 427.

[5] Dauthendey denied this, *cf.*, *Verdensaltet*, pp. 27, 28: "It is not true that an artist feels and creates unconsciously."

works. However, he felt thoughts at times to be "ponderous collossi of the mind,"[6] and found his own imagination richer than any of the ancient systems of thought.[7] To him love was infinitely more powerful than wisdom,[8] and the presence of the beloved answered all questions of heaven and earth.[9]

To the reader of the extensive published work of this writer[10] the question suggests itself: How can Dauthendey be characterized? As early as March 3, 1893, Dauthendey reported to Villinger and Loewenthal the critics' difficulty in classifying his poetry.[11] The question of classification has been previously treated. Carl Mumm in his painstaking study of Dauthendey's style[12] came to the general conclusion that this poet is *sui generis*. Basing his judgment on stylistic details, Mumm suggests that on the whole Dauthendey is representative of the impressionistic style. However, it is very difficult to imagine a pure impressionist writing such plays as *Frau Raufenbarth, Madame Null, Menagerie Krummholz*, or the naturalistic sketches, "Barmherzige Schwestern," "Siebzig Jahre," and "Aus langer Weile." Humorous ventures such as *Die Ammenballade* and *Der Venusinenreim* are surprisingly out of place in any impressionist category. After all, one must admit that such classifications are inadequate when applied to a writer of original genius. As Arthur Schnitzler felicitously phrased it: "Every poet is at once a realist as well as an expressionist, a naturalist as well as a symbolist, else he is no poet at all. To be sure, one of these conceptions of art and the world predominates, according to his temperament, his endowment, the

---

[6] "Wahrheiten wollte ich suchen," *Kaßler Allgemeine Zeitung*, XXXVII, 269, October 5, 1921, p. 5. *Cf.* also *Die ewige Hochzeit, Gesammelte Werke*, IV, p. 188: "Mehr als Erde ist oft ein Gedanke schwer."

[7] *Gedankengut aus meinen Wanderjahren, Gesammelte Werke*, I, p. 300.

[8] "Vom Ishiyama den Herbstmond aufgehen sehen," *Die acht Gesichter am Biwasee, Gesammelte Werke*, III, p. 191; "Das Wissen der Menschen," *Insichversunkene Lieder im Laub, Gesammelte Werke*, IV, p. 296.

[9] "Gern höre ich Vögel mit runden Kehlen," *Der brennende Kalender, Gesammelte Werke*, IV, p. 212: "Verwundert seh' ich die zagenden Menschen/ Noch Fragezeichen zum Nachthimmel tragen;/ Ich leg' meinen Kopf in den Schoß der Geliebten,/ Und gelöst sind für Himmel und Erde die Fragen."

[10] The collected works consist of two novels, three volumes of *Novellen*, twelve dramatic writings, fourteen volumes of poetry, several volumes of autobiographical writings, and omit three dramas, two volumes of poetry, the two recent books of letters, *Mich ruft dein Bild* and *Ein Herz im Lärm der Welt*, as well as a number of youthful works to be found only in magazines and the unpublished Nachlaß.

[11] *Ein Herz im Lärm der Welt*, p. 108.

[12] *Op cit.*, p. 310.

times and his mood. But as soon as one of these predominates to such an extent that the others suffer considerably or that one or the other perishes completely, it is an indication of lack of talent and originality."[13]

That there is a homogeneity in Dauthendey's extensive writings, is, however, evident. Mumm's statement that Dauthendey's philosophy is "childishly primitive" is surprising in view of his careful, systematic study of the poet's works.[14] Mumm wrote his thesis hoping to bring system into the chaos created by the opposing camps, ranging all the way from the most ardent admirers who see in Dauthendey the prophet of a new art to those who deny him any poetic originality at all. To do this objectively he studied the poet's style, aiming "to reach, on the basis of a wholly inductive analysis of the linguistic and stylistic characteristics, generalizations which are valid for large expanses within Dauthendey's total production. These tend to correct the reader's preconceived notion (vorherige "innere Anschauung") and perhaps to contribute to a more uniform attitude toward the poet."[15]

On the basis of this analysis Mumm traced the various changes and divided the poet's life outwardly into three periods, which he calls respectively, the periods of "dynamic color," "of hyperbolic impressionism of figures of speech," and "of a tendency toward simplification" evident during the last years of the poet's life.[16] However, these periods were not merely milestones in stylistic development, but were conditioned by changes in Dauthendey's view of life. Even from the point of view of a purely stylistic study, I believe an analysis of *Verdensaltet; Det nye sublime i Kunsten,*

---

[13] *Buch der Sprüche und Bedenken. Aphorismen und Fragmente.* Vienna, 1927, pp. 185, 186.

[14] A similar misunderstanding is to be found in Johannes Alt's revision of Biese's *Deutsche Literaturgeschichte,* Munich: C. H. Beck'sche Verlagsbuchhandlung, III, p. 193. *Cf.* also Eugen Geiger, who calls Dauthendey "quite unphilosophic," *Der Bund,* Bern, LXIV, p. 379, August 15, 1913. Maurice Muret speaking of *Des großen Krieges Not* says: "Les poèmes de Max Dauthendey ont, du moins, ce mérite d'être excempts de toute prétention philosophique." *La littérature allemande pendant la guerre,* Paris: Payot, p. 216. M. G. Conrad, however, in discussing the philosophic passages of *Gedankengut aus meinen Wanderjahren* called them: "der wichtigste Beitrag zur Enthüllungsgeschichte der weltschöpferischen Dichterseele, der seit Wagners und Nietzsches Hingang erschienen ist," *Deutsches Literaturblatt,* December 1, 1913, no. 12, p. 10.

[15] *Op. cit.,* p. 4.

[16] *Cf.* Mumm's summary in *Auszug aus der Dissertation: Max Dauthendeys Sprache und Stil.* 1925.

Dauthendey's early exposition of his "new intimate art" and philosophy, to be essential to an understanding of the poet, since the little volume furnishes the key to his early literary endeavors. Dauthendey repeatedly insisted on the philosophic undercurrent of his works,[17] and claimed that even matters of style were interrelated with his philosophy of life. It would, therefore, be very unfair indeed to consider stylistic devices employed by this poet as mere mannerisms. Synaesthesia, paradoxical epithets, and other devices were used to depict the intimate life of the universe as it revealed itself to the poet.[18]

The title of his bulky biography, *Gedankengut aus meinen Wanderjahren,* was in part no doubt an answer to those who had thought Dauthendey unable to express philosophical ideas.[19] If his formulation of his philosophy in this work has been regarded as a failure,[20] it is due in no small degree to the yardstick applied by the critics. To compare his Weltanschauung with that of classic philosophical systems is manifestly as unfair as it would be to censure him for his inadequate systematic preparation. Dauthendey's philosophy is based on personal experience, with a minimum of seasoning from the thoughts of others. To appraise it adequately, it must be studied in this light. It is, of course, evident that in such a case many ideas were bound to be rediscovered which had long been known. Unconsciously, also, a great deal went into the poet's view of life that was derived from outside sources, so that we shall have to take his claim to originality with a grain of salt, sincere as it undoubtedly was.

When on October 11, 1915, Dauthendey confided to his Java

---

[17] *Gedankengut aus meinen Wanderjahren, Gesammelte Werke,* I, p. 325: "This philosophy in time took firm root in me and then really became the basic note of all my song books and prose books which were written within the last twenty-two years (*i.e.* previous to 1913). Even internal rhyme and my use of changing comparisons and similes of nature which constantly astonished the critics, is the result of that liberated world view and has its origin in a heart which feels itself creator and created and not merely slavish subordination to traditional concepts." *Cp.* also pp. 366, 367.

[18] The prominent place of Max Dauthendey in the shaping of the literary philosophy of affirmation of life of the turn of the century is well brought out by Elisabeth Darge, *Lebensbejahung in der deutschen Dichtung um 1900.* "Deutschkundliche Arbeiten," 1934, A., Allgemeine Reihe, Band 1, *passim.*

[19] *Loc cit., Gesammelte Werke,* I, p. 396.

[20] Michael Gebhardt considers the philosophical passages of *Gedankengut aus meinen Wanderjahren* "verfehlt." *Lebensläufe aus Franken,* III, Würzburg, 1927, p. 66.

diaries that "things seem to exist between heaven and earth which man's reason has fortunately been unable to plumb[21] he expressed a life-long belief in the importance of emotions as opposed to reason. Reason occupies a minor niche in Dauthendey's scheme of things; feeling is the corner stone of his philosophy. It soon became evident to the poet that pure reason would not be able to uphold his philosophy: "The caution of reason never permits man to fuse with the feast of the universe as deeply and heartily as feeling does. Only the strongest of men succeed in maintaining themselves against reason in feeling, and those are the most artistic of men."[22]

Müller-Freienfels has given a pattern of a man governed by emotions, which is helpful in understanding Dauthendey's philosophy: "To be sure," he says, "the purely emotional man hardly succeeds in completing systems of philosophy. Usually he does not go beyond attempts; often he becomes at home in other systems which he changes only according to his needs. Philosophy is to him the expression of his emotional life, perhaps also a reflective reconciliation of tormenting emotional needs."[23]

In studying Dauthendey's Weltanschauung we must not, therefore, expect to find words used with philosophic accuracy. Very often they are of his own coining. They are especially difficult to render into adequate, felicitous English. Many of these expressions are compounds of the word "Welt"[24] and show how he stressed the universal range of his philosophy.

Believing his philosophy to be the warmest under the sun,[25]

---

[21] *Aus fernen Ländern, Gesammelte Werke*, II, p. 336.
[22] *Gedankengut aus meinen Wanderjahren, Gesammelte Werke*, I, p. 713. *Cp.* with this his father's indoctrination of the boy, "Der Verstandesgeist bahnt den Weg, dann erst kann der Herzgeist die Wunder des Weges in Frieden genießen." *Der Geist meines Vaters, Gesammelte Werke*, I, p. 276.
[23] *Persönlichkeit und Weltanschauung*, 2nd edition. Leipzig, 1923: Teubner, p. 166.
[24] Such expressions are: Weltallfestlichkeit, Weltallgemeinsprache, Weltallverkehrssprache, Weltallverstehen, Weltallzeichensprache, Weltferne ("world-detachment"), Weltfestgeist, Weltnähe ("world-proximity"), Weltseele, Weltunergründlichkeit, Weltzusammengehörigkeit. "Welt" compounds are much more numerous in Dauthendey than those with "Leben" which seem to predominate in the affirmative poetic philosophy of his contemporaries. *Vide*, Elisabeth Darge, *op. cit.* Concerning the affirmative nature of his philosophy Dauthendey says: "Sobald man den Schöpfer absetzt und jedes Geschöpf als seinen eigenen Schöpfer einsetzt, dann wird eine große Fülle von lebenbejahenden, lebenbejubelnden und lebengründenden Dichtungen entstehen." *Gedankengut aus meinen Wanderjahren, Gesammelte Werke*, I, p. 309.
[25] *Loc. cit.*, I, p. 367.

Dauthendey constantly strove to make it available for the common man and hence couched his ideas in words readily understood by the audience he addressed. Thus he explains "Das Gras wachsen hören," the first title of *Das Lied der Weltfestlichkeit* to his friend Rademacher: "I had to put a popular title at the head, since the song is written for our people and all peoples, and therefore I could use the philosophical title only as a subtitle."[26] His meaning, however, is at times elusive in the frequent juxtaposition of such terms as "Weltnähe" and "Weltferne," "Sein" and "Nichtsein."[27]

While continually emphasizing the "newness" of his philosophy, Dauthendey felt that feeling universal festivity "is native to man; it is not a theory, but a natural condition which everyone may perceive in himself."[28] The poet, however, was impressed by the necessity for discovering this natural condition to mankind by translating his belief into active life. Only through realizing this natural feeling of universal festivity could humanity develop its potentialities. Only through acceptance of this panacea could humanity become of age.[29] At last even the most stupid would be swept along and would have to fall in line, "since the immediate future of humanity leaves no other alternative for progress but the one road of realizing that we are all creators of the constantly progressing creation which we call life."[30] Dauthendey's main object in expounding his view of life in *Gedankengut aus meinen Wanderjahren* was thus "simply to recall to our consciousness our innate and only temporarily lost connection with the universe, with the festive life of the universe."[31] At last one would accept the new philosophy calmly. One would wonder, then, why one had not always been aware of it. That, we are told in *Verdensaltet*, is the way with all new ideas.[32]

---

[26] Letter of August 5, 1917, Tosari. *Ein Herz im Lärm der Welt*, p. 202.

[27] Other polar concepts employed by Dauthendey in *Gedankengut aus meinen Wanderjahren*, are "Wirklichkeit—Unwirklichkeit," p. 368; "Ruhe und Betrachtung—Tätigkeit," p. 335; "das ewig festlich Unabänderliche—das ewig sich festlich Verändernwollende," p. 331; "Angebetete—Anbeter," p. 811; "Ewigkeit—Endlichkeit," p. 337; "Allmacht—Ohnmacht," p. 337.

[28] *Op. cit.*, p. 396. Similarly Dauthendey claimed that feelings associated with the "new intimate art" had always existed but had lain dormant until the key was furnished, *Verdensaltet*, p. 43.

[29] *Op. cit.*, p. 395.
[30] *Op. cit.*, p. 316.
[31] *Op. cit.*, p. 815.
[32] P. 42.

However, although living and preaching his theory by word and deed, Dauthendey was at no time a militant apostle. It never occurred to him to wish to impose his philosophy upon anyone.[33] In conversation, to be sure, he often turned to his favorite ideas and presented them with great enthusiasm. Arthur Kahane, the well-known dramaturgist, has given us a vivid picture of the almost unconscious yet fervent manner with which Dauthendey broached his ideas even to strangers.[34]

Toward the end of his life Dauthendey became much more zealous. "A new dawn has come" he proclaimed in Nietzschean fashion. "Let humanity everywhere be freed from the shackles of imperfection." "Let all attain ultimate knowledge." "May the spirit of festivity no longer remain hidden from anyone."[35] One may say of him as Wilhelm Wundt did of Gustav Fechner, the great champion of panpsychism,—he "not only wishes to convince through argument, but has something of the spirit of the prophet who would like to free mankind from deep-rooted errors and make them share the joy of the new knowledge of God and world, which had revealed itself to him."[36]

It is the object of this work to explore the poet's philosophy of life through a consideration of all the available published and unpublished material.[37] Every character, certainly every creative character, has an inner consistency. One need not go so far as Schiller in *Wallenstein* and claim to be able to derive the entire man from an inner "kernel," but one must nevertheless admit that

---

[33] *Gedankengut aus meinen Wanderjahren, Gesammelte Werke,* I, pp. 500, 501.
[34] *Tagebuch des Dramaturgen.* Berlin, 1928: Bruno Cassierer Verlag, p. 196.
[35] Angebrochen ist die helle Zeit. Rund die
Menschheit sei befreit von Unfertigkeit.
. . . . .
. . . zum letzten Wissen sollen alle dringen.
. . . . .
Geist der Festlichkeit keinem mehr ver-
borgen bleibe.
"Das Lied vom innern Auge," *Das Lied der Weltfestlichkeit, Gesammelte Werke,* V. p. 549.
[36] Gustav Fechner: *Das Büchlein vom Leben nach dem Tode.* Leipzig, Insel-Verlag, Insel-Bücher, no. 187, pp. 7, 8.
[37] Joseph Ferdinand Schneider's excellent study, *op. cit.,* confines itself primarily to the collected works. Of two searching recent studies Elisabeth Darge's (*op. cit.*) sketches Dauthendey's position among the life-affirming poets about 1900 while that of Wilhelm Annecke: *Max Dauthendey als Dramatiker* (Dissertation, Würzburg, 1934: Verlag Konrad Triltsch) traces the position of love in Dauthendey's ideology as expressed in his dramatic works. Other attempts to evaluate Dauthendey's philosophy (*vide* bibliography, *infra, passim*) were too cursory to prove of help.

expression flows from a mental and emotional *habitus* which is compounded of experiences and pre-natal dispositions, and is none other than individuality. This being the case, the expressions of a poet can, if properly fitted together, be made to produce a mosaic that is comprehensible as a unit. If these expressions deal with intelligible ideas, they will furnish in outline, at least, an intelligible Weltanschauung.

Since so very little that is accurate is generally known of the poet's life and since a knowledge of its main features is absolutely essential to an understanding of the development of his philosophy, I have wherever possible introduced the pertinent biographical details, and have tried to present the subject in chronological order. More specifically it is the purpose of this investigation not so much to distil a philosophic system from the poet's works as to discover his poetic Weltanschauung. This I have sought in the poet's various attempts to analyze his own ideas, and in the ideology of his poetic works.

II
EARLY INFLUENCES

A number of the basic concepts of Dauthendey's view of life are a legacy from his early upbringing.[1] His love of his native country, for example, was but natural to one born in idyllic Würzburg, whose praises he never tired of singing. Of his native city he said: "Even the most dispassionate and life-weary of men must when strolling through the city and its surroundings be made happy by the stream of light and air which penetrates earth and heaven. The wise cheerfulness of Greece, the delicate beauty and earthly virility of Japan, both of which I learned to know with body and soul, I find united here in Würzburg. In this city it is easy to think, easy to laugh and easy to work. Here love is easily awakened; here the longing and fervor of love are deepened."[2]

With the exception of *Ultra Violett, Reliquien,* and *Des großen Krieges Not,* practically all of the numerous nature poems from *Singsangbuch* to *Weltspuk* are culled from Würzburg and its immediate surroundings. Of the novels, *Josa Gerth* was inspired by the country house on Neue Welt, while the dramas *Das Kind, Ein Schatten fiel über den Tisch, Madame Null* and *Frau Raufenbarth* all have Würzburg for their scene. In *Die Heidin Geilane* the Würzburg of the martyr Kilian relives. To Würzburg Dauthendey returned from all his wanderings. It was the answer to his costly quest for a home for his poetic muse. The early trips to Mexico and Greece which devoured his patrimony were necessary if only to prove to the poet the irresistible attraction of his native city, and when he was confined in Java during the World War, it was longing for this city that was partly responsible for undermining his health and for his premature death.

Moreover, while on his journeys, he was frequently reminded of Würzburg. It is probable that his sympathetic understanding of foreign countries and peoples was increased when he could in some manner recall his native city. When a Cook's Tour around

[1] Elisabeth Dauthendey ably supplements the poet's own account of his youth as presented in *Der Geist meines Vaters. Das Bayerland,* XLI, 5, 1930, p. 149.
[2] *Der Geist meines Vaters, Gesammelte Werke,* I, p. 198. *Cp.* also "Ein Morgen auf meinen Heimatbergen," pp. 128, 129 *infra,* and *Gesammelte Werke,* I, p. 687, II, pp. 375ff., IV, pp. 232, 419, and V, pp. 542, 591.

Max Dauthendey.

Josa Gerth.

Roman

Dresden und Leipzig.
E. Pierson's Verlag.

Title Page of *Josa Gerth*.

the world in 1905, 1906, took him to Japan, Kobe recalled to him Würzburg's "Käppele."[3] Such discoveries of resemblance contributed not a little to the empathy which made Dauthendey feel attuned to the soul of the Orient.

The natural brilliance of Würzburg aided, no doubt, in developing the poet's highly trained sense of color and gave concrete embodiment to his later thought of "world festivity." "Never did my native air become unfaithful to me," Dauthendey says in *Der Geist meines Vaters*. "Always, it gave me peace to work, if only my desire was genuinely urgent."[4] And most of his works were written there, could only have been written there.[5]

The sentiment of patriotism which became one of Dauthendey's basic concepts, he found exemplified in his father[6] who after

[3] *Der Geist meines Vaters, Gesammelte Werke*, I, p. 143. *Cp.* also p. 117 and *passim*.
[4] *Gesammelte Werke*, I, p. 290.
[5] *Vide* "Chronological List of Works," pp. 148ff. *infra*.
[6] The poet's father, Carl Albert Dauthendey (November 1, 1819-September 5, 1896) introduced daguerreotype photography into Germany and Russia. His was an exact, methodical mind, enlightened in matters of religion and imbued with the pride of the scientific conquests of his century. The contrast with his son could not have been more striking. To the father even poetry had to have a practical aim. Naturally the few poems he wrote were highly conventional and of a didactic and occasional nature. Among these (In the following I am quoting from an unpublished manuscript of Carl Albert Dauthendey used by his son in writing *Der Geist meines Vaters*—referred to by the poet in the book of that title, *Gesammelte Werke*, I, pp. 11, 12—a manuscript now in the possession of Mrs. Dauthendey—) there have been preserved "Am Verlobungsmorgen," "Am Hochzeitstage," "Bei einer Durchreise," etc. Their general character may be seen from the following "Mahnungen und Gedenksprüche für meinen Max, bei seiner Abreise nach Leipzig," Würzburg, October 14, 1891:

In sein Notizbuch

Pfleg' immer zu notieren,
Was Du behalten mußt.
Vergessen gleicht Verlieren,
Und beides ist Verlust.

Willst Du ein Werk ausführen, was schon besteht,
So scheu nicht Zeit noch Kosten einen Meister anzusehen,
Denn nichts, was man im Leben fertig schaut,
Ist ohne Lehrgeld jemals aufgebaut.

Willst Du ein Werk beginnen, das neu nach Form und Zweck,
So bringe Deinen Plan, der reif schon in Gedanken,
Erst auf Papier und prüfe, ob er rechnerisch das verspricht,
Was Du gedacht. Dann sparst Du viel und täuschst Dich nicht!

In Not und Gefahr, wachse Dein Mut,
Gegen Verführung Dein männlicher Wille!
Kämpfe für Wahrheit in heiliger Glut,
Und wenn Du betest, so bet' in der Stille!

having lived in Russia for years, returned to his native Germany to satisfy his home-longing. Moreover, his mother, descendant of a German-Russian émigré family,[7] returned to Würzburg as conscious of her German affinity as her early émigré forebears had been.

Ancestor worship was cultivated by Dauthendey's father.[8] His boundless admiration for Casparus Dauthendey, first of the German branch of the family, found characteristic expression in his "Taufrede bei der Geburt meines ersten Sohnes Caspar, als damaliger einziger Stammhalter unserer Familie. Mit Bezug auf unseren berühmten Vorfahren Casparus Dauthendey": "Casparus Dauthendey! Hochgefeierter vor 300 Jahren! Du mit soviel Lorbeeren geschmückter Förderer der Wissenschaft! Sei heute im Geiste hier anwesend! Siehe hier den letzten Sprossen Deines Stammes der, Dich zu ehren, auf Deinen Namen getauft werden soll.—Laß ihn der Erbe Deines Geistes sein! Erneue durch ihn den Ruhm Deines Namens, etc."[9] Ancestor worship is advocated by

---

When reading *Der Geist meines Vaters* one is reminded very strongly of Sir Edmund Gosse's *Father and Son*. Of imaginative characters, Felix Jäger in *Ein Schatten fiel über den Tisch* is modeled after Dauthendey's father.

[7] Dauthendey's mother (née Karoline Friedrich, May 11, 1837-July 11, 1873) was of a very frail, poetic nature, considerate, devoted and God fearing (*Der Geist meines Vaters, Gesammelte Werke*, I, pp. 24, 27). Her parents, as well as her grand parents had lived in Russia, particularly in St. Petersburg, in a German colony, tradition having it that their progenitors, weavers and organ builders (*op. cit.*, p. 8), and members of the Herrenhut sect (*op. cit.*, p. 320), had emigrated to Russia during the time of Peter the Great. There seems to have been also a strain of Spanish or even Arabic blood in this family branch (*op. cit.*, p. 274). The mother's tender care and understanding and her encouragement of the boy's poetic nature must have had a very great influence during his early impressionable years. The chalky atmosphere of the Franconian town, however, was unsuited to her delicate health, so that she had to spend her summers on the Neue Welt near Würzburg where the boy could visit her on weekends. It was there that she died when the boy was hardly six years old, as he has so touchingly told us in the last poem of *Reliquien* entitled "Das Geisterhaus" (*Gesammelte Werke*, IV, pp. 131, 132).

[8] *Der Geist meines Vaters, Gesammelte Werke*, I, pp. 282ff.

[9] According to an undocumented family tradition (*loc. cit.*, p. 33; also Elisabeth Dauthendey: "Das Ahnenbild," *Literarische Beilage des "Würzburger General-Anzeiger,"* May 24, 1930, no. 11, p. 3) Dauthendey's ancestors were French émigrés (Dauthenay is a current French name) whom the Huguenot persecution in 1572 drove to Scotland whence they emigrated to Germany. At any rate, the first German forebear of whom we have any record is the Casparus Dauthendey to whom the invocation quoted above is addressed. (I am copying it from the manuscript mentioned in footnote 6.) He was a brilliant mathematician and geologist at the court of Ulrich, Duke of Brunswick, and the author of numerous scientific treatises, among others of *Consignatio vieler mercklichen u. gedenckwürdigen Historien, welche je und je auff die Parelia oder Neben Sonnen, derer fünff den 23. Martij dieses 1618*.

Dauthendey as one of the twelve beatitudes in *Das Lied vom Herdbau der Weltfestlichkeit*[10] and together with love and patriotism it is one of his three "adorations."[11] It finds its noblest expression in *Der Geist meines Vaters,* the monument erected to his ancestors, and in "Der unbeerdigte Vater" of the collection of novellettes entitled *Lingam,* a story of filial piety among the Chinese. It proved to be another sesame to his profound understanding of the Oriental mind.

Dauthendey's sister Marie[12] early in his life drew his attention to the beauties of nature and helped develop the poet's latent color sense, which was to become a prominent characteristic of his tenet of "world festivity." In a letter of May 25, 1891, Dauthendey, then in his twenty-fifth year, enthusiastically voices his indebtedness to her: "With hands and eyes she pointed out to me the colors and beams round about us, and her imagination was inexhaustibly inventive. Every tree, every flower, every cloud she endowed with a soul. In the evening we two walked outside the village, and there her nature perception was so warm and delicate that I could only listen in astonishment. Only now do I know who in my earliest youth first made me comprehend the soul of the world and who taught me to open my eyes to the fairy world. The early development of my color sense was largely due to her. She nurtured me with images and animated the most drab corners with phantasies. My sister Lisa[13] later gave me the touch of seriousness which enabled me to arrange the motley abundance, and took pains to see that my world did not dissolve into intangible mists."[14]

Jahres . . . zu Braunschweig gesehen worden, 1618; *Confutation oder Wiederleg. und Umbstossung vieler bey jetzigen Zeiten vermeindten Landmessern falscher Nachmess,* 1639; *Fundamentum Geographicum. Wie nemblich die Erdkugel an ihr selbsten einzutheilen, etc.,* 1639; *Idea cometarum nova, und gründliche Beschreibung des neuerschienenen Cometens, im Jahr Christi 1618, . . . 1619,* of which the last is preserved at the University Library, Tübingen, in a bound volume entitled "Alte antique astronomische Piesen," while the former three may be consulted at the library at Wolfenbüttel. Maps by Casparus Dauthendey are to be found in a number of German libraries.

[10] As "Elternliebe," *Gesammelte Werke,* V, pp. 642, 643.
[11] *Der Geist meines Vaters, Gesammelte Werke,* I, p. 282.
[12] *Loc. cit.,* pp. 190, 201.
[13] *Cp.* Introduction, footnote 2, p. 1, *supra.*
[14] *Ein Herz im Lärm der Welt,* p. 15. Josa Gerth in the novel of that name is a composite of Max and Marie Dauthendey and furnishes an excellent account of Dauthendey's thoughts about 1890.

The unity of all inanimate and animate nature belonged to the author's earliest ideas and found expression in his childhood poems. He had been steeped in fairy-tale lore by his step-sister Marie. The elder Dauthendey abhorred these evidences of what he considered weakness;[15] to him the word "elves" conveyed no meaning.[16] It was from the anthropomorphic elements of such fairy-tales, no doubt, that the son soon peopled his world with sprites and endowed with life what to his enlightened father was certainly inanimate. A number of poems written from 1880-1890 bear witness to this fact.[17] In the poem, "Das Geisterhaus," Dauthendey has revealed his early intimacy with flora and fauna:

> Denn mehr verwandter als die Menschenherzen
> Waren die Herzen mir der Tiere und der Pflanzen.[18]

There is a charming instance of his communion with so-called lifeless nature in a vivid description of his Würzburg room: "Mein Stüberl," written as early as 1888:

> Und einsam, ist gar nit,
> Wir versteh'n all einand'
> Die Bücher, die Bleamerl,
> Die Bilder an d' Wand,
>
> Die schwätzen und plaudern,
> Denn auch die hab'n ihr Sprach;
> Und red'n am laut'sten,
> Von vergangene Tag'.[19]

This was, of course, long before his belief in atoms and the all-pervading life-force had replaced the earlier forms of anthropomorphism.[20]

---

[15] Many passages of *Der Geist meines Vaters* bear witness to the elder Dauthendey's difficulty in understanding children. Miss Rostosky gives the following description of Dauthendey's father: "I remember Dauthendey's father very well. We children stood in awe of him. He found it impossible to associate with children and he frightened us. We always objected violently when we were to be taken to Kaiserstrasse to the Dauthendeys. There was a tension in the air which oppressed us." (Unpublished manuscript.)

[16] *Der Geist meines Vaters, Gesammelte Werke*, I, p. 184.

[17] *Vide* "Meine ersten Gehversuche auf der steilen Dichterlaufbahn," *infra*, pp. 128 ff.

[18] *Reliquien, Gesammelte Werke*, IV, p. 132.

[19] "Meine ersten Gehversuche auf der steilen Dichterlaufbahn," *infra*, pp. 138, 139.

[20] *Der Geist meines Vaters, Gesammelte Werke*, I, p. 437.

Dauthendey's early religious feeling inspired by his native city, "luxuriating in churches"[21] never quite left him and became the greatest solace of his last days, when even his philosophy of "world festivity" no longer met the test of the troublous war times.

In early childhood there was nurtured in him that belief in superstition which was certain to aid in the development of his view of life. He later called himself a "number fanatic,"[22] twenty-three being his "fateful number,"[23] and he thoroughly believed in the prophetic nature of dreams,[24] in premonitions, mental telepathy[25] and common folk superstitions. Many passages in the imaginative works[26] and particularly the references in the works of autobiographic nature prove convincingly the poet's preoccupation with the supernatural, which he later found to be another facet of the Oriental mentality.

As a youth Dauthendey did not clearly know whether he belonged to Russia or to Germany.[27] His father's Russian cigarettes, the manufacture of which demanded the spare time of most of the children, the samovar, the Russian costumes the boy was forced to wear much to his discomfiture and the amusement of his play

---

[21] He called Würzburg "kirchenüppig," *Gedankengut aus meinen Wanderjahren, Gesammelte Werke*, I, p. 303.

[22] "Zahlenfanatiker," *Der Geist meines Vaters, Gesammelte Werke*, I, 14; *id. loc.* for the influence of the numbers 11, 19, 23; p. 184 for the numbers 13, 23. Two Americans, James and Theodosia Durant (*Vide*, p. 38 *infra*) first called Dauthendey's attention to number mysticism, *loc. cit.*, p. 18. *Cf.* letter of May 28, 1914 (Bandoeng), *Gesammelte Werke*, II, p. 153, for the influence of the number 13. While discussing his nineteenth wedding anniversary, Dauthendey referred to the numbers 19 and 23. Curiously, this latter reference is deleted from the published letter, Garoet, May 3, 1915, *Mich ruft dein Bild*, pp. 279, 280.

[23] *Der Geist meines Vaters, Gesammelte Werke*, I, p. 14: "The fateful number twenty-three accompanied me through my whole life. Twenty-three years after my mother's death my father died, and I may say that the twenty-third of each month always presents to me some weighty piece of news, a change of fate, a special bit of fortune or an exceptional case of misfortune."

[24] *Das Lied der Weltfestlichkeit, Gesammelte Werke*, V, p. 571. Early in life Dauthendey began to note down his dreams. Among his published works they are particularly abundant in the Java diaries where he occasionally interprets them. Frequent reference to these dreams is made by Ignaz Ježower, *Das Buch der Träume*, Berlin, 1928: Ernst Rowohlt. *Cp.* also letter of October 23, 1902, to Mrs. Dauthendey, *Mich ruft dein Bild*, p. 43.

[25] This phase has been studied by E. Hitschmann in an article entitled "Telepathie und Psychoanalyse," *Imago*, IX, 3, 1923, pp. 368-382.

[26] *E.g.*, the number symbolism in *Der Drache Grauli*, supernatural elements in "Das Iguanodon," "Im blauen Licht von Panang," the obsessions portrayed in "Das Giftfläschchen" and "Himalayafinsternis."

[27] *Der Geist meines Vaters, Gesammelte Werke*, I, p. 80.

mates, the observance of Russian holidays and the use of the Russian tongue between father and mother created a distinctly Russian atmosphere. Nevertheless, our author assures us "There was not a drop of Russian blood" in his veins.[28] As late as October 1910 he became enraged because Michael Georg Conrad "destroyed his wish" to be a native of Würzburg and a German poet and tried to make of him a "thickblooded" Slav.[29]

We can hardly expect the sensitive youth to have felt particularly attracted to school. Only his brother's failure in the exit examination of the Realschule, entailing the loss of special military privileges, led Dauthendey on to the greatest exertions to pass his examinations.[30] He frequently referred to his hatred of a school which taught only the stilted German of compositions and stunted any original ideas,[31]—a hatred surprisingly common among the poets of that period. These feelings he epitomized near the end of his life in a letter to Georg Rademacher: "No time of my life was so stupid as my school years. I always think that, although the young Greeks were intelligent and naturally original and artistic, they never had to sit still in medieval schools. The less hampered a man's education is, the stronger and fuller of worldly wisdom does he become. . . . I hope that our grandchildren will

[28] *Op. cit.*, p. 81.
[29] Letter of October 20, 1910, to Mrs. Annie Dauthendey, *Mich ruft dein Bild*, p. 209. The reference is no doubt to a review of *Weltspuk, Lieder der Vergänglichkeit* by Michael Georg Conrad, *Bayerische Landeszeitung, Würzburg*, volume XXVI, No. 210, 1910, p. 3. Dauthendey must have been particularly offended by the following paragraph: "Unter den üppigen, verschwenderischen Farben spürt man wohl den kräftigen, heißen Pulsschlag des Dichters, aber dieser Pulsschlag ist doch von einer merkwürdigen Gleichförmigkeit, von einer gewissen Zähigkeit und Dickflüssigkeit des Blutlaufes. Etwas Befremdendes in der Temperatur rührt wohl von slawischer Blutsverwandtschaft her." He also compares *Weltspuk* to the "fatalistischen, rhapsodischen Rhythmus eines russischen Steppensängers" and ventures to say that Dauthendey's passion is "nicht blutvoll . . . nicht vollmenschlich, nicht national genug."
[30] I append here an unpublished note by Dauthendey concerning the chronology of his school life: "Mit vier Jahren Spielschule bei Frl. Johanna (2 Jahre). Mit sechs Jahren 1. Klasse Institut Fischer (bis neuntes Jahr). Prüfung in der Lateinschule durchgefallen. Bis zum zwölften Jahre wieder Institut Fischer. Vom zwölften bis zum achtzehnten Jahre Realschule. Vom achtzehnten bis zum neunzehnten Jahre. Privat. Einjährigen Examen."
[31] *Gedankengut aus meinen Wanderjahren, Gesammelte Werke*, I, p. 323. In Mrs. Dauthendey's diary there is an entry of April 28, 1908: "Erzählt von der Schulzeit, nur Aufsätze interessierten ihn, nachdem er tagelang mit vor Vergnügen rotem Kopf dagesessen. (Schlechte Orthographie.) Dann bekam er doch eine schlechte Note, weil er es angeblich abgeschrieben."

have only parental wisdom in their early years and no superfluous schooling, which atrophies heart and mind. How I should like to see the death of school!"[32] It was, perhaps, his dislike of schooling, and his desire to develop his own original genius, that led Dauthendey into naïve evaluation of his own philosophy.

That he described many of his thoughts as "new" is evidence of his unfamiliarity with the history of common philosophical trends, "Without flattering myself," he said, "I may well call myself the poetical herald of a new emancipating philosophy."[33] Thoughts of a "new" philosophy, to be sure, had a wide currency among the life-affirming poets of the turn of the century.[34] To Dauthendey, however, newness implied originality. Thus *Verdensaltet, Det nye sublime i Kunsten*,[35] deals with the "new" intimate art and with the "new" form of the sublime. He was thoroughly convinced of the importance of *Das Lied der Weltfestlichkeit* and compared this poetic summary of his Weltanschauung to the teachings of Christ, calling it "the greatest philosophical poem which has been written for humanity for a long time.[36]

Whatever detailed knowledge Dauthendey had of philosophers and philosophical systems, was derived largely through his friend, Arnold Villinger. He was, to be sure, familiar with Schopenhauer's *Welt als Wille und Vorstellung,* which he considered lucidly written and easily understood,[37] and with Nietzsche's philosophic prose.

As early as 1890 Dauthendey read Schopenhauer enthusiastically[38] and was particularly impressed by the explanation of the

[32] Letter of February 9, 1918, Tosari, *Ein Herz im Lärm der Welt*, p. 217.
[33] *Gedankengut aus meinen Wanderjahren, Gesammelte Werke*, I, p. 325.
[34] *Cp.* Elisabeth Darge, *op. cit., passim.*
[35] *Vide* Chapter IV.
[36] *Mich ruft dein Bild,* p. 435.
[37] Schopenhauer is referred to repeatedly in the Nachlaß, also *Verdensaltet*, pp. 49, 50, *Gedankengut aus meinen Wanderjahren, Gesammelte Werke*, I, p. 300, and in various letters. Mention of Nietzsche occurs in *Verdensaltet*, pp. 54, 55, *Gedankengut aus meinen Wanderjahren*, pp. 399, 400, 404 and in several letters. Thus, in a letter of July 12, 1891, to Siegfried Loewenthal, while criticising his brother-in-law, a man apparently much addicted to the use of worn-out clichés, he says: "Von der tiefen Wahrheit des Ausspruches von Nietzsche, der das Motto unserer Zeit ist: 'Es wird umgewertet!'—keine Ahnung." *Ein Herz im Lärm der Welt*, p. 42. Hegel is mentioned once in a reference to color, *Verdensaltet*, p. 70. Spinoza and Emerson are mentioned only casually in *Fünfuhrtee, Gesammelte Werke,* III, p. 201.
[38] Letter of June 5, 1891, to Siegfried Loewenthal: *Ein Herz im Lärm der Welt,* p. 16.

concepts "schön" and "erhaben."[39] That his reading was not entirely desultory, but that it stimulated him to further thought, is proved by a reference to Schopenhauer in the unpublished Nachlaß, dated June 8, 1891, "Just as Schopenhauer explains the perception of art, of the beautiful, only through a complete forgetting of one's own will, of the desiring, hoping and willing ego, so also the feeling of love may be explained. The loving heart may be called purely unegotistic in its love when it can subordinate its desire even to the disappointments and renunciations, the painful aspects of love, when without will itself, it lives only for the will of the other heart."[40] Dauthendey's preoccupation with Schopenhauer during his sojourn at Quille, Bohuslän, Sweden, he later referred to humorously in *Bänkelsang vom Balzer auf der Balz,* as follows:

> Wenn Eul und Kauz verliebt nachts schrie,
> Trieb ich statt Lieb' Philosophie,
>
> Welt ohne Will', nur Vorstellung,
> Gab meinen armen Nächten Schwung.[41]

However, with the exception of a stylistic influence, Dauthendey's indebtedness to Schopenhauer was slight. For a poet of the affirmation of life, little could be gleaned from a philosophy of pessimism. The thread of human sympathy which winds through Dauthendey's works,[42] had its origin in his own delicately attuned soul and needed no stimulation. Although a surpassing interest in Oriental thought characterized both Dauthendey and the great expounder of the philosophy of the will, the poet ascribed his interest to a spiritual affinity with the Orient. The reading of such books as *Max Havelaar* as a school boy was his first impulse in that direction. Finally, far from accepting the Oriental Nirvana, the negation of the will, as a solution of life's problems, Dauthendey

---

[39] Letter of June 22, 1891, *op. cit.*, p. 28.
[40] "Wie Schopenhauer das Erkennen der Kunst, des Schönen nur durch ein völliges Vergessen des eigenen Willens, des verlangenden hoffenden und wollenden Ichs erklärt, so kann auch das Gefühl der Liebe in die Erklärungen einbegriffen werden. Das liebende Herz wird nur dann rein unegotistisch liebend genannt werden können, wenn es sein Verlangen, auch den Enttäuschungen und Entbehrungen, den Schmerzen der Liebe unterordnen kann, wenn es völlig willenlos nur dem Willen des andern Herzens lebt."
[41] *Gesammelte Werke,* IV, pp. 586, 587.
[42] E.g., in *Messina im Mörser, Die Untergangsstunde der Titanic,* "Siebzig Jahre."

succeeded in finding a niche for it as the "Weltferne" of his philosophy of Weltfestlichkeit, which is an affirmation of life rather than a glorification of passiveness and dissolution.

Dauthendey's familiarity with at least the terminology of Nietzsche is seen in *Bänkelsang vom Balzer auf der Balz*, in which his friend, the Swedish author Gustaf Uddgren[43] (=Balduin) is described as an "Übermensch."[44] The influence of Nietzsche upon the poets of the turn of the century was inescapable. As Elisabeth Darge has well pointed out, Nietzsche was so much the intensified expression of his cultural epoch that everyone had to settle accounts with him whether he wanted to or not.[45] Although he was familiar with Nietzsche's works, and although there are numerous references to well-known clichés such as "godt og ondt,"[46] "overmennesket,"[47] "fornægten af 'Vilje til Livet,' "[48] etc., Dauthendey's mature view of life is as little indebted to Nietzsche as to Schopenhauer. With Nietzsche he believed in an eternal recurrence of things, differing, materially however, from the theory of the author of *Zarathustra* on this subject.[49] Theories of the superman and the slave are totally at variance with Dauthendey's "Weltallzusammengehörigkeit." Dauthendey's vindication of war is confined to his Java seclusion, and is a product largely of war psychosis. His innate pacifism is rather to be judged by his elation at being found unsuited for military training.[50] With Nietzsche, but unlike Bruno Wille, Dauthendey valued the writings of the ancient Greeks,[51] although it was rather through first-hand reading of a few Greek masterpieces than through Nietzsche's philological approach.

Dauthendey emphasized his unfamiliarity with the works of the Orientals, ascribing his understanding of Oriental thought proc-

[43] *Vide*, p. 41, *infra*.
[44] *Gesammelte Werke*, IV, p. 579.
[45] *Op. cit.*, p. 29.
[46] *Verdensaltet*, pp. 54, 63, 64.
[47] *Ibid.*, pp. 54, 55.
[48] *Ibid.*, p. 49.
[49] *Gedankengut aus meinen Wanderjahren, Gesammelte Werke*, I, pp. 337, 338.
[50] Letters of June 12, 13, 14, 1891, *Ein Herz im Lärm der Welt*, pp. 19-21.
[51] Hans Mack, *Bruno Wille als Philosoph*. Dissertation. Gießen, 1913: Christ & Herr, p. 39. For the importance of the Greeks to the poets of the affirmation of life of the turn of the century, *cp*. Elisabeth Darge, *op. cit.*, who finds it expressed best by Dauthendey, p. 196.

Cover of *Bänkelsang vom Balzer auf der Balz.*

esses simply to a spiritual affinity.[52] He seemed to find his own mature philosophy confirmed rather than enriched by new elements from the Orient.

Of theosophy the poet claimed little knowledge[53] beyond an early imperfect acquaintance with Blake and occultism. Of the latter he at that time "did not understand anything," and he "had no mind," no longing for it, as he had "for warm life and love."[54] Although he studied the books of the Cabbala and found them very poetic,[55] they likewise had little bearing on his developing philosophy.

There is no direct evidence of first-hand familiarity with the works of Francis of Assisi, Giordano Bruno, or Leibniz, much as his philosophy may be tangent to theirs in certain phases. Dauthendey's acquaintance with Bruno Wille antedates most of Wille's philosophical books. It is quite possible, of course, that he absorbed ideas for his panpsychism from thoughts current in the Friedrichshagen circle, to which he had access in the early nineties.[56] This panpsychism drew largely on Fechner, whose works must have been quite familiar to Villinger.

The superstructure of Dauthendey's Weltanschauung is then in the main a rediscovery or an unconscious elaboration of thoughts gathered in his long conversations with his philosopher-friend Villinger. Fundamentally, therefore, his system is not a cosmic philosophy in the stricter sense, but rather a Lebensanschauung with ethical and pragmatic coloring. Like Fechner's, it is predominantly "anschaulich."[57] Dauthendey lacked the inclination as well as the training and the power for acute thinking, so necessary to one who would enrich the world with a new, rigid philosophical system. His belief in imponderables precluded a search for ulti-

---

[52] *Gedankengut aus meinen Wanderjahren, Gesammelte Werke*, I, p. 326.

[53] Unpublished letter of April 9, 1917, regarding W. Leadbeater's *Einfaches Lehrbuch für Theosophie* and Annie Besant's *Die alte Weisheit:* "Es sind meine ersten theosophischen Bücher, die ich im Leben lese. Mit Ausnahme des Blake, im Jahr 1893 in London habe ich nie wieder Theosophie in der Hand gehabt. Aber solche Bücher lesen sich gut vor großer Natur."

[54] Diary entry of March 15, 1918, *Aus fernen Ländern, Gesammelte Werke*, II, pp. 666, 667.

[55] Unpublished note to Richard Dehmel, written October 12, 1896.

[56] *Cp. Ein Herz im Lärm der Welt*, pp. 78, 86.

[57] Reinhold Liebe, *Fechners Metaphysik. Im Umriß dargestellt und beurteilt*, p. 44.

mate truths, while his deep-rootedness in the direct perception of the senses made any coldly logical deductions impossible. It is in this spirit that we must examine the poet's philosophy:

> Wir alle bleiben blinde Erdenkinder,
> Doch da blind alle, ist der Schmerz gelinder.[58]

[58] Unpublished Java poem: "In den Wolken."

III
ATOMISTIC BASIS

Although it is quite feasible to derive a Weltanschaung from Max Dauthendey's works, as one can indeed from the works of every genuine poet, he facilitates the task by devoting several works to an elaboration of his thoughts. The first of these, *Verdensaltet,* was written in 1893, when very little had as yet appeared from his pen and when his ideas were still in the process of experimentation. It was written in collaboration with his Swedish friend, Gustaf Uddgren.[1] Although published and unpublished letters guide us in delineating the further course of his thoughts, nothing appeared in print until 1910 when, in the autobiographical *Gedankengut aus meinen Wanderjahren*[2] and to a lesser extent in *Der Geist meines Vaters*[3] he defined his mature philosophy at length and with much repetition. Later in 1917, shortly before his complete conversion to the idea of a personal god, the poet in a few days produced *Das Lied der Weltfestlichkeit*[4] which epitomized the cardinal thoughts of his Weltanschauung in two long

---

[1] *Vide,* p. 41, *infra.*

[2] In 1911 Dauthendey first thought of writing these reminiscences, but he did not begin to write them until a year and half later. Since he had been so often misunderstood and for the majority of the critics and reading public was still the author simply of *Ultra Violett* and similar examples of youthful extravagance, he purposed to write the story of his life and works up to that time, embedding them in the literary and philosophic currents of the period from 1890 to 1900, and, incidentally, to expound his philosophy of life. In this autobiography we learn of Dauthendey's meeting his student friends, Loewenthal and Villinger. We are introduced to Villinger's philosophy, which made such a great impression on Dauthendey and which was to color all of his subsequent writings. The long conversations with Villinger are reproduced "nicht im Wortlaut, aber im Sinn." *Gedankengut aus meinen Wanderjahren, Gesammelte Werke,* I, p. 377. We read of Dauthendey's life as a free-lance in Berlin, meet the representatives of the day: Dehmel, George, Hansson, Uddgren, Wille and many others, and accompany Dauthendey on his trips to Sweden, England, Paris, Mexico and Greece. Throughout the work there are constant allusions to his philosophy of "world festivity." These passages in the original version are accentuated by means of spaced type. (2 volumes, Munich, 1913: A. Langen. Quotations in this study are from *Gesammelte Werke,* I.)

[3] *Der Geist meines Vaters. Aufzeichnungen aus einem begrabenen Jahrhundert.* Munich, 1912: A. Langen. Quotations in this study are from *Gesammelte Werke,* I.

[4] Tosari, 1918. The work was written between March 19 and March 30, 1917. It was first published in a limited Java edition and was later incorporated in the *Gesammelte Werke,* V. Its genesis can be traced in various letters of *Mich ruft dein*

but slightly incongruous poems. I shall in the following pages attempt analyses of the "Gedankengut" of these works, while drawing upon the imaginative works for additional examples and specific restatements, in an effort to demonstrate that although seemingly heterogeneous to the casual reader, Dauthendey's works really form an organic whole. Even apparently extraneous elements are thus found to have their place in the edifice of his thoughts.[5]

It was in Würzburg in 1890, a crucial year in Dauthendey's development, that he made the acquaintance of the young medical students, Siegfried Loewenthal and Arnold Villinger. The latter, particularly, was greatly interested in philosophy,[6] and through his studies in physics and chemistry had become acquainted with atomic theories,[7] which he sought to use as a foundation for a

---

Bild and *Ein Herz im Lärm der Welt*. As Schneider has pointed out (*op. cit.*, p. 337), *Das Lied der Weltfestlichkeit*, besides elaborating former ideas, strives to fix the poet's cardinal thoughts in easily remembered couplets, reminding one in their structure of the poems of Angelus Silesius. The poem consists of two parts, *Das Lied vom innern Auge* and *Das Lied vom Herdbau der Weltfestlichkeit*, the former consisting of twelve (unnumbered) "heavens," the latter of twelve "chambers." The order is somewhat incongruous as may be seen from the following juxtaposition:

Zwölf Himmel	Zwölf Kammern
1. Elternliebe (3)	1. Gesundheitsliebe (11)
2. Kindesliebe (4)	2. Gattenliebe (3)
3. Gattenliebe (2)	3. Elternliebe (1)
4. Nächstenliebe (5)	4. Kindesliebe (2)
5. Vaterlandsliebe (10)	5. Menschenliebe (4)
6. Arbeitsliebe (7)	6. Gesetzesliebe (7)
7. Gesetzesliebe (6)	7. Arbeitsliebe (6)
8. Liebe zur Natur (8)	8. Wissenschaftsliebe (9)
9. Liebe zu der Wissenschaft (8)	9. Kunstliebe (10)
10. Liebe zu der Künste Heiligkeit (9)	10. Vaterlandsliebe (5)
11. Liebe zur Gesundheit (1)	11. Weltallliebe (8)
12. Liebe zur Weltfestlichkeit (12)	12. Die Liebe zu dem Weltgeist und Gefühl (12)

[5] Helmut Wocke, discussing Dauthendey's view of the world says: "Es ist einheitlich —und voll köstlicher Widersprüche, einheitlich durch seine Widersprüche. "Weltfestlichkeit," in *Neue Jugend und neue Dichtung*, I, Albert Langen, Munich, p. 34.

[6] In an unpublished letter to Arnold Villinger of March 5, 1910, Dauthendey speaks of his philosopher friend's "unerhört scharfsinnigen Begabung" and of his "Hang die Welt zu erklären und zu begründen."

[7] Among the Würzburg professors, A. Fick (September 3, 1829-August 21, 1901; after 1868 professor of physiology), particularly, was interested in atomic theory. According to his biographer, Friedrich Schenk (*Pflügers Archiv für Physiologie*, XC, pp. 313 ff.; *cf.* also A. Fick, *Gesammelte Schriften*, I, pp. 1-42), he enjoyed "sowohl infolge seiner vortrefflichen Charaktereigenschaften als auch wegen seiner

systematic panpsychism. He had read the writings of the important classical and modern philosophers and took great pleasure in explaining the elements of philosophic systems to Dauthendey, who, lacking training in this field, often experienced difficulty in following him. Like most youthful philosophers Villinger sought to explain the essence of things, to leave little or nothing unexplained. What method could be more convincing than to adhere strictly to the findings of science?

Villinger was at that time engaged in writing a summary of his ideas. However, it was not completed until 1895 and was not published until 1896 under the ambitious title: *Das Buch vom Wesen aller Dinge*.[8] Although this volume appeared three years after Dauthendey's own exposition of his "new" philosophy, *i.e.*, *Verdensaltet, Det nye sublime i Kunsten*, it embodied the subject matter of their daily conversations in 1890 and furnished the germ for Dauthendey's own Weltanschauung.[9]

In a letter of June 18, 1891, Dauthendey apprized Siegfried Loewenthal of Villinger's rejoicing at having found a support for his atomic theory in a lecture by Professor Fick. Of his own opinion after reading the lecture, Dauthendey says modestly: "Unfortunately I cannot, like you, judge about such scientific matters, since I lack counter proofs; and if a thing is represented quite lucidly, it naturally appeals to me."[10] Professor Fick's lecture may, therefore, be considered a logical, academic statement of Villinger's fundamental premises.[11] Professor Fick's purpose is to prove the apodictic nature of the statement that "The whole mass

---

Erfolge in Lehr- und Forschertätigkeit bald der größten Hochachtung und des größten Vertrauens seiner Kollegen in der engeren Fakultät und auch den weiteren Universitätskreisen . . ." (*Gesammelte Schriften*, I, p. 7).

[8] Dresden and Leipzig, 1896: E. Pierson's Verlag. Contents: I. Teil: Das Leben in der "leblosen" Natur. II. Teil: Erklärung der Vorgänge im Menschengehirn. III. Teil: Entstehung der Organismen. Schluß: Der Welt Rätsel und Ende. I am greatly indebted to Dr. Villinger for sending me his only copy of this book, all my efforts to locate a copy in European and American libraries having proved futile. Considering the rareness of the volume, I may perhaps be excused for quoting freely. Reference to this book is made by Dauthendey, *Gedankengut aus meinen Wanderjahren, Gesammelte Werke*, I, pp. 319, 323.

[9] *Gedankengut aus meinen Wanderjahren, Gesammelte Werke*, I, p. 371.

[10] *Ein Herz im Lärm der Welt*, p. 23.

[11] The reference in the letter referred to in footnote 11 is undoubtedly to an article entitled "Die stetige Raumerfüllung durch Masse" which appeared in *Verhandlungen der phys.-med. Gesellschaft zu Würzburg*, N.F., XXV (Würzburg, Stahel, 1891). I quote from Adolf Fick, *Gesammelte Schriften*, I, pp. 189 ff.

of the world is divided into amounts of finite size, of which each occupies in every moment a definite mathematical point without extension" and incidentally that the "interaction of the masses, *i.e.*, the change of their velocities according to a change of their mutual distances in observance of definite laws, is absolutely nothing but influence into the distance."[12] The scientist summarizes his lecture, the substance of which, by the way, he admits is tangent to thoughts held by du Bois-Reymond and Bouissinesq,[13] as follows: "I hope in these observations to have given good reasons for holding that only one conception of the nature of matter makes experience possible, *i.e.*, makes it possible to bring all manifestations into a uniform, lawful connection. This conception, to repeat once more, is that matter exists in finite amounts divided into mathematical points, which move in such a manner that changes of their velocity (hence also changes of their kinetic energy) are related according to certain laws to change of their relative position (or the potential energy of the system). A material point according to this conception is naturally not by any means an atom in the sense of chemistry. Such a chemical atom is rather to be considered a very stable system of perhaps many millions of material points. One's idea of an electrical particle corresponds best, perhaps, to the conception of a simple material point. If one understands these particles to interact according to Weber's law, it is possible to conceive the structure of stable systems, in which the individual particles whirl about each other with tremendous speed, as Weber himself has shown."[14]

Proceeding from such scientific hypotheses as these, Villinger, in his slender volume attempted to solve problems that had puzzled philosophers throughout the ages. His work is divided into three main parts which deal respectively with life in so-called "lifeless" nature, with the nature of mental processes, and with the origin of organisms.

The first chapter is concerned primarily with chemistry and physics; in these domains of science an atomic theory is built up and fortified by means of numerous pictorial representations. A close analogy is indicated between molecular and celestial movements. From the rotation of molecules Villinger sought to explain

[12] *Op. cit.*, p. 189.
[13] *Op. cit.*, p. 188.
[14] *Op. cit.*, p. 199.

chemical, physical, and even psychical phenomena. The atoms are the carriers of an all-pervading will:

In its essence everything is the same, everything is will, just as you are, O man.

. . . .

Man, you are, what everything beside you is,—will. And when you die you become what everything beside you is: will.

Everything longs just as you long, everything mourns, everything drinks moments of love, just as you mourn, just as you love.

Man, all wills strive for contentment, from eternity all wills have been striving for contentment, and contentment of all wills is the riddle of the universe, is the aim of the universe.[15]

Furthermore, these atoms are endowed with life, "they feel, just as we feel, they love whatever is kindly disposed toward them; they avoid whatever is inimical to them. If they have to choose, the smallest opposition, the smallest advantages determine the choice. If two atoms possessing the same form but unequal mass rotate in a corresponding manner, with the same rotary speed, they both feel discontent because the peripheral parts of the greater atom move too rapidly for the smaller one, hurrying past it, pulling it along. Because the smaller atom holds back the greater one, Hydrogen and the atoms of higher specific weight avoid each other, *e.g.*, an atom of silver and an atom of hydrogen."[16]

In spite of its formidable title, the booklet was not intended to set forth the theory in its final form. However, although Dauthendey was apprized of later changes[17] in his friend's position, these were not used by him, since his own elaboration was based essentially on the early conversations and on the notes used in preparation for *Das Buch vom Wesen aller Dinge*.

With the enthusiasm so well portrayed in *Gedankengut aus*

[15] *Op. cit.*, p. 142.
[16] *Op. cit.*, p. 37.
[17] Dr. Villinger has continued his interest in atomic theory and its bearings on philosophy. He published a greatly revised version in 1910: *Grundzüge einer Weltanschauung*. Leipzig: J. A. Barth. In a letter of June 21, 1930, he told me that he was engaged on a new study in pure physics which would take issue with the more recent theories of the atom and serve to support ideas of his first books in the light of present-day research. Concerning Dr. Villinger's second book, Dauthendey wrote him March 5, 1910 (unpublished letter), Munich: "I anticipate with great pleasure receiving the *Grundzüge einer Weltanschauung*, for it is essential that the present loose thoughtlessness of all concepts cease, and that a scientifically trained energetic brain establish a new and fresh viewpoint similar to that of the *Buch vom Wesen aller Dinge.*"

meinen Wanderjahren,[18] the young medical student concluded the first part of his treatise: "Even through this framework there flows the rosy light of the knowledge that there is life in 'lifeless' nature; that it loves, longs; that it hates and avoids; that it feels just as our human brain feels."[19]

Dauthendey adopted two important phases of this theory without questioning their validity: (1) All atoms are sentient beings; (2) Atoms are carriers of an all-pervading will. He made no attempt to prove these statements. To him they were axiomatic. There is evidence in early unpublished notebooks that he tried to define concepts, such as "longing," "pain," or "joy," in Villinger's pseudo-scientific manner: e.g., "Longing is the will-to-move of a mass particle that is gently aided by a remote particle towards which it now rolls." "Pain is the obstruction of the will-to-move of a mass particle through the disturbing movement of another." "Joy is the complete reinforcement of the will-to-move of one particle through another."[20]

While discussing his preliminary studies for *Verdensaltet, Det nye sublime i Kunsten,* Dauthendey wrote to Richard Dehmel: "I base my ideas mainly on Noldy's (*i.e.,* Arnold Villinger's) theory. Every atom is a sentient being. The corollaries of this are mighty."[21] It is with the corollaries that Dauthendey is chiefly concerned in his later expository writings. While acknowledging fully his indebtedness to Villinger, Dauthendey states in *Gedankengut aus meinen Wanderjahren,*[22] that this indebtedness only furnished him with a point of departure for his own thoughts, which then evolved during the years from 1890 to 1913, when for the second time he reduced them to writing. Thus he characterizes the initial ideas as a seed which later developed into a gigantic ash tree,[23] and again as the initial gold piece of his later (philosophic) riches.[24]

---

[18] *Gesammelte Werke,* I, pp. 373 ff.
[19] *Das Buch vom Wesen aller Dinge,* p. 40.
[20] "Sehnsucht ist der Bewegungswille eines Massenteiles, welches leise durch einen entfernten Teil gefördert wird und nun diesen entgegenrollt." "Schmerz ist die Hemmung des Bewegungswillens eines Massenteiles durch die störende Bewegung eines andern." "Freude ist die volle Bestärkung des Bewegungswillens eines Teiles durch einen andern." *Cp.* also *Verdensaltet, Det nye sublime i kunsten,* p. 70.
[21] Unpublished.
[22] *Gesammelte Werke,* I, p. 395.
[23] *Op. cit.,* p. 371.
[24] *Op. cit.,* p. 372.

The influence of Arnold Villinger may then be stated briefly as follows: He acquainted Dauthendey with the elements of atomic theory and structure. In innumerable talks about philosophy and philosophic systems—and these he was fond of holding up to scorn, characterizing them as mere verbal wrangling,[25]—he tried to convince the poet of the non-existence of a personal God.[26] The proof of the non-existence of God is not elaborated in *Das Buch vom Wesen aller Dinge,* although it is immanent in Villinger's atomic theory. As a substitute for the godhead, the atoms were to be considered as sentient beings,—an idea which furnished the basis of a systematic panpsychism. Naturally, this theory did not appeal to the poetic youth at first, but when he was told that it involved a new responsibility, namely, that of being the creator and the created simultaneously, he accepted it with his customary enthusiasm.[27]

Neither in Dauthendey's reports of his conversations with Villinger in *Gedankengut aus meinen Wanderjahren,* nor in Villinger's books is there any evidence of the idea of "world-detachment" and "world-proximity," which occurred to Dauthendey suddenly in 1897.[28] The concept of "world-festivity"[29] also is a later and apparently original thought with Dauthendey. Mention of it in his works does not occur until *Das festliche Jahrbuch, Erster Gesang,*[30] which was written in 1898, after a temporarily pessimistic attitude toward life had produced *Die schwarze Sonne*[31] and after the Mexican venture[32] had failed for lack of the

---

[25] *Op. cit.,* p. 300.
[26] *Op. cit.,* pp. 373 ff.
[27] *Op. cit.,* p. 377.
[28] *Vide infra,* pp. 78 ff.
[29] *Vide infra,* pp. 84 ff.
[30] *Pan,* IV, 4, 1898, pp. 215-219, and *Blätter für die Kunst,* series 4, IV, 1897-1899, pp. 104-106.
[31] Mexico, 1897: Hijas de J. F. Jens.
[32] While in London in 1894 Dauthendey met an enthusiastic artist, James Durand, and his equally gifted wife, Theodosia, two Americans who like many of their co-expatriates of that day thought Europe necessary for their spiritual well-being. They belonged to a secret cult and initiated Dauthendey into the rudiments of Occultism. The writings of the mystics formed the topic of continuous, involved conversations. In an age when the Worpswede colony sprang up in Germany and when Bellamy's *Looking Backward,* a work Dauthendey read avidly, made a sweeping conquest of America and Europe as the latest Utopia, these American friends conceived the idea of founding an artist colony. They first planned to locate it at Geneva, later in South Carolina, and eventually decided on Mexico. The projected colony aroused great enthusiasm among their Paris friends. Notices appeared in French and American

very fortitude which thoughts of "world-festivity" would have inspired.

Other elements of Dauthendey's own philosophical scheme developed only gradually, many of them merely a rationalization of

---

periodicals. Of these I have located "The Foundation of a Colony of Selfsupporting Artists" in *Arena*, vol. XVII, pp. 642-651, and "Fondation d'une colonie d'artistes subvenant eux-mêmes à leurs besoins" in *La Plume*, Volume IX, 1897, pp. 10-15. Dauthendey's translation: "Gründung einer Kolonie sich selbsterhaltender Künstler," I was able to consult in the Nachlaß at Traben. The poet wanted to take along to the land of the Sun, at least as souvenirs, the best books, statues, paintings and music that Europe and Asia had produced. He procured a plaster of Paris cast of the Louvre Venus de Milo, also a statue of the ancient Egyptian Sun God, Osiris, and one of an Indian Buddha sitting on a large lotus flower. He also filled portfolios with reproductions of works by Dürer, Rembrandt, Leonardo da Vinci, and Michelangelo, chests with reproductions from many European museums, and boxes with replicas of the friezes of the Parthenon. (*Raubmenschen, Gesammelte Werke*, III, pp. 902; *Gedankengut aus meinen Wanderjahren, Gesammelte Werke*, I, p. 729; *Bänkelsang vom Balzer auf der Balz, Gesammelte Werke*, IV, pp. 649, 650; *cp.* also Franz Blei, "Erinnerungen an Max Dauthendey," *Roland*, XXIII, 26, June 25, 1925.) Of books he included the Edda and the Nibelungenlied, the Bible, Homer, the Koran, and the Indian Vedas. To supplement this "extract of universal culture," hunting guns, fish nets, and spy glasses, all necessary to the founding of the colony, were provided. It never occurred to the naive authors of the plan to inquire of their respective consuls or the Mexican government whether such a scheme would prove advisable or at all practicable. The American couple preceded the Dauthendeys to Mexico. Dauthendey and his wife spent a few weeks in May and June at Pouldu, Bretagne, which they left June 11, 1897, embarking from Southampton on June 14 for New York on the "Prinzregent Luitpold von Bayern" of the North German Lloyd. They arrived in New York on June 24. In the ship's register they inserted their profession as "artistes," which led to the various mistakes elaborated in the novel *Raubmenschen*. (*Gesammelte Werke*, III, p. 627.) While in New York they stayed at the Holland House, a hotel formerly located near Madison Square (*cf., New York Times*, June 25, 1897, XLVI, No. 14,306, p. 2). Before leaving they paid a short visit to Dauthendey's sister at Philadelphia (*cp.* Rennewart's trip to Philadelphia in *Raubmenschen*).

On arrival at the Mexican capital nothing was to be seen of the Durands. Not until a week had passed did Dauthendey meet them quite casually. The first blush of adventure had passed, however. On first setting foot on Mexican soil Dauthendey realized that this land would never yield a German song to him. "No sooner had I set foot on the tropical mainland at Vera Cruz, Gulf of Mexico, no sooner did I see the first cocoanut palms on an avenue of the little harbor city, than it suddenly dawned upon me: Here I shall never write a German song." (*Gedankengut aus meinen Wanderjahren, Gesammelte Werke*, I, p. 713.) "Rather would I be a stonecutter, street cleaner and beggar at the church-doors of Europe than remain in a country whose nature, palms and volcanos, whose agave-farms, sugar cane and coffee trees would never inspire a German song." (*Ibidem*, p. 717.)

Although the authors of the plan had called themselves men "not easily daunted," "being prepared for failures at the first," and had compared themselves to Hercules "ready to perform the labors of life," (*Arena, loc. cit.,* p. 643), Dauthendey soon developed an aversion to the undertaking and the founding of the colony came to naught.

his experiences or an elaboration of his basic concepts. Villinger's attempts at scientific proofs must have seemed too mechanical to Dauthendey to be incorporated into his Weltanschauung. The young medical student had, *e.g.*, even sought to explain love in terms of the atomic will:[33] "Here the secret of love is exposed in its simplest form," he enthusiastically states, "the wills approach each other, and therefore they love each other; and in love they strive towards union.—Everywhere, where love is experienced in the world, be it as longing, as ecstasy, as pleasure, as laughter, as harmony . . . , it is the same correspondence of wills which reigns between attracting poles of magnets.—And everywhere, where hatred or vexation or fear or jealously or sadness or pain are present in the world: there the wills contradict each other."[34] This to Dauthendey naturally seemed inadequate; from an early time he was much concerned with the proper niche which love would occupy in his philosophy, until finally it assumed the most important position of all.[35]

[33] *Das Buch vom Wesen aller Dinge*, p. 16.
[34] One is reminded of Goethe's *Wahlverwandschaften*. Ernst Haeckel held a similar view in *Die Welträtsel*, which did not, however, appear until 1899. *Volksausgabe*, 171-180. Tausend, Stuttgart: Alfred Kröner Verlag, p. 91.
[35] *Vide infra*, pp. 195 ff.

IV
VERDENSALTET

While in Berlin in 1893 Dauthendey met Gustaf Uddgren,[1] a Swede who had traveled extensively in Europe and the United States, whom he described as a "young blond Viking prince, with an iron will and a heart of honey."[2] Uddgren was a newspaper correspondent and a poet, was very much attracted by the new impressionistic writers, and considered Dauthendey to be one of the foremost exponents of the new literary art. He invited his friend to go with him to the west coast of Sweden. The latter, anxious to escape financial worries and to find the necessary seclusion for artistic creation, gladly accompanied him. This trip Dauthendey described at length in *Festliches Jahrbuch*,[3] *Gedankengut aus meinen Wanderjahren*,[4] and *Bänkelsang vom Balzer auf der Balz*.[5] Of the imaginative works *Der Drache Grauli* and *Maja* recapture the atmosphere of the Northland.

To Richard Dehmel Dauthendey wrote: "I spent five months there in the golden solitude of nature. First in Sweden at the

[1] (1865-1927), best known in English speaking countries for his studies of Strindberg. Author of *Balders återkomst o.andra dikter*, 1895; *Acherontia. Prosadikter*, 1902; *Kring rosenbusken. Ungbohêmen. Två novelleter*, 1906; *August Strindberg. Början till en biografi*, 1909, 1912; *Andra boken om Strindberg*, 1912; *Fredrikson. En konstnärsmonografi*, 1912; *Stockholms-bohême. Skildringer ur konstnärslifvet*, 1912; *Flamman son släcktes. Komedie i 3 akter*, 1913; *Stora starka seglare*. Skägårdsroman, 1913; *Grossman mot hela världen*, 1917; *Skuggan som stal hans hjäl. Skildring ur den internationella konstnärsbohêmen*, 1917. Uddgren introduced Dauthendey to the Danish reading public by an article entitled "Den tyske 'Farve' digter M. Dauthendey" (*Politiken*, Torsdagen den 3dje August 1893, Nr. 215, p. 1.) He also translated Dauthendey's prose poem "Schwarz" ("Sort," *Politiken, loc. cit.*) and "Doppelleben" ("Dobbeltliv. Skitse fra Danmark." *Politiken*, Onsdagen, den 16de August 1893, Nr. 228, p. 1, accompanied by a brief article on M. Dauthendey signed by G[ustaf] U[ddgren] and illustrated by a line drawing of the German poet). The translations brought forth as parodies: "Sort," *Avisen*, Lördag den 5te August, 1893, Nr. 217, p. 3, and "Dobbeltsyn, Skitse fra Benegalien af M. Dauthentisk," Dannebrog, 2. Aargang, Nr. 357, Tirsdag den 22. August 1893.

[2] Letter of March 3, 1893, *Ein Herz im Lärm der Welt*, p. 110. Cp. also *op. cit.*, p. 116 and particularly pp. 120, 121. Shortly before his death Uddgren, in an interview granted to the present writer, laughingly alluded to Dauthendey's calling him "der junge Schwede" in *Gedankengut aus meinen Wanderjahren* (*Gesammelte Werke*, I, p. 480 and *passim*). He was actually two years older than Dauthendey.

[3] *Achter Gesang, Gesammelte Werke*, IV, pp. 563-569.

[4] *Gesammelte Werke*, I, pp. 471 ff.

[5] *Gesammelte Werke*, IV, pp. 584-588.

gray and bare Viking coast and later at the Isefjord with its soft green beech trees and gentle silvery strand. As a winter abode Stockholm is ideal for me."[6]

To understand Dauthendey's poetry of this period adequately, one must be familiar with the west coast of Sweden. For miles and miles it consists of huge, rounded rocks which give the impression of primeval monsters, Dinosaurs, or gigantic elephants.[7] Villages are very few and are scattered so that the houses of any particular village may be widely separated. To one bent on discovering the language of inanimate as well as animate life, there could hardly have been a more ideal background.

Dauthendey came to Quille to the house of Uddgren's father, the local preacher, and for months lived practically in solitary communion with nature.[8] There he believed he learned the language of the birds and bees, of the trees, bushes, flowers and blades of grass. This close proximity to nature is reflected in all his imaginative work of that time, the "Stimmen des Schweigens" of *Ultra Violett*[9] and a number of unpublished notebooks of prose excerpts. "The intense enjoyment of nature which I daily absorb at the coast and in the mountains, forced me to compose that way,"[10] Dauthendey wrote to Richard Dehmel, indicating thus the innate compulsion and the intuitive nature of the poems of that period.

However, the poet did not confine himself to furnishing practical examples of "the new intimate art." Together with Uddgren

---

[6] Unpublished letter of November 16, 1893, Stockholm: "Ich habe fünf Monate ganz in goldener Natureinsamkeit gelebt. Erst in Schweden in der grauen öden Vikingerküste. Dann am Isefjord im weichgrünen Buchenwald an weichsilbernem Strande. Stockholm ist als Winteraufenthalt für mich eine Idealstadt."

[7] Korfiz Holm gives a good description in *Herz ist Trumpf*, pp. 203 ff.

[8] For a description of Quille (also spelled Kvile), see letter of April 5, 1893, to Siegfried Loewenthal, *Ein Herz im Lärm der Welt*, pp. 113, 114, and the letter to Arnold Villinger, of April 1893, *loc. cit.*, pp. 114, 115.

[9] The chronology of *Ultra Violett* appears on the title page of a copy of the original edition in the possession of Annie Dauthendey. There Dauthendey on May 15, 1896, while on the island of Jersey, supplied each poem of *Ultra Violett* with date and place of writing. Everything up to "Stimmen des Schweigens" was written in 1891 and 1892, mainly at Würzburg, Berlin, Munich. All the poems of "Stimmen des Schweigens," however, were written 1893 in Sweden or Denmark. The poems inspired by the poet's seclusion in Quille are as follows: "Abend" (March), "Faulbaumduft" (May), "Kuckuckruf" (May), "Amselsang" (May), "Morgenduft" (April), "Vollmond" (April), "Wolkenschatten" (April), "Totes Feuer" (April), and "Regenduft" (April).

[10] Letter referred to in footnote 6.

he elaborated a work previously started at Berlin (1893) under the German title *Weltall*. This manuscript, Uddgren, with the aid of a Danish lawyer, translated into Danish and published as *Verdensaltet, Det nye sublime i Kunsten*.[11]

Since *Verdensaltet*[12] represents Dauthendey's earliest statement of his credo, I may perhaps be excused for giving a rather full account of the book. That Dauthendey himself considered it of great importance is obvious from the numerous enthusiastic references in letters of that time.

"I have not only given an essay or a discursive composition, but the foundation for the longed-for new art, so that I may say I re-establish the sublime,"[13] he writes to Siegfried Loewenthal. "Having discovered the new technique and the new ideal, I feel mature to write great sublime poems . . . I believe the religion which we educated ones now have, written down for everybody and given to the people, to be a necessity, a benefit for him who gives it and a greater benefit for those who no longer can believe in the old ideals and who have no new ones."[14]

In an unpublished letter to Siegfried Loewenthal[15] he characterizes the last two parts of *Verdensaltet, i.e.*, "Den sublime Kunst," as a "new universal religion." In a letter to Otto Goetze[16] he describes this as "a simple, elevating contemplation of nature, founded on the sublime essence of the eternal force and mass of the universe. Perhaps these thoughts will not affect you so deeply as they do me. However, I believe that when you read my first book of the natural religion, you too will feel as deeply as I do."

---

[11] Copenhagen, 1893: A. Christiansen's Kunstforlag. *Oversaettelse*. Of the two collaborators C. G. Uddgren is mentioned first, although the first part was written by Dauthendey prior to his meeting Uddgren for the first time.

[12] The book is very rare. It was printed in a very small edition and is out of print. For this study I was able to consult the copies in the Royal Library at Stockholm and in the National Library at Copenhagen, apparently the only two copies available in libraries.

[13] Letter of July 17, 1893, *Ein Herz im Lärm der Welt*, p. 118.

[14] *Loc. cit.*, p. 119.

[15] Undated, written before July, 1893.

[16] Unpublished letter of August 2, 1893, Gjepperup: "Und zugleich arbeite ich jetzt an einer neuen Religion. An einer einfachen erhebenden Naturandacht, gestützt auf das Erhabene der ewigen Kraft und Masse des Weltalls. Diese Gedanken werden Dich vielleicht als zu neu oder absonderlich nicht so erregen, wie mich. Aber ich denke, wenn ich meine erste Dichtung des Erhabenen geschrieben und Du mein Buch der Naturreligion lesen wirst, Du ebenso tief mit mir fühlst." Reference to Otto Goetze is made in *Gesammelte Werke*, I, p. 422.

In the unpublished letter to Siegfried Loewenthal, referred to above, Dauthendey wrote: "I have written to Mrs. Besant. I am thinking of winning her as a speaker for the new religion. If I receive the hoped for prize of 500 marks for my novel, I shall go to Tolstoi to impart my ideas to him."[17]

Being thus convinced of its value, Dauthendey left no stone unturned to have the book appear in German. Although he submitted it to his friends, with a view to publication, and although for a long time the manuscript lay in the *Zukunft* office[18] and was submitted to other publishing houses, his wish was never fulfilled. In 1913 the ideas of the tract were paraphrased and those still held by Dauthendey at that time were incorporated into *Gedankengut aus meinen Wanderjahren,* so that there was no longer any need of its appearance in German.[19] The original German version is found in the Nachlaß. Dauthendey apparently had misplaced it when writing *Gedankengut aus meinen Wanderjahren,* since he states there that he must have lost it during his travels.[20] The account of *Verdensaltet* in *Gedankengut aus meinen Wanderjahren*[21] is based mainly on memory, for Dauthendey there speaks of the book's having appeared in Swedish, whereas it actually appeared in Danish,—a mistake he would certainly not have made had he had the translation before him. That this is not a mere slip is shown by the fact that he emphasizes that the German original was destined to appear in Swedish by a Danish publishing firm.[22]

The appearance of *Verdensaltet* was almost unnoticed by the critics.[23] Dauthendey, however, writes of its enthusiastic reception among his friends. He claims, *e.g.,* that Hemning Jensen, the

---

[17] "Ich habe mich in Beziehung gesetzt mit Mrs. Besant ... Ich denke sie als Rednerin für die neue Religion zu gewinnen. Bekomme ich den erhofften Preis für meine Novelle, 500 M., dann reise ich zu Tolstoi um ihm meine Ideen mitzuteilen."

[18] Letter of April 5, 1893, Quille, to Siegfried Loewenthal, *Ein Herz im Lärm der Welt,* p. 114.

[19] In view of the above I cannot subscribe to M. Gebhardt's statement that Dauthendey must have considered the book of small importance, since it never appeared in German, *op. cit.*, p. 60.

[20] *Gesammelte Werke,* I, p. 558.

[21] *Loc. cit.,* pp. 557, 558.

[22] *Loc. cit.,* p. 558. Similarly Jens Peter Jacobsen is not mentioned in *Verdensaltet,* although Dauthendey expressly states that he is, *id. loc.*

[23] I know of only one newspaper review, by G-g N., *Aftenbladet,* Stockholm, March 9, 1894. The tenor of this criticism is somewhat ironical, because of the self-assurance of the co-authors.

Danish poet and philosopher, was so moved on being introduced to the thought content of the booklet that he exclaimed: "That is the future, the great, mighty thing which we all feel in our yearnings. But you have comprehended it, your poetry really is the new form of the sublime."[24] George Brandes, to whom the poet sent the book, was not impressed.[25] This is all the more surprising since the great Danish critic had taken up the cudgels for Jens Peter Jacobsen, whom Dauthendey acknowledged as his prose master.[26] Brandes probably classed the fledgling poet among those imitators of Jacobsen to whom he had sounded the following note of warning[27] "I do not believe that Jacobsen's prose will form a school, if only because of its exquisite distinctiveness. He resembles some of the greatest colorists of the world, as *e.g.*, Correggio. These have reached the acme in their field. One step more would lead to morbidity or affectation. What a poet may and should learn from them is to become himself."[28] However, to interpret *Verdensaltet* justly we must visualize the state of mind of the poets at the time, their exuberant enthusiasm, genuine sincerity and comparative innocence of other writings on aesthetics. What they lacked in knowledge of abstract works, however, was well counterbalanced by thorough first-hand acquaintance with representative works of art foreshadowing their ideals.[29] Wagner's music, *e.g.*, had made an indelible impression on Dauthendey as a youth. In 1888 he saw *Parsifal* performed at

[24] Unpublished letter of August 16, 1893 to Siegfried Loewenthal. "Gestern war ich zum Abendessen bei Hemning Jensen, dem alten Dichter und Philosophen des jungen radikalen Dänemark. Ich sagte ihm die Gedanken über die Weltallreligion und die neue erhabene Kunst. Erst wurde er ganz still, dann aber ganz plötzlich erschüttert rief er ganz erregt: 'Das ist die Zukunft, das Große, Mächtige, die wir alle in Sehnsucht empfinden, aber Sie haben es gefaßt, Ihre Dichtung ist wirklich das neue Erhabene'."

[25] According to Gustaf Uddgren, in an interview granted to the present writer.

[26] *Gedankengut aus meinen Wanderjahren, Gesammelte Werke, I, pp.* 403, 406.

[27] Translated from *Menschen und Werke*. 2. durchgesehene und ergänzte Auflage. Frankfurt a.M., 1895, p. 42.

[28] According to Dauthendey's letter of August, 1893, addressed to Siegfried Loewenthal, Brandes prevented Jörgensen's publishing an article directed against Dauthendey's poem "Drosselsang." *Ein Herz im Lärm der Welt*, p. 123. A partial translation entitled "Droslens Sang" had appeared in Uddgren's article "Den tyske 'Farve' digter M. Dauthendey," *vide* footnote 1. It is the second verse of the original "Amselsang," *Ultra Violett, Gesammelte Werke*, IV, p. 52.

[29] In one of Dauthendey's unpublished notebooks (Nachlaß, Traben) of about that time, there occurs the significant self-reminder: "Prüfe die Gewalt eines Gedankens an der Gewalt der größten Kunstwerke!"

Bayreuth and later attended practically all Wagnerian operas at Munich, even though much of the stage business appeared to him as childish.[30] Wagner aimed at a synthesis of poetry and music in his great tone dramas: Dauthendey strove for a synthesis of all the arts through synaesthesia. Byron's *Manfred,* which Dauthendey saw performed in Munich in 1892[31] and Maeterlinck's *Les aveugles* and *L'intruse,* both of which latter plays he translated in 1891, prepared the way for his future treatise. Herman Gorter's *Mei, een gedicht* (1889) and Frederik van Eeden's *De kleine Johannes* were read eagerly by Gustaf Uddgren upon his return from America and he transmitted his enthusiasm to Dauthendey.[32] Of Belgian poetry, however, Dauthendey disclaimed any influence in a letter to Richard Dehmel, who had assumed such an influence on Dauthendey's "Gesänge der Düfte."[33] The magic of Leoncavallo[34] and Mascagni[35] did not fail to impress Dauthendey in Berlin in 1892. Grieg's "Åses Death" the authors considered superior even to Wagner's "Waldweben."[36] While Dauthendey's natural talent for the pictorial arts was fanned by visits to the treasure houses of art in Dresden (1886) and Munich (1884, 1887), the art of Edvard Munch[37] seemed to approach most closely the new intimate art. Frequent visits to Ola Hansson and Laura Marholm at Friedrichshagen[38] introduced Dauthendey and Uddgren to a literature consonant with their ideal, which was already concretely embodied in such works as Hansson's *Sensitiva Amorosa.*

Verdensaltet, Det nye Sublime i Kunsten is "dedicated to poets and artists." It deals with "Intimate Art" ("Den intime Kunst")

---

[30] *Gedankengut aus meinen Wanderjahren, Gesammelte Werke,* I, p. 442.
[31] *Op. cit.,* p. 437.
[32] Dauthendey later translated several poems of Gorter, and published them in *Pan,* III, 4, 1897, p. 253. Gorter is mentioned in *Gedankengut aus meinen Wanderjahren, Gesammelte Werke,* I, pp. 482, 486. In *Reliquien, Gesammelte Werke,* IV, p. 106, lines 6-12, there is a parallel to a scene from van Eeden's *De kleine Johannes.*
[33] The letter of November 16, 1893, referred to in footnote 6. I have quoted the pertinent excerpt in *The Germanic Review,* IV, 1 (January, 1929), p. 83, where the letter is incorrectly dated 1897.
[34] *Ein Herz im Lärm der Welt,* p. 60.
[35] *Idem,* p. 79.
[36] *Verdensaltet,* p. 35.
[37] *Ein Herz im Lärm der Welt,* pp. 98, 99, also *Gedankengut aus meinen Wanderjahren, Gesammelte Werke,* I, pp. 452 ff.
[38] *Gedankengut aus meinen Wanderjahren, Gesammelte Werke,* I, p. 448. *Ein Herz im Lärm der Welt,* pp. 16, 27, 35, 77, 82, 90.

and "Sublime Art" ("Den sublime Kunst"). The former is subdivided into chapters called "Artistic Creation" ("Den kunstneriske skaben," pp. 9-23) and "Intimate Art" ("Den intime Kunst," pp. 25-43), the latter into "The Old Form of the Sublime" ("Det sublimes gamle form," pp. 47-56) and "The New Form of the Sublime" ("Det sublimes nye form," pp. 58-77).

Although "Den kunstneriske skaben" purports to be an analysis of artistic creation, it is more specifically a statement of the processes of the brain of an impressionist. Impressionists try to convey to our brains through the medium of their works, we are told (p. 11), the pleasant and unpleasant sensations of their own brains, the totality of the effect depending on the spectator's ability to experience the sense impressions. By various examples, the authors try to prove that there is a scale, at the extremes of which there are pleasure and displeasure (Lyst eller Ulyst, Veeller Vel-Fornemmelser),[39] each sensation swinging like a pendulum from one extreme to the other. To the authors of *Verdensaltet* there were no other possible vibrations (pp. 12, 13). Thus the color-impression "sky-blue" might be defined as "mild" (p. 14). The corresponding sensation for sound would be a chord on a harp; for smell, the fragrance of almond blossoms; for taste, the flavor of sweet milk; for touch, the lukewarm dampness of a cave. Hence the various senses, each traversing the scale of sensations of pleasure or displeasure, at any particular point may resemble each other and may be used interchangeably (p. 15), to produce the same effect, just as any one of our five fingers can strike the C on the piano. This is an attempt to justify synaesthesia in literature, couched in an analogy, a method perhaps familiar to the authors through the reading of Gustav Fechner, who likewise employed analogies somewhat indiscriminately.[40]

---

[39] Fechner devotes much space to the elucidation of feelings of "Lust" and "Unlust," and since parallel thoughts occur there, it is not unlikely that the authors of *Verdensaltet* may have been familiar with the scientist-philosopher's point of view, perhaps through Arnold Villinger. *Cp.*, e.g., "Die Weltfragen der Lust und Unlust" in *Die Tagesansicht gegenüber der Nachtansicht* (Leipzig, 1904), second edition, pp. 130-154), and chapter II of *Vorschule der Aesthetik. Erster Teil.* (Leipzig, 1876, pp. 7-12). A reference to "Lust" and "Unlust" in paragraph 38 of Schopenhauer's *Welt als Wille und Vorstellung* was familiar to Dauthendey through his reading at Würzburg. *Cp.* chapter III, p. 26. "Lust" and "Unlust" are translated here as "pleasure" and "displeasure."

[40] Johann Kuno Fiedler: *Die Motive der Fechner'schen Weltanschauung.* Halle (Saale), 1918. P. 25. *Cp. Gedankengut aus meinen Wanderjahren, Gesammelte Werke*, I, p. 271, *et passim*.

Memories are defined as vibrations of the brain which have been retained from an earlier impression. Artistic impressions may be rendered either directly or from memory (p. 16). In the latter case they may be either chronological, when they are inferior to direct impressions, or combinational, when through the alignment of impressions far removed from one another a stronger effect can be attained than through mere copying of direct impressions.

Such new combinations may be composed of similar elements, such as the combination of tones to form chords, of colors or lines to yield new shapes or forms, of odors to produce new perfumes; or, new associations may arise through a re-combining of different sense impressions, such as, sounds and colors, or colors and odors. The best vehicle to express these thoughts the authors believed to be fairy operas (p. 18), and "Sündflut" and "Dornröschen" of *Ultra Violett,* as well as *Sehnsucht,* were attempts to embody these thoughts concretely.

Thus artists take feelings of pleasure, the "beautiful," and feelings of displeasure, the "ugly," and combine them so as to create increased feelings of pleasure or displeasure or a blending of them. As examples are cited Böcklin's "Sea Monster," on whose back there grow seaweeds and who has fins instead of feet, and Stuck's "Lucifer," a demonic dark apparition with staring, clear cat eyes and hard, sharp pupils. Examples from the realm of music are the composers Wagner, Mascagni, and Leoncavallo, who unite pure tones and dissonances to produce therewith exceedingly strong vibrations in our brains. Poets similarly describe elves and mermaids, delicate transparent creatures with butterfly wings and lithe rosy female bodies with shiny fishtails, such combinations calling forth a doubly strong feeling of pleasure (pp. 18, 19).

Here also there is adduced a proof of the superiority of a work of art over a scientific discovery (pp. 19ff.). The first experience of fossils or Newton's falling apple as scientific problems, was analogous to the process of artistic creation. The results of later confirmation of these phenomena, however, are considerably weaker than the original effect, whereas reproductions of the strange and marvelous in the arts have an effect much more lasting on the human mind. It will be noted that the logic of the authors was at times somewhat colored by their ardor.

Three main divisions of literature and art are next singled out for discussion (pp. 22ff.), the idealistic, realistic, and mystic. Idealistic art depends on memories of impressions which through a process of combination give rise to memorable works of art, characterized by vividness and a tendency toward the transcendental, but lacking the strength of direct impressions. The *Nibelungenlied*, Wieland's *Oberon*, Goethe's *Faust* are listed as examples of this technique, as are also elves, angels, sphinxes, or centaurs in the visual arts, and the works of Wagner, Mascagni, Leoncavallo in music. Realistic art, on the other hand, lacks the unexpected combinations and hence the transcendental aspect of idealistic art. A synthesis, the authors declare, is attempted in the paintings of Uhde, whose *Christ* they cite as an example, and in those of Böcklin, which also combine a direct copy of nature with transcendental ideas. This technique is characteristic of the works of the so-called mystics. "From all these divisions of art," we are told in the concluding sentence of the first part of the treatise, "from memory associations (idealisms), from the direct copying of an impression (realisms), or from the outward combination of the two (mysticism), we now feel the beginning of a new art: The intimate art." (p. 23).

Whereas "Den kunstneriske skaben" had aimed to give a description of artistic creation and proof of the analogy of the various senses, the second half of "Den intime Kunst" concerns itself with a minute description of the "new" intimate art, an art which strives to employ all the sense impressions,—sound, color, light, taste and touch (p. 27).

Only outward impressions either direct or indirect, are capable of producing feelings of pleasure or displeasure. If the artist wants to impart his most intense feelings of pleasure or displeasure, he tries to reproduce the impressions in the work of art with the greatest possible intimacy.

The authors next show that an artist cannot work unconsciously. They describe an artist in creative mood standing in a morning landscape: "He notices at first only feelings of pleasure or displeasure, the effect of the landscape or of the remembrances it calls forth. He tries to arrest the intense feelings. He begins either to paint or to capture them in sounds or in words, to compose or to write" (p. 28). Thus he "seeks the fitting expression for the colors of the twilight or the shadows, etc. But as soon as he does that, the cause of the feelings of pleasure or displeasure has become clear in his consciousness." "The stronger, therefore, the power of reception is schooled in the artist, the more intensively can he render in his work the most delicate perceptions of his brain." (p. 29).

However, it is not sufficient simply to reproduce the great direct impression for eye or ear. "One should tell us how the silver gray vibrates, and which perception this awakens in us, whether it vibrates with sad indefiniteness or gleams or caresses mildly, in which color birds sing, and in which tones or odors colors vibrate or give forth fragrance, and how the coolness and dampness of the twilight press upon us and awaken feelings of color or sound or odor in us" (pp. 29, 30).

Intimate art thus was no longer to be concerned with such concepts as "man," "character," "fate," "tragic action" (p. 31). We live only colors or sounds. Stronger vibrations of the molecules produce stronger shadings of pleasure or displeasure. This observation the co-authors of *Verdensaltet* illustrate by the effect of smoke in a street: ". . . We suddenly experience displeasure. If we have formerly observed the impression of the odor of smoke, this reaction appears now as a memory combination of a great fire, a former event with unpleasant feelings. If we have no memories of such an experience, the smoke acts purely physiologically and oppresses our breathing, influences our mood and our thoughts, and may gradually develop into a feeling of dejection, determining our actions during the next minutes" (p. 32).

Such inner events called forth by the surroundings each artist may observe in himself. "A *color*, such as the sharp brilliance of a flower, the reflection of a sheet of water, or a *sound*, such as the cracking of a whip, the chirping of a bird, or an *odor*, such as the dampness of a musty room, the fragrance of a forest, or a *taste*, such as that of a sour or a sweet fruit, or a *feeling*, such as the touch of a cold pavement, walking on a soft carpet or soft dewy grass," may color and change our basic mood. "When now there appear stronger impressions, *e.g.*, a thunder storm, a piercing flash of lightning, sudden sunshine, a rainbow, etc., these may completely change our basic mood and with this change new wishes and hopes or doubts may appear or may influence our actions. It is with these silent invisible novels that intimate art concerns itself" (pp. 32, 33). Each individual reacts, of course, differently. Reactions depend on varying susceptibilities to sounds, colors, etc. (p. 33). In other words, each individual experiences his own novels (p. 34).

Creative works partially illustrative of this theory of art are the works of Hansson (p. 34), Wagner (p. 35), and Grieg (p. 35), and, particularly, those of Munch.[41] In *Sensitiva Amorosa* Hansson (pp. 34, 35) described "how a tendency, a distaste, or a mood can change through the influence of a sound, a facial expression, or some peculiar movement of the body, and how the pleasant or unpleasant association aroused through it can determine our feelings and actions." Wagner similarly in *Waldweben* and *Siegfried* produces the same effect on our five senses with the aid of music. "The notes of the violin tremble, pointing on high; one hears a humming of bees and flies, one sees the hot bright trembling summer air above the wild meadow, one feels the warm vapor from the dark earth, one breathes in the cool fragrance of strawberries,—all the tones burn in the vibrating glow of the sun" (p. 35). Grieg to the co-authors of the pamphlet was even more effective. Of his music they say: "Each chord drags behind it a weakness just like the mourning cloth of a black dress, the odor of faded funeral wreaths and the odor of a death room" (p. 35). To the painter Edvard Munch the authors devoted three pages, declaring that he had represented every vibration of color, even the last and weakest: "In his continual effort to hold fast the transitory, fickle shadings under the continual changes of light, Munch can paint only with perfect technique" (p. 37).

In literature the authors distinguished between intimate novels and intimate poetry. The intimate novel concerns itself with

[41] Jacobsen, the exemplar of the new art, to whom Dauthendey had dedicated *Josa Gerth* and whom he called his only prose master (*Gedankengut aus meinen Wanderjahren, Gesammelte Werke,* I, p. 558) is not mentioned here, although Dauthendey expressly stated some years later in the biographic *Gedankengut* that he was mentioned (*vide* footnote 23). How close a parallel there exists between the two poets may be seen from an excerpt by Hans Bethge, *Jens Peter Jacobsen* (Berlin, Axel Juncker, p. 83): "One may call Jacobsen a mystical pantheist. He revealed to us the pollen of the soul in man and thing. The hairs on the hands are endowed by him with soul, likewise the person's walk and the lines of the shoulders and also the sounds and colors of nature, the human voice, water, etc., everything that exists, —has a soul and contains a deep, mystical undertone. In a letter from Dresden dated 1873 he speaks of the splendor in the colors of a sunset and says that the bleeding red, the golden yellow and the fading gold lay there as a long silent ribbon and if the ear had been able to hear what the eyes saw, it would have become a clear, long drawn-out tone."

moods in the observed person, and depicts his feelings as influenced either by nature or by the proximity of other persons.[42] The intimate poet, however, seeks to experience "the joys of all the colors and their sadnesses; the lamenting violet blue, the brutal scarlet red, the slender, singing May-green and the resonant golden yellow. He renders all the shadings of the odors: the eager in the goading jasmin odor, the poignant sharpness in the odor of orange blossoms, the snowmelting warmth in the breath of roses, and the thunderstorm odor of the heliotropes" (p. 39). Similarly, among sounds the intimate poet describes "a bird's cry as flashing red lightning, the song of the thrush as blue silver vines, the splashing of water cascades as yellow fireflames. Likewise the sensations of warmth or cold: purple-red summer heat, tea-rose colored evening coolness, steelblue dewy dampness, etc." (p. 40).

A more succinct statement of this technique is to be found in Dauthendey's letter to Siegfried Loewenthal, dated Gjepperup, July 17, 1893: "When one hears a musical selection no-one asks: 'What is meant by that, what idea is expressed by this symphony?' That is incidental, just as one does not ask when enjoying a sunrise or a view from a mountain: 'What idea is expressed by this event, this morning glow?' We should simply enjoy the *pictures,* the sounds of pleasure and displeasure, which always ring in our brain unconsciously, when we enjoy the fragrance and the color of roses or jasmin, or hear the cuckoo's call, or breathe the fragrance of rain. These sounds of pleasure and displeasure which constitute the entire mood, and which stream towards us from roses and jasmin, the poet wants to awaken in the reader through the sad and joyful pictures which he draws, and thus arouse the same stimulation to pleasure and displeasure that roses and jasmin exert."[43]

Naturally a new style is demanded by the new intimate art. It can no longer employ the rhythm or rhyme of earlier poetry. The delicate shadings which are only weakly recognizable in the most intimate sense impressions can be rendered only in short quick sentences, in the one, embracing word in which the whole

---

[42] Dauthendey had attempted to do this in *Josa Gerth. Cp.* letter of October 18, 1891, *Ein Herz im Lärm der Welt,* p. 60: "Der Grundgedanke, daß sie (*i.e.,* Josa Gerth) durchs Leben wandelt und die Gestalten anderer an ihr beeinflussend vorüberziehen, ist geblieben."

[43] *Ein Herz im Lärm der Welt,* p. 119.

feeling is concentrated. (p. 40). In a letter of April 17, 1893, to Villinger and Loewenthal, Dauthendey wrote from Quille: "I try to become more and more concise in my poetry. The smallest superfluous word must disappear. I try to render sensations only with strong direct impressions, such as our senses receive."[44]

The co-authors of *Verdensaltet* knew very well that their theories would not be welcomed with open arms, and realized that to many these theories might seem insufficiently founded. But, had not this also happened to Wagner, Böcklin, and more recently to Munch? Gradually the importance of the new art will be realized. Finally it will become the natural thing, however much frowned upon at first (p. 42).

The poetry of the new intimate art can be enjoyed only if one surrenders himself to it completely. It does not aim to be didactic. It is to be produced from the depth of man's soul. It must likewise be enjoyed "in utter solitude,—such as when one lies dreaming in the grass and looks out into the blue, sitting close by another in the twilight, holding another's hands, very quietly, without conversation or thoughts, and only the twilight, the other's warm breath, warm hands, only the gray solitude speaking."[45]

The feelings with which the intimate art is concerned always existed. But the authors believed they had rediscovered them and had recalled them to our consciousness, opening to us a world which had previously lain within the realm of the unconscious. What the new intimate art strives to give is essentially "what an evening landscape, a nightingale, a rose give us" (p. 42).

While the first part of *Verdensaltet* gives a minute description of "Den intime Kunst," the new intimate art, the second part, entitled "Den sublime Kunst," endeavors to give the main tenets of the "new" universal religion which forms the foundation of the new intimate art. The authors were convinced that artists are indeed bound to a view of life, that they could not create lasting works of art nor have ideals concerning art without a philosophy of life. This Dauthendey later elaborated as follows: "Whoever maintains that artists are not bound by a view of the world, that they write, compose, paint, sculpture simply what pleases them, to him I should like to answer that the creations of artists

[44] *Op. cit.*, p. 116.
[45] One is reminded of Herman Gorter's *Mei, een gedicht*, familiar to both Dauthendey and Uddgren, which celebrates solitude as the highest ideal.

have always depended on the view of the world cherished by their nation and the era to which they belonged."[46]

As noted above[47] Dauthendey, in one of his letters to his Würzburg friends, remarked on the lucidity of Schopenhauer's style. He was particularly entranced by the descriptions of the concepts of "beautiful," "ugly," and "sublime." The concept of the sublime the co-authors believed to have disappeared entirely from the mental horizon of their contemporaries. Although both Kant and Schopenhauer had carefully delimited the concept, "erhaben," giving copious examples of it, Dauthendey and Uddgren did not have the circumscribed philosophers' definition in mind when writing the second part of *Verdensaltet*. In past ages, they argued, the sublime had been inspired by belief, first in gods, such as is evidenced in Greek art, then in the Trinity, as in the art of the Middle Ages (p. 64). Goethe's *Faust* and Byron's *Manfred* were among the last representative master-pieces inspired by a sublime art. With Schopenhauer's negation of the will, Darwin's theory of evolution, and Nietzsche's revaluation of the concepts of good and evil, the death blow had been dealt to religious belief and no substitute had been found. The formulation of a new metaphysics now became imperative if enduring master-pieces were to be created.

In the first part of "Den sublime Kunst," entitled "Det sublimes gamle form," "The old form of the sublime," the authors attempted to show how modern naturalism and realism failed to produce lasting contributions to art. A long preliminary discussion of atomism shows clearly Dauthendey's indebtedness to Villinger. We learn that in the entire universe there is a single great flux—the eternal life power of the eternal mass, power and mass being inseparably united (p. 59). Man, far from being an exalted being, like all other manifestations is only an accidental

---

[46] *Gedankengut aus meinen Wanderjahren, Gesammelte Werke*, I, p. 428. *Cp.* also *op. cit.*, p. 430: "The artist, however, was always bound by the philosophy of his period even when it was inimical. He always had to adapt himself to the philosophy of his era." The latter reference seems to be at variance with Dauthendey's claim to originality. However, he considered himself an innovator and believed that he was promulgating the philosophy basic for the new literature. *Cp.* also W. Dilthey, "Das Wesen der Philosophie," in *Die Kultur der Gegenwart* (Paul Hinneberg, editor), VI, 1924, p. 50: "Bis in die Melodie der Verse, in den Rhythmus der Gefühlsfolge ist die innere Form jeder wahren Dichtung durch die Bewußtseinsstellung des Poeten und seines Zeitalters bestimmt."

[47] Chapter III, page 26. *Cp.* also Dauthendey's letter of April 17, 1893, *Ein Herz im Lärm der Welt*, p. 117.

combination of atoms (p. 59). The atoms of which everything is composed are eternal. We have belonged to the same eternal mass from the remotest times and shall continue to belong to it throughout eternity (p. 60). Only when we become absorbed in the thought that we have always been part of the eternal life and mass do we begin to love eternal man (p. 60). Eternal force and eternal mass supplant the former bases of the sublime, humanity, creation, godhead. Since these concepts were invalidated by science, it seemed logical to found the new ideal on the atomistic findings of modern science.

A belief in the new bases of the sublime engenders a love for colors and sounds. The eternal sublime is no longer to be sought behind nature. "It is directly in the vibrations of colors, directly in sound waves, etc.," (p. 62). This belief inculcates the greatest love for everything that aids life. A pragmatic, hedonistic attitude is thus introduced when we learn that that which aids life because it benefits us and gives us feelings of joy is to be especially prized. A premium, then, is put on artists, since their creations exert a beneficial influence on their fellow-beings. This influence is most effective when artists select their subjects from the domain of the infinite sublime, the ideals of their time. Then they originate master-pieces (p. 64).

The realistic period in literature is characterized by a selection from Dostoyevsky's *Crime and Punishment*. With Raskalnikoff the authors agreed in valuing the importance of even such a menial task as cleaning sewers, but unlike him they naturally upheld the greater importance for society of the works of Raphael and Pushkin. Zola, Ibsen, Strindberg are evaluated briefly, and it is noted that not one of these authors occupies himself with "the eternal,—the strongest expression, under which the sublime in its new form 'eternal mass and eternal force' appears to our consciousness—with eternal nature, the eternal colors and eternal tones, with the most powerful movements of the sublime."[48]

The new sublime art is, therefore, founded on the emotional life of tones and colors, which are not mere ideas in our brains but are actual vibrations of pleasure and displeasure of the eternal

---

[48] Pp. 66 ff. A similar thought is voiced by Rjäbinin in Garschin's *Künstler*, as quoted in act II of Gerhart Hauptmann's *Einsame Menschen*. Dauthendey was familiar with Hauptmann's drama, which he praised in letters to Siegfried Loewenthal of June 18 and 22, 1891, *Ein Herz im Lärm der Welt*, pp. 24, 27.

mass about us. (p. 71). The artists of the new sublime art must teach us to experience all the degrees of vibration of colors and sounds from the strongest to the weakest. It is in nature unspoiled by trivial associations that one finds the emotional life portrayed to the fullest.

Although one no longer believes in a personal God nor in personal immortality, the concept of immortality is by no means dead. There is no absolute death, there are only forms which change, atoms which change places in creation. However, the universe, "the eternal mass," is everlasting, and it is from a love for the universe, for nature, that the new sublime art will grow. The sublime art is not a copying of nature nor of men, as in realistic or naturalistic art; it consists, rather, in depicting the eternal emotional life, *i.e.*, all nuances of the joy and sorrow of the universe (p. 73). Sublime art is thus concerned with "the rejoicing of the colors of the day, the lament of twilight, the chorals of the stars, the mighty life of spring, etc." (p. 75). It can be attained only through enthusiasm for the emotional life of the universe, indeed, "the new ideal of the sublime art is identical with the emotional life of the universe" (p. 77).

It appears, therefore, that in the philosophical passages of the second part of *Verdensaltet* little of a basic nature is said which cannot also be found in Villinger's thoughts as imparted to Dauthendey. To recapitulate, we are here apprized of an atomic surge endowed with eternal force. All atoms are sentient beings. Man has belonged to the eternal mass from time immemorial and will continue to do so *ad infinitum*. There is no master over him. He possesses everything and is possessed in turn by everything. There is no absolute death. There are only forms which change their pattern. Colors and sounds are the language of the universe. Strangely enough there is no reference to love, which later assumed the most prominent place in Dauthendey's metaphysical edifice.

In the restatement of *Gedankengut aus meinen Wanderjahren* we further learn that each atom experiences joy or sorrow and is an eternal ego with reason and emotion.[49] The atoms are not to be considered mere points from which there issue undirected forces. They are rather to be imagined as little suns and planets.[50] Each atom may contain a universe. One is reminded of Leibniz'

[49] *Gesammelte Werke*, I, p. 307.
[50] *Op. cit.*, p. 611.

monads. Unlike these, however, Dauthendey's atoms are not windowless, shut in, and activated according to a pre-established harmony. More nearly do they resemble the atoms of Fechner's metaphysical system and more closely those of Bruno Wille. There are also parallels to the philosophy of Giordano Bruno, but the latter's supreme governing principle of reason as contrasted with Dauthendey's paramount principle of emotion indicates an essential difference. The parallelism with Bruno is particularly apparent in the language in which thoughts are couched, as in the long lists of illustrative examples.[51]

When the authors of *Verdensaltet* declared the dethronement of man, whose form they thought "merely an accidental combination of atoms" (p. 59), and who, to them, was "merely the cleverest being with the greatest number of brain cells and not one who towers over other beings with an immortal soul" (p. 71), they voiced for the first time in Dauthendey's writings the concept of the equality of all natural phenomena, which assigned the same exalted or humble place to the smallest particle of matter no less than to man. This poetical, metaphysical "Communism," as Schneider very aptly calls it,[52] occupied Dauthendey throughout the remainder of his life. It is expressed in his repeated dictum that we are not slaves, the chattels of a single superior being, but that we possess everything and are in turn possessed by everything,[53] a thought analogous to Byron's

> Are not the mountains, waves and skies, a part
> Of me and of my soul, as I of them?[54]

[51] *Cp.* Giordano Bruno in *Von der Ursache, dem Prinzip und dem Einen.* Leipzig, 1902. "Philosophische Bibliothek," Band 21, p. 36: "Also ein toter Leichnam hat noch eine Seele? Also meine Schuhe, meine Pantoffeln, meine Stiefel, meine Sporen, mein Fingerring und meine Handschuhe sollen beseelt sein? Mein Rock und mein Mantel sind beseelt? . . ." *Cp.* Dauthendey: *Das Lied der Weltfestlichkeit, Gesammelte Werke*, V, p. 551:

> Geist ist aller Weltensame, Geist ist
> nicht der Mensch allein. Geist ist
> Staub. Und Geist ist Stein. Geist
> ist Laub und Holz und Bein.
> Alles Dasein, wie es heißt, alles Dasein,
> das ist Geist.

[52] *Op. cit.*, p. 335.

[53] *Gedankengut aus meinen Wanderjahren, Gesammelte Werke*, I, p. 312. See also variant forms, *op. cit.*, pp. 316, 326, 329, 330, 334, 351, 352, 371, 376, 813, 814, *et al.*

[54] Dauthendey had attended a performance of *Manfred* in Munich in 1892, *Gedankengut aus meinen Wanderjahren, Gesammelte Werke*, I, p. 431. The quotation also occurs in Schopenhauer's *Die Welt als Wille und Vorstellung*, paragraph 34, and was thus doubly familiar to Dauthendey.

Disregard of this leveling thought may lead to dire results, Dauthendey indicates in his description of the plight of the doomed passengers of the Titanic in *Die Untergangsstunde der Titanic:*

> Sie dünkten Schöpfer sich noch immer und blieben,
> ach, Geschöpfe bloß,[55]

which ends on the following note:

> Das Schicksalsbuch, darin ich weiterlas,
> Es schlug mir neue Bilder auf und Seiten.
> Doch zwischen neuen Zeilen ich es nie vergaß,
> Daß Menschen ihrem Tun den Untergang bereiten.
> Wenn nicht die Demut mit beim Werke saß.[56]

In language modeled after the Bible, the poet exhorts his readers to reveal to the proud, the tyrants, and the haughty, as well as to the humble, downtrodden and those weary of life, that everything and nothing belongs to them in the universe and that they shall enjoy everything as guests as well as furnish everything as hosts at the inexhaustible feast of their creative force.[57]

Dauthendey strove to embody his thoughts of the universal equivalence in numerous forms, perhaps most consistently in *Sehnsucht* and in *Sun*. In the latter the sounds of nature occur side by side with the soliloquies and dialogues of the human rôles, thus carrying this concept to its logical conclusion.

He believed disregard of this world-integration (Weltzusammengehörigkeit) to be responsible for the apparent estrangement of humanity from its original festive condition, from a solidarity which although natural in children is lost by human beings when grown. This thought he enunciates in *Gedankengut aus meinen Wanderjahren*[58] by way of summary, "He who believes himself superior, better, and nobler than the animals and plants and the earth and all things, simply because he is a human being, forfeits the connection with the world and with his own primeval state."

---

[55] *Gesammelte Werke,* IV, p. 721.
[56] Pp. 727. *Cp.* also, "Sommerelegie," *Weltspuk, Gesammelte Werke,* IV, p. 347:
> Gleich sind aller Dinge Endgeschicke,
> Aller, welche sich zu leben trauen.

[57] *Gedankengut aus meinen Wanderjahren, Gesammelte Werke,* I, pp. 351, 352. *Cp.* also "Häcksel und die Bergwerksflöhe," *Geschichten aus den vier Winden, Gesammelte Werke,* III, p. 289.
[58] *Gesammelte Werke,* I, p. 815.

V
SYNAESTHESIA

In his early poetic works—*Ultra Violett, Sun, Sehnsucht*—Dauthendey succeeded in erasing all barriers erected by a narrow aesthetics. Never had the dogmatic dicta of Lessing's *Laokoon* been more flagrantly violated. Thomson, Bodmer, Breitinger, Ewald Kleist, Heinse himself, were mild offenders compared with the Dauthendey of *Ultra Violett* and of the early dramolets. Rather than delimit the provinces of the arts, he deliberately erased their boundaries, since at bottom, he argued, the effects produced by them were identical. It must be emphasized, however, that he used this literary method not as a mere stylistic device, the result of deliberate mental constructions, but in a very sincere effort to formulate what he himself experienced. Impressions of odors, colors, and sounds became deeply ingrained in him, and, clamoring for synaesthetic combinations rather than for cool, realistic treatment, they combined to form poems.[1] Dauthendey had found it impossible to get at the core of things through hackneyed personifications: "The gods and knights of romanticism were to remain far behind." Instead, he "wished enthusiastically to reveal in completely new poems the romance of the formerly undiscovered life of the landscape, the language of things as such, without their entering into human form, without their assuming fairy-tale form."[2]

However, the language of everyday proved to be too defective to render the most intimate longings of natural phenomena. These Dauthendey believed could be truly expressed only through recourse to synaesthetic analogies. Only thus could the emotional language of the universe—sounds and colors—be expressed. Far from wishing to be modern or different at any cost, as his early critics thought, Dauthendey merely strove to impart through synaesthesia the intimate thoughts and the essence of all things. The logic of this procedure he had attempted to demonstrate in the first part of *Verdensaltet*. Although there had not been any deliberate effort by other artists to portray the underlying lan-

---

[1] Letter of March 3, 1893, *Ein Herz im Lärm der Welt*, pp. 108, 109.
[2] *Gedankengut aus meinen Wanderjahren, Gesammelte Werke*, I, p. 310. *Cp.* also *op. cit.*, p. 437.

guage of inanimate as well as animate life, there were nevertheless tendencies in the works of some of Dauthendey's contemporaries —Jacobsen, Maeterlinck, Ola Hansson, Przybyszewski,[3]—which approximated Dauthendey's conceptions. That he had a well-developed sense of color perception has been noted above, also the great influence of his sister Marie in stimulating his interest in colors. His Würzburg university friends, Villinger[4] and Loewenthal shared his interest in colors. In Uddgren, also, Dauthendey found a kindred spirit. Of him he wrote to Richard Dehmel: "Uddgren I like particularly well. His poems[5] are very intense color perceptions, and not only that, but he also throbs with an unusual sensitiveness."[6]

Dauthendey's letters of that period contain frequent references to his intense experience of colors. "Bells ringing and sunshine! What more does man desire: Sounds and colors, a world of satisfaction!" he exclaims, only to find that one "desires the enjoyment to be doubled, that one wants to feel that the reflection, the echo, moves another heart, and wants to revel with it again in enjoyment."[7] His painstaking work on *Josa Gerth* taught him that he "must still learn diligently to see, in order to be able to hold all the colors even to their last trembling echos."[8] The insistent spell of the multifarious colors taxed his carefully schooled

[3] Stanislaus Przybyszewski appears in Dauthendey's drama à clef *Maja* as Loge. Dauthendey found his way to him through Ola Hansson (*Gedankengut aus meinen Wanderjahren, Gesammelte Werke,* I, pp. 458, 460). Przybyszewski later defined Ola Hansson's use of synaesthesia as follows: "Symbolism is a bit of nature transformed into nerve vibrations, a bit of nature, which does not confine itself to a visual, auditory or tactile impression, but an impression, which flows down to the focus (Knotenpunkt) of all senses so as to cause the whole brain to vibrate from there." *Zur Psychologie des Individuums,* chapter II, "Ola Hansson," p. 37. Berlin, F. Fontane: 1897.

[4] Villinger probably had Max Dauthendey in mind when discussing those gifted with special aptitude for color-sensations in *Das Buch vom Wesen aller Dinge,* p. 86: "Besondere Anlagen für Farbenempfindungen äußern sich in einem guten Gedächtnis für Gesehenes: solche Menschen denken an Gesehenes, falls sie nicht musikalisch (im weitern Sinne) sind, erzählen von Gesehenem: von Natur, von Gemälden . . . : sie beschreiben genauer Gesehenes: sie lieben die Natur, Gemälde, und zwar besonders farbenprächtige: sie haben ein gutes Personengedächtnis: sie haben Verständnis für Farben: sie kleiden sich gerne mit harmonischen Farben. Sie können sich mit sich selbst unterhalten, in der Erinnerung und Kombination ihrer stillen Farbenempfindungen, ohne sich zu langweilen."

[5] Particularly *Balders Återkomst och andra Dikter,* Stockholm, 1895: Andreens Boktryckeri. *Balders Återkomst, Episk Dikt* was written in Berlin in 1892-1893.

[6] Unpublished letter, undated, probably *Verdensaltet* period.

[7] Letter of June 24, 1891, *Ein Herz im Lärm der Welt,* p. 29.

[8] Letter of December 19, 1891, *op. cit.,* p. 68.

M. DAUTHENDAY, PARIS STUDIEN IN STILISIERTEN ROSEN

Designs for Embroidery by Max Dauthendey, *Dekorative Kunst*, IV, 1899, p. 204.

verbal technique to the limit. Discouraged at his lack of progress he confessed: "I always begin to stammer and stumble with language when I perceive most passionately. Then everything sways in me, and words are not to be found in that chaos. I should then like best of all to take a brush full of colors and paint everything I feel in glowing flames."[9] Dauthendey not only used colors to express his feelings, but often sought inspiration from colors in themselves. Thus he enthusiastically recounts his procedure in writing *Sehnsucht* in a letter of December 18, 1892, "I bought myself six marks worth of aniline dyes. Daubing about with them, I gather inspiration for the various moods-in-color of my drama, *Sehnsucht*. It is delightfully pleasant to look at this beaming and blossoming and to become sated with it."[10]

Synaesthesia seemed to furnish the key for unlocking the psychic life of the universe. Color vision, *audition colorée, farbiges Hören,* or synaesthesia,[11] as it is known in its most comprehensive

---

[9] Letter of August 23, 1891, *op. cit.*, p. 52. During the nineties it was not unusual for poets to try to recapture the spirit of painting in words. As Richard Hamann points out (*Der Impressionismus in Leben und Kunst.* Köln, 1907, p. 95) the *Blätter für die Kunst* are replete with these attempts. In the first part of *Ultra Violett*, written before Dauthendey's close communion with nature on the west coast of Sweden, there are no less than seven recreations of paintings in words. The original art works are listed in the rare first small printing of *Ultra Violett*. Since mention of them is omitted in the easily available reprint in *Gesammelte Werke*, it might be of interest to enumerate them here: "Paradies" (p. 11), by Viggo Petersen; "A Vespero" (p. 12), by Gerolamo Cairato; "Das heilige Feuer" (p. 15), by Otto Sinding; "Die Welle" (p. 17), by Julius Exter; "Frühling" (p. 38), by Ludwig von Hofmann; "Wintersonne" (p. 40), by Hans Olde; and "Flucht nach Egypten" (p. 42), by xxx. A comparison with reproductions of the originals shows Dauthendey's keen sense of observation for coloristic details. Naturally these preliminary efforts did not long occupy the future master of direct nature impressions.

[10] Deleted from the published version, *Ein Herz im Lärm der Welt*, pp. 80 ff. "In meinem Zimmer sieht es jetzt aus wie bei einem Dekorationsmaler. Denkt Euch, ich habe mir für sechs Mark Anilinfarben gekauft. Und nun schmier ich Anregung für die verschiedenen in Farben wühlenden Stimmungsbilder meines Dramas *Sehnsucht*.—Ach, es ist so köstlich, so wohlig, dies bunte leuchtende Blühen zu schauen, und sich zu sättigen."

[11] Erika von Erhardt-Siebold, *PMLA*, XLVII, no. 2 (June, 1932), pp. 580, 582, defines synaesthesia as "that curious faculty of harmony between the senses, whereby a given strong impulse not only causes the sense actually stimulated to respond, but compels other senses to vibrate simultaneously." D. F. Fraser-Harris in *Coloured Thinking and Other Studies in Science and Literature* (Brentano's, N.Y., 1928, pp. 1-31) states (p. 1) that "the linking together of any two kinds of sensation is called synaesthesia; of all the possible synaesthesiae, the linking of color and sound is the commonest." He distinguishes between "colored *thinking*" ("chromatic mentation"), on the one hand, and "colored *hearing*," on the other hand.

form, "that curious cross-circuiting of the senses" as J. E. Downey calls it,[12] is still for the most part viewed with suspicion, as the peculiar province of decadents. Nevertheless, evidences of the phenomenon may be found in everyday life. Thus we often hear of a "loud" tie, a "dark" sound, we see "red," etc.[13]

Friedrich Mahling in a study called "Zeugnisse aus der schönen Literatur"[14] gives a cursory treatment of synaesthesia. He mentions among those who use it in varying degrees E. T. A. Hoffmann, Tieck, Goethe in the Eckermann conversations, Eduard Mörike, Otto Ludwig, Grillparzer, Ganghofer, Gerstäcker, Hartleben, Löns, Gottfried Keller, Gautier, Huysmans, Rimbaud, Baudelaire, Ghil, Verlaine, Maupassant. Curiously enough, he omits Max Dauthendey.[15] In her discussion of this subject Erika von Erhardt Siebold[16] subjects English literature to a very searching study, incidentally citing many examples from French and German Romanticism.[17]

[12] *Creative Imagination. Studies in the Psychology of Literature*, N.Y., 1929; Harcourt, Brace and Co. P. 92. *Cp.* also her article: "Literary Synaesthesia," in *The Journal of Philosophy, Psychology and Scientific Methods*, Vol. IX, 18: August 29, 1912, pp. 490-498.

[13] The literature on synaesthesia is voluminous. In 1927 there appeared as the outgrowth of the "Farbe-Ton-Kongress" held at Hamburg, a special volume devoted to it: *Farbe-Ton-Forschungen*, Volume I, by Georg Anschütz, Heinrich Heinz, Friedrich Mahling. The bibliography of this work (pp. 398-432) lists about 650 separate studies. To this very extensive list may be added the following pertinent contributions: Hermann Bahr: *Kritik der Moderne*, III, Berlin, 1895: S. Fischer. S. S. Epstein: "Sinnesvikarität in der Poesie." *Die Gesellschaft*, 1895, pp. 661-671. D. F. Fraser-Harris: *op. cit.* Carl Mumm, *op. cit.* Franz Rauhut: "Das Romantische und Musikalische in der Lyrik Stephan Mallarmés," *Die neueren Sprachen*, Beiheft no. II, Marburg a. d. Lahn, 1926. Luise Thon: *Die Sprache des deutschen Impressionismus*, Munich, 1928: Max Hueber Verlag. G. L. van Roosbroeck: "Decadence and Rimbaud's Sonnet of the Vowels," *The Romanic Review*, XVI, 2 (April-June), 1925, pp. 122-135, also in *The Legend of the Decadents*, Institut des Études Françaises, Columbia University, 1927, pp. 21-39. Erika von Erhardt Siebold, *op. cit.*

[14] *Farbe-Ton-Forschungen, op. cit.*, pp. 350-362.

[15] Dauthendey's name is also absent from the bibliography mentioned above.

[16] "Synaesthesien in der englischen Dichtung des 19. Jahrhunderts. Ein ästhetisch-psychologischer Versuch." *Englische Studien*, Leipzig, 53. Band, 1919-1920, pp. 1-157, 196-334. Carl Mumm's discussion of Dauthendey's synaesthetic examples takes its departure from this well-known study. Luise Thon's account of Dauthendey, *loc. cit.*, is in turn indebted primarily to Carl Mumm's dissertation.

[17] Synaesthesia was very common among the German Romanticists, both in theory and practice. Special studies are: Hermann Petrich: *Drei Kapitel vom romantischen Stil*. Leipzig, 1878; Walter Steinert: *Ludwig Tieck und das Farbenempfinden der romantischen Dichtung*. Dortmund, 1910; Ludwig Wagner: *Über Joseph Görres Sprache und Stil*. Strassburg, 1914 (pp. 16-20); Paul Margis: "Synaesthesien bei E. T. A. Hoffmann," *Zeitschrift für Ästhetik und allgemeine Kunstwissenschaft*, V. 1.

A typical psycho-chromaesthete, as Fraser-Harris calls a person endowed with the faculty of colored thinking, has his associations fixed at an early age. Other characteristics are "the unchangeableness of the color thought of," "the extreme definiteness in the minds of the possessors," "the complete non-agreement between the various colors attached to the same concept in the minds of colored thinkers," "the unaccountableness of psychochromes" and lastly, "the hereditary or at least inborn nature of the condition."[18]

To a certain extent these conditions seem to obtain also for synaesthetes, although, as Fraser-Harris points out, a psycho-chromaesthete is not necessarily a synaesthete.[19] Similarly, Mahling insists that "Belege" from the belles-lettres should be used in a methodical treatment of *audition colorée* with great reserve,[20] as frequently they are merely the result of artificial construction and are not genuinely experienced.

Under chromatic mentation,[21] Fraser-Harris treats sound-, taste-, odor-, touch-, temperature-, and pain-photisms, while syn-

---

Heft, 1910. The employment of images suggested by one sense to illustrate the effect of another is a common device in a certain kind of modern prose. In cursory reading I have noted the following instances which are not listed elsewhere: "There is a romantic sweep and glow to the score, there are colors of purple and gold in the instrumentation . . . ," Olin Downes in a review of a performance of *Tristan und Isolde*, *New York Times*, November 7, 1930, p. 33. "Aus seinem Munde steigt die silberne Melodie wie eine Fontäne ins Blau, funkelnde Töne in allen Farben, doch zumeist rosa, hellgrün und lila," Frank Thieß, "Tropische Dämmerung," in *Der Kampf mit dem Engel*, Stuttgart, 1928: J. Engelhorns Nachfolger, p. 231. " 'A wonderful voice—it's like a big red poppy or a great yellow orchid!' cried Eugene," Theodore Dreiser, *The Genius*, New York, 1927: Boni and Liveright, thirteenth printing, p. 147. "Dann aber drang der warme Alt ihrer dunkelblauen Stimme in ihn . . .," Stefan Großmann, *Chefredakteur Roth führt Krieg*, Berlin, 1928: Paul Zsolnay, p. 164. " 'Ach,' sagte Gertrud und starrte in das Abendrot hinein, 'die schönsten Farben sind doch die schönste Musik,' " Eduard von Keyserling, *Abendliche Häuser, Gesammelte Erzählungen in vier Bänden*. Berlin, S. Fischer, 1922, p. 64. ". . . in so großen symphonischen Akkorden rauschten diese Farben daher." Richard Muther, *Geschichte der Malerei*, III., *18. und 19. Jahrhundert*. Berlin, 1920, p. 337. "Het was als zongen de lichte stralen," Frederik van Eeden, *De kleine Johannes*, 's Gravenhage, 1922, p. 185. "Die Edelsteinriemen, die glitzernden Brustschmucke und Stirnbinden aus Edelmetall kreischten Lichtgesänge, umtobt, umheult von der Farbenorgie der Perlen, Amethyste, Bernsteine, Opale, . . ." Eduard Stucken, *Die weißen Götter*, II. Berlin, Deutsche Buch-Gemeinschaft, 1931, p. 71.

[18] *Op. cit.*, pp. 18-20.
[19] *Op. cit.*, p. 2.
[20] *Op. cit.*, p. 349.
[21] A striking example of chromatic mentation in Dauthendey's works is the association of "gray" with Richard Dehmel, letter of February, 1893, to Villinger and Loewenthal, *Ein Herz im Lärm der Welt*, pp. 100, 101. It was this adjective

aesthesia proper he subdivides into light- or color-, taste-, odor-, touch-, temperature-, and pain-phonisms. Further divisions are, of course, possible, such as the fragrance of moon light, for which he ventures the term "light olfaction." Erika von Erhardt-Siebold in "Synaesthesien in der englischen Literatur des 19. Jahrhunderts," gives detailed subdivisions. Of particular interest for this study are her sections on "Ton-Farbe."[22]

To a certain extent Dauthendey was familiar with the pseudoscientific lore concerning synaesthesia. In a letter of June 5, 1891, he enthusiastically quotes a newspaper article about Maeterlinck in whose works "feelings are inhaled, odors are tasted, sounds are seen, and every sunbeam is heard."[23] Dr. Wicking and Dauthendey's *alter ego*, Josa Gerth, in the novel of that name, discuss colors and compare each color with a shrill or soft tone. They also discuss vicarious sense impressions.[24]

We obtain a glimpse into Dauthendey's poetic workshop in an unpublished contemporary notebook, where he describes his color technique as follows: "First mention the basic color of the poetic work, then paint the individual colors. But not all the indifferent ones; select only the most exciting of them. Do not describe the skeleton. Do not repeat what as a matter of course constructs itself in the imagination of the reader. Paint only that which is characteristic to an extraordinary degree. Like music the versification must sway with the mood. It must become faster, more concise, and more inclusive. Rhymed indifferently and in a gnarled fashion according to the intensity of the content."[25]

---

rather than a more colorful one which he repeatedly associates with Richard Dehmel although in the early nineties their friendship was exceedingly intimate, as appears from several unpublished letters in the Dehmel-Archiv. Thus Dauthendey's first timid letter of January 24, 1893: "Sehr geehrter Herr, der mir befreundete Herr Przybyszewski, hat Sie mir empfohlen. Er glaubt mein Buch könne Sie interessieren. Ich erlaube mir es Ihnen zu senden. Mit hochachtungsvollem Gruß Max Dauthendey" contrasts sharply with the demonstrative letters written shortly after this: "Morgens vier Uhr . . . ich schlafe nicht und schwelge noch in Stimmung." "Es ist wie rote Musik in mir und um mich, ich horche und starre in meine Sehnsucht, und solch ein Drängen, und Gedanken schlagen Wurzeln und treiben Keime, und eine Schaffenslust! Diese Freundschaft ist wie Frühling in mein Blut gedrungen." *Cf.* also Dehmel's poem "Entbietung" dedicated to Dauthendey, published in *Lebensblätter* (Berlin, Verlag der Genossenschaft Pan, 1895, p. 63).

[22] *Loc. cit.*, pp. 83-85, 109, 110, 125, 153.
[23] *Ein Herz im Lärm der Welt*, p. 15.
[24] *Josa Gerth, Gesammelte Werke*, III, p. 497.
[25] Nachlaß, Traben: "Erst die Grundfarbe der Dichtung nennen, dann die Einzelfarben malen. Aber nicht alle gleichgültigen, nur die erregendsten unter ihnen

Examples of the use of synaesthetic analogies dominate *Ultra Violett,* although there are also a number in *Reliquien* and in *Sun* and *Sehnsucht.* They have been studied from stylistic principles by Carl Mumm, and it is, therefore, unnecessary to repeat that type of analysis here. Instead, a few representative instances culled mainly from *Ultra Violett* will suffice to show how Dauthendey's dictum: "Tones and colors are the emotional language of the universe" was carried out:

Ultra Violett: "Oben schmettert das Licht in Posaunen, die Sonnenbrände wirbeln und über die Laubkronen brausen die grünen Feuer" (p. 11). " . . . dasselbe nachdenklich schweigende Blau" (p. 11). "Die Sonne fällt zur Erde. Gellend zerspringt ihr Licht" (p. 12). " . . . gellende Strahlstöße, fletschende Goldbrunst" (p. 12). " . . . das rote Dunkel stöhnt im Laube" (p. 13). " . . . die gelbe Wut" (p. 13). "Alles, alles singt in Farben und Düften" (p. 14). "Ihr Gesang müde, rot wie das Abendlicht" (15). " . . . gläsernes Schweigen" (15). " . . . dies . . . knirschende . . . Rostrot" (p. 16).

Reliquien: " . . . dein rötestes Lachen" (p. 112). " . . . jungblaue Triebe" (p. 112). "Um mich brennt rot die Angst als letzter Schein" (p. 130).

Die ewige Hochzeit: " . . . wie blanker Stolz" (p. 196). "Mit roter Geigen Genuß" (p. 198).

Striking as these instances are, the effect heightened by the use of strange or paradoxical epithets, they are not intended to be mere adornments of style, and hence cannot be fathomed by a purely stylistic approach. Rather, they are intended to conjure up the artist's mood when he first contemplated a scene, completely surrendered to the effect it produced on his senses. These synaesthetic renderings thus represent the same experience recorded by different instruments. To one initiated they supposedly invoke the original mood. Illustrative of this early striving after the emotional language of the universe are a number of unpublished notebooks of this period.[26] The notebook habit was characteristic of the Naturalistic writers. While with them, however, notes were taken with the utmost attention to accuracy of detail, so that

---

aussuchen. Und das Gerippe nicht beschreiben. Das, was schon in der Phantasie des Lesers sich alltäglich konstruiert, nicht wiederholen. . . . Nur das außerordentlich Charakteristische malen. Versmaß muß mit der Stimmung wie Musik wanken. Und schneller, knapper und gedehnter werden. Gleichgültig und knorrig gereimt je nach der Wucht des Inhalts."

[26] *Gedankengut aus meinen Wanderjahren, Gesammelte Werke,* I, p. 334.

they resembled photographs, Dauthendey's notebooks represent a day-by-day record of his communion with nature, the language of natural phenomena themselves, as he believed. An excerpt from such a notebook will illustrate their uniqueness. It is part of a sequence written in March, 1894, during Dauthendey's trip to London in the company of Gustaf Uddgren. In the style advocated by *Verdensaltet* it renders the moods engendered in the poet by the approach to the English coast:

Sonnabend Mittag 17. März.

Blaurosiger scharfer Streif die englische Küste. Das Wasser schwül malvengrün schleimgrün beinfahl.—

Heliotropblauer, dunkelschärfig glüht die Küste. Schwarze Segelboote, scharf mit scharfen Segelflügeln, stehen lautlos, schwinden lautlos. Ziehen stumm schwarz durch das laute hackende Sonnensilber. Mattweiß schwüle Wolkendämmer.—

Sonnenruhe.

Im schrillen weißen Feuerregen das Mittagmeer.—

Durch die silberne siedende Flut stechen steifschwarze Segelbote—

Wolkenwellen dumpfweiß lagern am Horizont. Silberfrisch das Wasser. Blankbleich der Sonnenhimmel. Dröhnend stößt der Kiel schwarz und schwarz Taue und Mast vorwärts. Öde Wellen waschen im nackten Wühlen.

Just as in Eichendorff's life the year 1808 is particularly rich in synaesthetic references, which later cease almost entirely, a fact which led Josef Nadler to think that it was merely a literary mannerism,[27] so also in Dauthendey's life instances are particularly abundant for the years 1890-1893. The paucity of examples of synaesthesia in Dauthendey's later life[28] seems to suggest that

[27] *Eichendorffs Lyrik. Ihre Technik und ihre Geschichte.* Prag. 1908. P. 31.

[28] Thus, in a letter to Gertraud Rostosky, September 7, 1915, (*Das Literarische Echo*, XXIII, 10, p. 584), in a discussion of Javanese music: "Diese Musik ist so traumhaft. . . . Das ist die Musik, die man hören würde, wenn Mondschein Musik würde, wenn Tautropfen Musik würden, wenn Orangenduft Musik würde, und wenn die zarte Tanzbewegung schöner nackter Javaninnen Musik würde und auch wenn ein angezündetes Feuer Töne, flackernde und gereizte, in Musik abbrennen würde." In "Ameisenarbeit," an unpublished poem written February 13, 1917, there occur several instances of literary synaesthesia:

"Heimweh's Qualen,
Im Herbste singen es die Farbenstrahlen."
"Die Sterne droben singen mit den Strahlen,"
"Wir wissen, daß der Rosen Röte singt,"

cf. also "Ablehnung des Paradieses," *Berliner Tageblatt, Abendblatt,* June 12, 1928:

"Licht in den Steinen, Licht im Klang,
Der Garten aus dem Geist des Lichtes sang."

they were not genuine physiologic experiences.[29] Neither, however, do they seem to have been deliberately constructed poetic devices. The poet's mouthpiece, Sun, speaks of the intuitive rather than the intentional quality of his analogies:

> Nie vertrauen sich mir die Lebensbilder der Dinge,
> Wenn ich sie zwingen will.
> Nur wenn ich einsam, still am Schweigen sauge
> Und tief allein all meine Sinne lauschen,
> Dann öffnen blühend sich
> Der Farben, der Düfte, der Töne Stimmen,
> Und ihre Bildermeere rauschen durch mein Auge.[30]

The utter lack of comprehension on the part of Dauthendey's first critics was due largely to a failure to understand what the poet had endeavored to do. Dauthendey graphically described the contempt in which his early poetry was held and his difficulty in trying to have his later works judged on their own merits. Critics continually invoked the rubber-stamp classification of the early reviewers of "Auferstehung,"[31] the first appearance in print of a work characteristic of his "new intimate art." With "Auferstehung" Dauthendey summoned upon his head the critical opprobrium which together with the later publication of *Ultra Violett, Sun, Sehnsucht,* and *Reliquien,* made him the laughing-stock of the nation,[32] the subject of numerous parodies and caricatures.[33]

---

[29] Walter Steinert came to the conclusion: "Die Vertauschung von Ton und Farbe scheint bei Goethe rein stilistischer Natur zu sein, d.h. keinem unmittelbaren psychologischen Zwang zu entspringen" (*Op cit.,* p. 18). June E. Downey was likewise led to the conclusion ("Literary Synaesthesia," *loc. cit.,* p. 497) "that while there is very slight evidence that the chosen poets experienced true synaesthesia, there is some justification in concluding that they enjoy, more than the ordinary reader, analogies between the senses." Similarly Arthur Symonds considers the use of synaesthesia in Baudelaire's *Les paradis artificiels* "quite natural, and any poetic mind, in a sane and normal state, easily imagines such analogies." (Baudelaire, *Prose and Poetry,* N.Y.: Albert and Charles Boni. P. 256).

That Dauthendey was easily swayed by impressions and that they enabled him to invoke analogous situations is evident from an excerpt from Mrs. Dauthendey's diaries of April 15, 1908, when Dauthendey was composing *Die geflügelte Erde,* two years after he had experienced the original impressions: "Während Max Indien schreibt, will er nur scharfes Essen haben, kein Kochfleisch."

[30] *Gesammelte Werke,* VI, p. 22.

[31] *Moderner Musenalmanach auf das Jahr 1893,* Munich, 1893, pp. 261-263; reprinted in *Ultra Violett, Gesammelte Werke,* IV, pp. 18, 19.

[32] *Gedankengut aus meinen Wanderjahren, Gesammelte Werke* I, p. 552. The vitriolic nature of the first reviews appears from the following excerpts. "Da hat ein Herr Max Dauthendey seine milde Hand aufgetan und uns eine A u f e r s t e h u n g

MAXIMILIAN DAUTHENDEY

SUN
DRAMA

SEHNSUCHT
DRAMA

BERLIN S.W.
BUCHDRUCKEREI MAX HAASE, ALTE JACOBSTRASSE 108

Title page of *Sun, Sehnsucht*

Gedankengut aus meinen Wanderjahren eloquently bears testimony to Dauthendey's long and weary striving to escape the fate of being forever judged solely on the basis of his youthful works.

---

beschert" says F. R. in the *Berliner Tageblatt* (1. Beiblatt, Nr. 38, January 21, 1893). "Es ist grober Unfug, so mit der Kunst umzuspringen, vernünftig denkenden Menschen solche Ungetüme von Bildern aufzudrängen. Wer so die seit Jahrhunderten giltigen Modelle der Kunst über den Haufen wirft, dem muß der mit den Musen angerufene Apoll in den modifizierten Worten des Heilandes zurufen: 'Mein Haus ist ein Bethaus, Ihr aber habt es zum Narrenhaus gemacht.'" While admitting the occasional aptness of synaesthetic experiences in poetry, the critic continues: "Herr Dauthendey sieht also alles Mögliche, und so muß man schließlich zu dem Resultat kommen, daß hier neben einer nervös überspannten Empfindsamkeit auch noch die Sucht hinzukommt, sich hervorzutun und durch das denkbar Ungewöhnlichste, die Aufmerksamkeit auf sich zu ziehen. Ich hätte diesem Meisterschaftsdichter keine so große Beachtung zugewandt, wenn er nicht typisch wäre für die ganze hier vertretene Lyrik." In a similar vein Constantin Brunner condemns Dauthendey in an article entitled "Unsere Lyrik und die 'Aufbrütesamen'" (*Der Zuschauer*, I, 1, February 15, 1893, p. 11): "Ich bin weit entfernt davon, auf den allgemeinen Prügeljungen mit einhauen zu wollen, sowie mir denn überhaupt jede Absicht auf Persönliches fern liegt. Mir ist es nur um den Typus zu tun, und insofern habe ich es allerdings als ein erfreuliches Zeichen begrüßt, als man einmal den Blödsinn hinstellte als das was er ist. Das aber muß gerade betont werden, daß es sich hier keineswegs um einzelne Sonderlinge, sondern um einen Typus handelt. . . . Da sind mir gleich zwei zur Hand: Max Dauthendey und Peter Hille, die viele andere um Haupteslänge überragen. Es dürfte schwer zu bestimmen sein, wer von den beiden den Vogel abgeschossen hat." Concerning "Auferstehung" Brunner says (p. 12): "Man achte in dem angeführten Beispiel auf den gänzlich entarteten Farbensinn, eine Erscheinung, die sich bei allen Aufbrütesamen findet und die eine symptomatische Bedeutung für die ganze Klasse hat." A fellow poet, Otto Ernst, in his article "Richtungs- und Klicquendichtung" (*Das Magazin für Litteratur*, LXIII, June 9, 1894, Nr. 23, column 708) joined the general condemnation of the poet of "Auferstehung": "Das Schlimmste in der soll- und mußmodernen Kunstmacherei leistet bekanntlich Dauthendey. Ich glaube aber, der Mann hat seine Herausgeber, Verleger und Bewunderer zum besten, und sie merken es nicht; ich würde mich wenigstens nicht wundern, wenn er sich eines Tages als loser Schalk entpuppte, der als Excentric-Clown auf dem überspannten Nervenseil die impotenten Empfindungsfexen genasführt hat. Wie mag er wohl im Stillen lachen, wenn er sieht, daß diese Leute eine verteufelt alte und bekannte Sache für 'modern' nehmen, daß sie gereimte 'Fälle' von vikariirenden Sinnesempfindungen oder besser: von vikariirenden Bezeichnungen als 'Gedichte' hinnehmen! . . . Diese Dauthendeyschen Experimente, diese Monstra an kunstfeindlicher, barbarischer Absichtlichkeit und die Aufnahme, die sie gefunden, sind von symptomatischer Bedeutung. Der Modernitätraptus ist nämlich wirklich so weit fortgeschritten und hat auch die respektabelsten Gehirne so verwirrt, daß man diese Stoppeleien e r n s t nehmen konnte! Man konnte sie ernst nehmen ohne das tiefste Bedauern für den Verfasser!" Theodor von Sosnosky comes to the rescue of the *Musenalmanach* by stating (*Deutsche Revue*, XIX, 3, July, 1894, pp. 117, 118): "Zur Ehre des Almanachs sei übrigens gesagt, daß die Ergüsse des Herrn Dauthendey auch das Alleräußerste sind."

[33] A first attempt to treat this phase is Alfred Richard Meyer's article "Dauthendey in der Karikatur" (*Max Dauthendey Gemeinschaft Rundbrief* Nr. 2, 1934, pp. 3-6), which is concerned with caricatures in the *Aeolsharfenalmanach* (1896)

That Dauthendey met with lack of understanding even in those close to him appears from the dramolet, *Sun*, written in Berlin during the summer of 1894.[34] Although the scene is set in a prehistoric village among dawn men ridden by tabus, it is evident that the dramolet is intensely personal. Sun obviously is the poet himself, the prophet of a new art, misunderstood by family, friends, and others alike. Even Bethe, his affianced, who apparently was modeled after Uddgren's sister, at last deserts the prophet, who almost succumbs to despair, but finds solace in intimate communion with nature, much as the poet had in the Swedish province of Bohuslän.

Richard Dehmel and Hermann Bahr stand rather isolated among German poets in appreciating Dauthendey's early poetic attempts, the former believing the "Farbenwortgewühle" to be the immediate language of Dauthendey's psyche,[35] while the latter tells how at times he read Dauthendey's *Ultra Violett* for hours with complete enjoyment, but at other times found the poems quite meaningless. Not until he met Dauthendey and learned that the close communion with nature in Sweden had conditioned these poems and that they represented the emotional life and language of natural phenomena, was he able to read them at all times with complete enjoyment and understanding.[36] He then gave Dauthendey the advice to write the biography of his poems first if he would be certain of their effect on his readers. This was, perhaps, the earliest suggestion to Dauthendey of *Gedankengut aus meinen*

---

of the "Allgemeine Deutsche Reimverein" (*i.e.*, Julius Stinde, Heinrich Seidel, Johannes Trojan, Julius Lohmeyer, Ludwig Pietsch), Martin Möbius's (*i.e.* Bierbaum's) *Steckbriefe* (1900), and Franz Blei's *Großes Bestiarium der Literatur* (Berlin, 1924). Other pertinent caricatures are the Danish ones mentioned in footnote 1 of chapter IV (p. 41), Hanns von Gumppenberg's *Das Teutsche Dichterroß in allen Gangarten* (1929, 13th and 14th editions, p. 84: "Am Brunnen," p. 85: "Taschenspieleraugen," p. 86: "Im Dunklen ist gut funkeln," p. 87: "Melancholie," p. 87: "In der Bibliothek," p. 89: "Das Gartenhaus") and Christian Morgenstern's *Palmström* (Berlin, 1920, p. 24: "Die Geruchs-Orgel," p. 25: "Der Aromat"). For caricatures of the poet himself *cf.* footnotes 25, 26, 27 of chapter I (p. 5).

[34] For a discussion of this play *cp. Gedankengut aus meinen Wanderjahren, Gesammelte Werke*, I, pp. 590-595, and Wilhelm Annecke, *op. cit.*, pp. 13-16.

[35] Richard Dehmel, *Ausgewählte Briefe*. Berlin, 1923: S. Fischer Verlag. P. 155. For his attitude concerning the emotional quality of color words *cp.* his *Bekenntnisse, op. cit.*, p. 23.

[36] *Renaissance, neue Studien zur Kritik der Moderne*. Berlin, 1897: S. Fischer. "Colour Music," pp. 59-66. Also in *Das Hermann-Bahr-Buch*. Berlin: S. Fischer, pp. 129-135.

Wanderjahren, the first title of which was "Die Geburtsstunden meiner Bücher."[37] What Dauthendey had failed to see was that synaesthetic experiences vary from individual to individual, constant though they may be in the same individual. When the poems of the *Verdensaltet* period invoked the original sensations in him, he failed to see that others would not necessarily be similarly affected. However, with a full understanding of the background of the poems, one may enjoy them as intimate revelations of delicately perceived moods of nature. When experienced in this light they no longer appear as the monstrosities his hostile critics believed them to be. Although the art as enunciated and advocated in *Verdensaltet* was but a transitional one in Dauthendey's career, it was essential for the development of his view of the world, and as such deserves a greater amount of attention than is usually accorded it.

[37] Compare excerpts from Mrs. Dauthendey's diary of August 13, 1911: "Nach dem Bade eingefallen, Buch: 'Die Geburtsstunden meiner Bücher.' Darin will er sein ganzes Leben wahrheitsgetreu beschreiben, soweit es mit der Entstehung seiner Bücher zusammenhängt. Er will darin alle seine Handlungen begründen, damit später nichts durch Kritik verdreht und entstellt werden kann."

VI
"UNIVERSAL LANGUAGE"

The main object of the "new" intimate art and of the "new" sublime art was to discover the emotional language of the universe. This idea never left the poet throughout his subsequent writings, and he returned to it with renewed vigor during the brooding self-centered years of his Java "captivity." It was the apparently bleak rocky coast-line of Bohuslän that first opened to him the secret of the universal language which he believed to be dormant in all of us. Francis of Assisi had considered the animate and inanimate world as his brethren, Giordano Bruno and Leibniz had endowed inanimate nature with life, Gustav Fechner, Alfred Lotze, Bruno Wille and Wilhelm Bölsche had attempted proofs of panpsychism. Max Dauthendey, apparently little versed in the views held by these philosophers, developed the idea of panpsychism to its logical conclusion by assuming an underlying universal language of all phenomena.

For a time Dauthendey seems to have broken his contact with nature when new worries overwhelmed the formerly carefree youth:

> Meine Augen voll Asche,
> Meine Ohren haben die Töne verloren,
> Bäume, Wind, Gestein,
> Eure Sprache fällt mir nicht mehr ein.
> Höre im Weltraum nur mich,
> Mein wildes, hungerndes Ich.[1]

However, he soon regained the magic gift and through the remainder of his life there are constant references to the universal nature language in his works. The gyrations of the swallows in the air,[2] the winding of the Main,[3] the sign language of doves and of the sun,[4] the magic formulas of the crickets,[5] of the ravens

---

[1] *Reliquien, Gesammelte Werke,* IV, p. 117.

[2] *Lusamgärtlein, Gesammelte Werke,* IV, p. 279. "Die Schwalben schossen vorüber tief dir zu Füßen."

[3] *Lusamgärtlein, Gesammelte Werke,* IV, p. 258: "Versonnen wie die Augenblicke, von denen keine Tafeln schreiben."

[4] *Weltspuk, Gesammelte Werke,* IV, p. 359, "Tauben und Sonne."

[5] *Op. cit., Gesammelte Werke,* IV, p. 217, "Die Grillen behexen die Sommernacht."

and of the sky,[6] the fire with its glowing gesture of love,[7] all have a language decipherable by him who would but take the trouble to do so. One need only hearken to the revelations of life about one. For in ourselves there are the forces of all lives. We can understand all lives if we but wish, and all manifestations can understand us.[8]

Two full-length novelettes embody the idea of "Weltallsprache," namely "Der Wildgänse Flug in Katata nachschauen"[9] and the story of Ata Mono and the Cryptomeria tree.[10] Of this tree he says: "Such a tree, which never moves and whose surroundings likewise never move and which knows only the changes of the seasons, has a remarkable memory. This, however, does not express itself in such a manner that its core ponders about what has been or what may happen, but the memory of a tree always lies exposed on its exterior. The grooves and the bark have noted down each day the very least of happenings with lines, incisions, gnarls, and furrows as if with a stenographic alphabet. Just as the tree stretched when it felt well in the world, and added bark and armor when it was threatened by the world, its covering furrowed and folded into a significant language."[11]

While entertaining new thoughts for the *Venusinenreim* during his trip around the world, Dauthendey wrote to his wife: "It is really true that at bottom everything in the household and on the street, everything which lives with man, voices its opinion about him in pleasure or aversion. A stone which likes you can call to you inaudibly in order that you may not stumble over it. A stone which hates you says nothing and takes care that you do not see it until you stumble over it. Similarly with doors: they like or hate to open and tell you about the arrival or passing of people if they like you. In the presence of whomever they do not like

---

[6] *Op. cit., Gesammelte Werke,* IV, p. 366, "Ein paar Raben schweben zur Stadt herein."

[7] *Der brennende Kalender, Gesammelte Werke,* IV, p. 223. For further examples cp. also *Lusamgärtlein, Gesammelte Werke,* IV, p. 262, "Eine Straße im Maiwald ohn' Ende"; *Der brennende Kalender,* IV, p. 215, "August"; *op. cit.,* IV, p. 225, "Fällt auch der Schnee tot ins Geäst"; *Weltspuk,* IV, p. 385, "Nachtschnee"; etc.

[8] *Gedankengut aus meinen Wanderjahren, Gesammelte Werke,* I, pp. 346, 347.

[9] For another treatment, cf. also "Im Kaiserpalast zu Kioto" *Die Geflügelte Erde, Gesammelte Werke,* V, p. 386.

[10] For another treatment, cf. also "Der alte Baum am Biwasee," *Die Geflügelte Erde, Gesammelte Werke,* V, p. 404.

[11] *Die acht Gesichter am Biwasee, Gesammelte Werke,* III, p. 146 (cf. also p. 145).

Cover of *Weltspuk*

they remain motionless and tell him unpleasant commonplace things which have passed in and out of the door. My book (*i.e., Venusinenreim*) will be rich if the entire world, even commonplace things, are allowed to express their daily passions and speak the way their hearts dictate."[12]

This belief is repeatedly expressed in Dauthendey's works. Thus, Kilian's murderer Notker is repulsed by every reed, stone, or house:

> Es zittert jedes Gras vor mir
> Der Stein auf dem ich niedersaß,
> Er zittert wie ein lebend Tier.
> Die Häuser sehn mich an voll Haß . . .[13]

Dauthendey believed that with the realization of true love knowledge of all imponderables would become almost effortless. The key to the universal language is found most readily through love. Whoever has realized true love and believes in the basic concept of the simultaneous condition of being the creator and the created, recognizes with little effort the secret writings of the universe.[14] Thoughts and feelings are the language which unites all manifestations, for all manifestations are in constant touch, all lives are representations of one and the same creative force, everything possesses the identical distal and proximal world.[15]

The idea of a universal language was henceforth never to leave Dauthendey. As late as April 26, 1915, he wrote to his wife: "I believe in nature and life, and I believe, as you know, in all sorts of signs and symbols around about us, in the universal language, which must surely exist. Heretofore people have been too much concerned with themselves and have not been aware of the sign language of the universe. I should like to persuade all people to take time to learn the universal language of signs. Not until they do will life be gentle and complete as it was in

---

[12] Letter of April 6, 1906, *Mich ruft dein Bild*, pp. 128, 129.
[13] *Die Heidin Geilane, Gesammelte Werke,* III, p. 848.
[14] *Gedankengut aus meinen Wanderjahren, Gesammelte Werke,* I, p. 811: "Wer das Liebesgefühl erkannt hat, wer sich als Mann mit seiner Frau als Angebeteter und Anbeter zugleich fühlt, dem offenbart sich die Weltallgeheimschrift in ihrer unendlichen Klarheit, ohne Wissen und ohne Denken, im einfachen herzlichen Festlichkeitsgefühl.

"Und die Frau wie der Mann sind in diesem Gefühl gleichwertig klug, gleichwertig weise, und sie gewinnen in der Liebeserkenntnis alles Wissen aller Unendlichkeiten ohne Grübeln."

[15] *Op. cit.,* pp. 360, 361.

paradise."[16] The same thought is reiterated in *Das Lied der Weltfestlichkeit* written in 1917:

> Erkenne auch die Weltallsprache rund.
> Denn sprechend sind sie, Stein und Gras und Hund.[17]

On September 27, 1915 Dauthendey wrote to his wife, "I should like to teach all men in songs what I have learned through my communion with the birds, what I know of their language, and of the trees, and of all sounds."[18] It was then that he wrote the intimate animal poems entitled "Lieder der Beschaulichkeit."[19]

On reviewing his boyhood schooling, Dauthendey remarked how happy a world this would be if instead of the humdrum language subjects taught in our schools, our children could be taught the language of the animals, plants, and things![20] The key to this language, to the "Weltallgeheimsprache"[21] of his youthful isolation in Bohuslän, he rediscovered during a similar seclusion on the island of Java. There he wrote the delicate animal stories of *Das Märchenbriefbuch der heiligen Nächte im Javanerlande*, which reveal a remarkable study of the psychology of animals, and an empathy which made him bear his isolation and which compensated him for the neglect suffered from his neighbors and compatriots.

[16] *Mich ruft dein Bild*, p. 275.
[17] *Gesammelte Werke*, V, p. 643.
[18] *Mich ruft dein Bild*, pp. 354, 355.
[19] Unpublished, in the possession of Mrs. Dauthendey.
[20] *Gesammelte Werke*, II, p. 270.
[21] *Gedankengut aus meinen Wanderjahren, Gesammelte Werke*, I, p. 811.

VII
"WORLD-PROXIMITY" AND "WORLD-DETACHMENT"

A very important concept in Dauthendey's Weltanschauung is the idea of "Weltferne" and "Weltnähe" which, for lack of more suitable terms, we may translate here as "world-detachment" and "world-proximity." We find first inklings of them in a letter written to Arnold Villinger, April 24, 1897, from which it appears that the concept had not occurred to the poet until that time: "I have been unable to write you . . . because our views no longer harmonize as they did formerly. I have had a hard winter full of great dissatisfaction with my ideas, although my outward life has been happy. Three weeks ago, while taking a spring walk, I arrived at the center of the universe, *i.e.*, I know that every living being is the center of the universe and every living being can say: I am everything. I say this not merely as a philosophical phrase but I try to realize it. I no longer consider my body, the five to six foot-high man, as my sole ego; it is the same to me as you or any other living being. I try to force my senses not to feel any bodily pain more strongly than sufferings of which I am told, and similarly with the joys. I, therefore, leave my body and live in the center of the universe. I recognize myself in everything I meet by feeling the joys and sufferings of all beings as strongly as the joys and sufferings of my own body. Being in this constant condition of uniform happiness, I no longer experience my body more strongly than a fiction. . . . While I am living thus I feel myself universal and immortal. For, because I assume or possess this stage of perception, to feel everything my own, I am eternal, even if my body, which now has become only the billionth part of myself fades away. I shall suffer no more in death than in seeing the death of plants or friends about me."[1]

This idea gradually matured in the poet and finds repeated expression in *Gedankengut aus meinen Wanderjahren,* Dauthendey's second accounting of his cargo of ideas. He there presents it as follows: World-detachment is the eternally festive immut-

---

[1] *Ein Herz im Lärm der Welt,* pp. 143, 144.
This is reflected in the poet's statement as recorded in one of Mrs. Dauthendey's diary excerpts of the time: "Universum, das bin ich!"

able; world-proximity, the eternally festive desire for change.[2] World-detachment stands for firmly anchored placidity and contemplation, for exaltation over life, whereas world-proximity represents activity.[3] In our profoundest, sublimest moments we return to world-detachment, to our non-entity, the apogee of the Greeks, the Nirvana of the Asiatics.[4] It resembles the center, whereas our everyday life corresponds to the periphery of a circle. Just as a radius is determined by both center and circumference, so there is a constant relation between our present form and the underlying eternal center. The temporary embodiments on the periphery are as inexhaustible as is the creative force of the common center of the universe. Since we are constantly experiencing world-proximity and world-detachment simultaneously, we are all omniscient, omnipresent, and omnisentient.[5] Neither world-proximity nor world-detachment is possible without the other, and both are inconceivable without the inexhaustible force which inheres in every atom.[6] We are everlastingly endowed not only with omnipotence but also with its opposite; our finite as well as infinite life fluctuates between eternity and finality.[7] Dauthendey's definition of world-detachment thus includes the theological concepts of soul and omnipotent God.[8]

Although we are constantly present and absent, real and unreal, in proximity to or at a distance from the core of the world, although theoretically we may at any moment raise ourselves to the central position of world-detachment,[9] it is only during our sublimest and most profound moments that we tarry for any length of time at the core of the universe.[10] Such moments are to be found, e.g., in the ecstasies of love, "the most profound moment of the world-festivity in each life and the highest, of a whole life."[11] It is thus that, because of the exuberant love consciousness of her soul, Talora in the eternal blue calm of her ethereal

---

[2] *Gesammelte Werke,* I, pp. 330, 331.
[3] *Op. cit.,* p. 335.
[4] *Op. cit.,* p. 330.
[5] *Op. cit.,* p. 333.
[6] *Op. cit.,* p. 337.
[7] *Loc. cit.*
[8] *Op. cit.,* p. 334. While in Java, Dauthendey used the term "Weltseele" as a synonym for "Weltferne," *Gesammelte Werke,* II. pp. 458, 459, 466.
[9] *Gedankengut aus meinen Wanderjahren, Gesammelte Werke,* I, p. 332.
[10] *Op. cit.,* p. 331.
[11] *Op. cit.,* p. 348.

garden appeared to hold daily communion with the distant Bulram "as if there were no proximity and no detachment in the universe."[12]

Among men Dauthendey believed the poet to be a natural adept in the transference from "world-proximity" to "world-detachment." "The contemplation of the world and the aloofness which are innate in him give him in his young years the calm, the depth, and the wisdom of an old man, while his creations make him strong and active, the creator of lofty eternal values. The poet is born complete within. He never develops within. His heart is a diamond which becomes neither brighter nor duller. Of all men he is the one born with balance, with that balance which others achieve only through life and age, or never achieve it, but strive toward it consciously or unconsciously. . . . A poet's heart is the most harmonious heart of the world."[13] The actual mechanism of the flux from proximal to distal life, Dauthendey did not elaborate. Here as elsewhere conviction and faith played a large rôle, obviating formal, logical deductions and proofs. The development of this part of his philosophy probably was the result to a large extent of Dauthendey's attempt to find an escape from the ardors of a troubled existence, an escape, to be sure, with ethical and pragmatic implications. By transplanting oneself to the distal core one can view life *sub specie aeternitatis,* with a cosmic perspective. Calmly contemplating the relative unimportance of the proximal manifestations and the eternal validity of the distal basis, one can fortify one's position in life and from this vantage point attack life's problems with renewed vigor when reprojected to the proximal periphery.

Later, during the Java period, Dauthendey began to doubt the frequency of such visits to the core of the universe and believed them to occur only at great intervals: "But the soul is omniscient, and it is in every manifestation of life; it knows everything, and unconsciously we, too, have long known everything. Sometimes we experience luminous moments of intuition of our omniscience, and then we say that we have a foreknowledge of something or have second sight, that we can prophesy or have had a meaningful dream. But that only means that for a moment we dwelt very close to the omniscient soul. . . . Such

[12] "Der Garten ohne Jahreszeiten," *Lingam, Gesammelte Werke,* V, p. 60.
[13] *Der Geist meines Vaters, Gesammelte Werke,* I, p. 298.

moments, however, are very rare; not everybody, even once in his life, visits his soul or is visited by it."[14]

It is only natural that doubting Thomases might ask, why should we not be able to change our form voluntarily if the foregoing be true? Does not our everyday experience deny the principle of a passage from world-proximity to world-detachment? Dauthendey disposes of this criticism by defining his concepts more closely. World-detachment and world-proximity in his scheme of life are eternally balanced.[15] Abrupt transitions are thus impossible, even forbidden by the eternal wisdom and serenity of the basic world core: "The detachment within us does not admit of any chaotic convulsions in the proximal world. We ourselves stand eternally supreme over folly."[16]

Although our proximal life is only temporal, death loses its sting in Dauthendey's Weltanschauung, nor do we need to make death more palatable by a belief in the Nirvana of the Asiatics, the melodic heaven of the Christians, or the sensuous heaven of the Mohammedans.[17] "Nothing will harm us when at the end of our human embodiment we allow death to approach our mortal form. For we have come from the transitory, from the unfathomable, and we return to the unfathomable. We therefore always belong to the unfathomable during every single second of life, because we came from it. *But we have likewise always belonged to reality because we have succeeded in attaining reality.*

"Since the possibility to enter the life of reality was once in us, we can very well assume that it existed thousands of times in us and that it continues to exist. We must learn to understand that we have already entered reality thousands of times and that many thousands of times we shall find the same possibility again. Unfathomable death does not hold us eternally, just as life, reality, does not hold us eternally."[18]

Hence Dauthendey's scheme of life also contains a belief in metempsychosis, the necessity for which he demonstrates by parallels. In "Zwei Reiter am Meer" we are told that "all leave-takings must be followed by a reappearance. Upon the separation

---

[14] *Gesammelte Werke*, II, pp. 458, 459.
[15] *Gedankengut aus meinen Wanderjahren, Gesammelte Werke*, I, p. 334.
[16] *Op. cit.*, pp. 334, 335.
[17] *Op. cit.*, p. 335.
[18] *Gesammelte Werke*, I, p. 510.

which death brings there follows the return, the hour of resurrection. Life does not permit itself to be buried indefinitely, even when dead. In death also there is the rhythm of waves. The land has its mountains and hillocks, the sea has its waves and billows, the sky its clouds and its placidity, and life, spent, also has its flux of going and returning."[19]

"You change from life to life, for you constantly desire to create, and this is your joy and your bliss,"[20] Dauthendey summarizes this thought. It is this festive volitional aspect which distinguishes his metempsychosis from other conceptions of transmigration of the soul. He himself called it a fusion of Christian and Buddhistic concepts, "but since it springs from creative joy and is without coercion, it is more, it is festive."[21]

Nor is this transmigration related to Nietzsche's eternal recurrence: "We ourselves have invented the game of creation and are continuing to play it endlessly, since it offers endless change. In card games the recurrence by chance of similar card combinations creates the illusion that games recur. But *no game is like another, no life which returns resembles any other.*"[22]

Our passing from life to life through the millenniums resembles the artist who produces one work after another: The artist-creator, too, enjoys immortality, "as his spirit stands behind all his works in godlike calm and contemplation."[23]

To Dauthendey it was possible for each manifestation of life to allow itself to die consciously or unconsciously, with or without coercion: If it no longer loves life, *i.e.*, no longer celebrates the feast of its life, it will allow its present incarnation to cease and with its inexhaustible vital or creative joy assume a new form.[24]

A child curious to know the fate of things Dauthendey would have enlightened as follows: "All men and all life can change forms, when tired of having been men, animals, or plants. But we never quite leave you nor the world. Perhaps your mother will become a cloud, perhaps your father will become a bolt of lightning, perhaps we shall become singing birds or perhaps together we shall

---

[19] *Geschichten aus den vier Winden, Gesammelte Werke,* V, p. 310.
[20] *Gedankengut aus meinen Wanderjahren, Gesammelte Werke,* I, p. 813.
[21] *Op. cit.,* pp. 328, 329.
[22] *Op. cit.,* pp. 337, 338.
[23] *Op. cit.,* p. 328.
[24] *Id. loc.*

become a flower in a flowerpot at your window. Perhaps we shall become a few moonbeams, perhaps a few sunbeams. Perhaps we shall be a piece of bread which you will eat, a draught of water which you will drink, a watch which ticks beside you, or a house and a garden in which you will dwell."[25]

[25] *Op. cit.*, pp. 342, 343.

VIII

"WORLD-FESTIVITY"

Another fundamental idea of Dauthendey's philosophy is that of world-festivity (Weltfestlichkeit). We find it first in the title of "Festliches Jahrbuch," a poem of which in 1898 Dauthendey wrote only the first and ninth of twelve contemplated cantos. The idea of world festivity was apparently original with Dauthendey and matured after his first sojourn in Bohuslän in 1893. In "Festliches Jahrbuch, Erster Gesang" the poet tells us how he discovered it in the stony loneliness of the Fjellbacka countryside:

> Ich hatte mich auf einem öden Stein geglaubt und
> Wurde es gewahr, es lebt noch um den letzten Stein ein Fest.[1]

His development of the idea was neglected in his preoccupation with financial difficulties. Later he became aware that in sorrow, also, there is festivity.[2]

To Dauthendey world festivity was no empty phrase. Did he not meet it in myriads of instances? Did not everything in nature down to the smallest inanimate object proclaim this life of happiness? One had but to look closely, listen attentively, to perceive this.

On the island of Koster, near Strömstad, *e.g.*, Dauthendey tells us he was surrounded by the joy of the summer sky, by the eternal festivity of the piercing blue summer sea.[3] He delights to reveal

---

[1] *Gesammelte Werke*, IV, p. 569. Elisabeth Darge, *op. cit.*, points out the underlying festive character of the philosophy of the life-affirming poets of the turn of the century, in a chapter entitled "Alltag und Fest," pp. 135-156. This festiveness too often, however, had a hedonistic basis and lacked the ethical implications of Dauthendey's Weltfestlichkeit. Several literary examples quite in Dauthendey's manner occur in Eduard von Keyserling's *Abendliche Häuser* (*Gesammelte Erzählungen in vier Bänden*, Berlin, 1922: S. Fischer, IV), p. 78: ". . . hier in der klaren Luft über der knisternden Schneedecke lag es wie ein festliches Erwarten"; p. 132: "Eine behagliche Heiterkeit klang durch diese letzte Abendstunde"; p. 145: ". . . hier und da blühte schon eine Kastanie in ihrer weißen Feierlichkeit mitten unter den grün verschleierten Birken." I find a parallel in Calvin Thomas' "The Choir Invisible," *Scholarship and other Essays*, N.Y., 1924: Henry Holt and Co., pp. 207-217.

[2] *Vide* pp. 91ff. *infra*.

[3] "Das Giftfläschchen," *Geschichten aus den vier Winden, Gesammelte Werke*, III, p. 250; *cp.* also p. 257, ". . . wo in der blauen Glocke des Himmels die Sonne täglich zu einem Fest geglänzt hatte."

the festive spirit of the universe in numerous other instances. The snow enlivens the wintry feast.[4] The moon is bedecked as if going to a feast[5] and illuminates all the clouds until they form a festive tent.[6] The flowers of his Würzburg days retain their festive mien even in the rain,[7] while those of his Tosari exile remind him of the innate festive spirit of all things:

> Sie haben Zeit aus ihrer Seligkeit zum
>   Unseligen hinzusehen,
> Sie schwelgen in dem Liebesfeste und merken kaum
>   mein ärmliches Vorübergehen.[8]

The crown of the fir dances in the sky.[9] The festive spirit resides in a mere stone, for even a stone knows longing[10] and when in the presence of lovers gleams festively.

Similarly we learn that the life of precious stones really begins only when they are worn by a beautiful woman, in festive illumination and in a festive spirit (festlichem Blut).[11]

But if a festive human heart can enliven nature, the opposite is also true, and Dauthendey counsels the gloomy reader:

> Der Wald ist uralt ein Liederhaus,
> Geh hin und singe dein Herz bei ihm aus.[12]

World-festivity, Dauthendey, the master of color impressions, found particularly revealed in colors. Whereas in the early works he had employed synaesthesia, the correspondence of colors, to voice the thoughts of so-called "inanimate" nature, for whose language ordinary modes of speech had seemed imperfect, he later increasingly used color to portray the festive aspect of the uni-

---

[4] "Fällt auch der Schnee tot ins Geäst," *Der brennende Kalender, Gesammelte Werke*, IV, p. 225.

[5] "Die Nacht saß auf den Tannen," *op. cit.*, p. 216.

[6] "Doch der Mond, der die Welt sich gern unwirklich macht," *Lusamgärtlein, Gesammelte Werke*, IV, p. 255.

[7] "Heller als Blitze im Gras alle Jungblumen jetzt funkeln," *op. cit.*, p. 249.

[8] Quoted from unpublished poem of March 20, 1917, Tosari, entitled: "Des Morgens bei den Blumen."

[9] "Der Liebsten Mund ist's Reiseziel," *Singsangbuch, Gesammelte Werke*, IV, p. 147.

[10] "Ich grübe mir gern in die Stille ein Grab," *Der weiße Schlaf, Gesammelte Werke*, IV, p. 416.

[11] "Nächtliche Schaufenster," *Geschichten aus den vier Winden, Gesammelte Werke*, III, pp. 336, 337.

[12] *Der brennende Kalender, Gesammelte Werke*, IV, p. 214.

verse. While synaesthetic references became fewer and fewer, color remained a distinctive characteristic of Dauthendey's prose and verse.

In the minute stage directions of his plays we note the skilful use of color in depicting the festive aspect of the universe. In *Die Heidin Geilane* we read: "In describing the costumes I proceed from the thought that the colors of the joy of life are to be emphasized in the clothing of the heathens, whereas in the clothing of the Christians, the colors are to be characteristic rather of the negation of life."[13]

Dauthendey, henceforth, with the realization of the principle of world-festivity, sought to use his highly developed chromatic experiences as a means to emphasize the festive spirit of all universal phenomena. No longer was there to be any "black" sun. The color adjective itself, used in innumerable infinitely fine gradations of shading, as well as the use of striking comparisons, seemed best adapted to produce the festive spirit the poet wished to call up. To impress the reader thoroughly with the festive aspect of the world, Dauthendey after his world tour,[14] increasingly adopted the method of repetition to gain the desired impression. Where, as a youthful freelance, he had literally daubed aniline dyes helter-skelter to produce orgies of color, he now strove to invoke the sense impressions by repeated daublike applications of the color words.

In the mature work of the poet there are numerous examples of the thematic use of variations of the basic color impression. Thus the blue haze over Penang had impressed Dauthendey during his short stay at that tropical port to such an extent that forever after he associated blue with it. "Eine Stunde in Penang" of *Die geflügelte Erde*[15] is, therefore, suffused with blue, with a recurring "blau, Bläue, bläulich, mondblau, geblaut." The novelette inspired by Penang is characteristically called "Im blauen Licht von Penang"[16] and likewise has variations of the adjective

---

[13] *Gesammelte Werke*, VI, p. 890. Cp. also particularly the detailed description of Catherine, at the beginning of each act of *Die Spielereien einer Kaiserin*, *Gesammelte Werke*, VI.

[14] *Mich ruft dein Bild*, pp. 112, 221. Duplication of a color adjective, as such, can be found as early as "Doppelleben," *Ultra Violett*, *Gesammelte Werke*, pp. 65 ff.

[15] *Die geflügelte Erde*, *Gesammelte Werke*, V, p. 276.

[16] *Lingam*, *Gesammelte Werke*, III, pp. 66, 67.

blue as its dominant color note. Gold pervades the description of Canton streets in the novelette "Der unbeerdigte Vater"[17] and more intensively in its counterpart, "Kantonstraßen" of his globe-encircling poetic journey.[18] Both of these go back to the impressions of gold which color Dauthendey's letter of March 4, 1906.[19] Gilded also are "Das Abendrot zu Seta,"[20] "Kiototempel" (at Seta),[21] and the Javanese "Geschichte des Wasserbüffels."[22] Red in daring splashes vivifies "Fahrt zum See Biwa,"[23] "Das Abendrot zu Seta,"[24] and "Palast des Großmoguls,"[25] while the rosy hue of Jeypore pervades "Die rosenrote Stadt."[26] Brilliant white, suggestive of tropical heat, dazzles the reader of "Schloß Amber,"[27] and of "Im Taj-Mahal Garten."[28] It is even more effective in Dauthendey's letter of May 7, 1914,[29] written while crossing the Red Sea at the beginning of his last journey. The sombreness of black speaks from the pages of "Auf dem Weg zu den Eulenkäfigen."[30] The magic influence of silver appears in the delicate "Mondscheinfahrt um den Kandysee," which may be quoted here to illustrate the cumulative effect of a visual impression:

> Ich fuhr eines Nachts in einem Rikscha rund um den
> See. Irgendwo hing der Mond wie ein S i l b e rpfund,
> war noch nicht über den Bergen aufgega n g e n,
> Aber die höchsten Palmen standen schon wie ver s i l -
> b e r te Spa n g e n; wie in der Werkstatt bei den
> Juweli e r e n, tat blaues Email den ovalen See wie
> ein Medaillon verzi e r e n.
> Und, hinterm Geäste r e g t e der Mond seine S i l b e r -
> feile, und das Mondlicht zerle g t e die Bäume mit
> Geschi ck in ein vielgezacktes Mosa i k.

[17] *Op. cit.*, p. 82.
[18] *Die geflügelte Erde, Gesammelte Werke*, V, p. 305.
[19] *Mich ruft dein Bild*, p. 112.
[20] *Die acht Gesichter am Biwasee, Gesammelte Werke*, III, p. 204.
[21] *Die geflügelte Erde, Gesammelte Werke*, V, p. 388.
[22] *Das Märchenbriefbuch der heiligen Nächte im Javanerlande, Gesammelte Werke*, II, pp. 838 ff.
[23] *Die geflügelte Erde, Gesammelte Werke*, V, pp. 403, 404.
[24] *Die acht Gesichter am Biwasee, Gesammelte Werke*, III, p. 209.
[25] *Die geflügelte Erde, Gesammelte Werke*, V, p. 116.
[26] *Op. cit.*, V, p. 93.
[27] *Op. cit.*, V, p. 104-106.
[28] *Op. cit.*, V, p. 126.
[29] *Mich ruft dein Bild*, p. 221.
[30] *Geschichten aus den vier Winden, Gesammelte Werke*, III, p. 314.

Wie beim S i l b e rschmied war man unter den Palmen
zu Haus; wie S i l b e rbarren und S i l b e rgefäße
Sahen die Schäfte und Blattscharen am Wege aus,
Als waren da Alleen hingestellt von riesigen S i l b e r-
pokalen. Und in langen Zügen standen die Kur-
ven ungeheuerer Ka k t e e n,
Gleich getriebenen S i l b e rurnen und S i l b e rkrü g e n.
Endlich kam der Mond groß über den Berg, um
im See die Nacht durch fruchtlos zu pflü g e n.
Ich fuhr unter der n a ck t e n S i l b e rfracht in Mondan-
dacht hin durch die mit Wohlgerüchen und mit
Zinn- und S i l b e rbildern bepa ck t e Nacht.[31]

To Dauthendey's great mediaeval predecessor, Walther von der Vogelweide, "Diu werlt was gelf, rot unde blâ." Of the same country-side Dauthendey says, "Rot, gelb und lila sind jetzt die Hügel."[32] Everywhere he turns, colors reveal the festive aspect of the universe. Their skilful use invokes it again from the poet's works. The kaleidoscopic use of colors appears in descriptions of temperate Sweden as well as in the riotous nature of Java. Two examples illustrating these extremes will suffice to show the poet's preoccupation with colors: the first, a description of Koster, the island off the Swedish west coast near Strömstad, the second a Javanese scene culled from *Das Märchenbriefbuch der heiligen Nächte im Javanerlande*:

I

Zwischen dem Heidekraut auf dieser Insel und bei den reichen wilden Rosenbüschen, die ganz überschüttet von r o s a Kelchen dastanden, als ich im Juni landete, liegen die seltsamsten Steine zerstreut; dort ein blendend w e i ß e r, wie ein großes Marmorei, dort ein g e l b e r, wie ein harter Honigbrocken oder wie ein Stück Bernstein, dort ein r o s e n r o t e r wie eine Fleischkeule von einem geschlachteten Tier, dort ein s c h w a r z e r flacher wie ein Rabenflügel oder ein runder wie ein Seehundkopf. Hinter den Wacholderfiguren und unter den schirmartigen kurzen Eichen, deren Kronen flach wie g r ü n e Teller auf dem Stamm wachsen, von den Seewinden wie mit einem Messer beschnitten,—bei diesen kleinen Eichen und großen Wachholderbüschen weiden glänzende r o thaarige Kühe und Kühe, w e i ß und s c h w a r z gesprenkelt, als hätten sie sich von der Nacht bemalen lassen mit dunklen Flecken und

---

[31] *Die geflügelte Erde, Gesammelte Werke*, p. 263.
[32] Poem entitled "Fort fliegt der Sommer," *Simplicissimus*, XVII, 26 (September 23, 1912), p. 408.

mit w e i ß e n Flecken vom Mond, mit g e l b e n und r o t e n Flecken von der Sonne. Und die wandernden Kühe mit ihren Flecken, auf der totstillen Insel bei den Flecken der f l e i s c hfarbenen s c h w a r z e n, w e i ß e n und b l a u e n Steine, wandern in der f e u e r b l a u e n Meerumrahmung, zwischen den g r ü n e n Sonnenflecken unter den Eichen, zwischen den r o s a Flecken der Rosenbüsche und im Weihrauchgeruch der Wacholderbüsche, wie vierbeinige kauende Götzenbilder.[33]

II

Und seltsam, die Wolken bildeten Figuren und Formen. Und mit der Zeit entstanden aus den Rauchwolken bunte Tücher an beiden Javanen. Und es begann an ihnen zu blitzen und zu funkeln. Und es war ganz sonderbar: sie bekleideten sich wie zwei Fürsten mit den kostbarsten handgemalten Stoffen. Aus Rauch gewobene b l a u e und k u p f e r r o t e Seide entstand, und die beiden Javanen, als sie nach einer Weile aufstanden, hatten die herrlichsten javanischen Königsgewänder an, die man sich nur denken kann. Der Alte trug eine v e i l c h e nfarbene Jacke, die war über und über mit r e g e n b o g e nfarbigen Perlen bestickt. Die w e i ß e n Perlen bildeten Blüten und Ranken am Saum der Jacke, und die Perlenstickerei bedeckte die ganze Brust. Er hatte außerdem eine seidene Hose an, die war wie aus den schönsten Gartenblumen zusammengestellt, aus r o t e n und w e i ß e n Nelken, aus b l a u e n Irisblumen und g e l b e n Irisblumen, aus Feuerlilien und Jasmin, aus w e i ß e m und l i l a Flieder, und die Säume unten um die Hosen waren dicke s c h w a r z r o t e Rosen, und dazwischen guckten gestickte G o ldkäfer hervor.[34]

To his wife, the poet wrote August 18, 1915: "All the stars looked like oleographs with entirely new, fresh colors. Just painted. Never in my life have I seen such a motley-colored world in one place."[35] The great profusion of colors in Java taxed the poet's descriptive powers to the limit and led him to painting as the only logical outlet of his pent-up chromatic visions. From early childhood Dauthendey had shown talent for drawing and painting and for a while had wavered between embracing painting or poetry as his chosen career. In aquarelles he could portray the last delicate color visions which seemed to defy verbal translation. A number of paintings were produced during the world

---

[33] "Das Giftfläschchen," *Geschichten aus den vier Winden, Gesammelte Werke,* III, p. 247.
[34] "Geschichte des Beovogels," *Das Märchenbriefbuch der heiligen Nächte im Javanerlande, Gesammelte Werke,* II, p. 773.
[35] *Gesammelte Werke,* II, p. 326.

trip in 1905, 1906, and these later served as the basis of Dauthendey's Oriental tales.[36] The poet was most productive in painting during the last years of his life in Java. His artistic work forms an interesting analogue to his poetics and has won acclaim wherever it has been exhibited. Thus Hermann Eßwein speaks of the exhibition at the Münchener Kunstverein in January, 1927, as "the triumph of the outsider." In his opinion "It was no playful creative urge which made Max Dauthendey take colored crayons and aquarelle brush in hand, but deep pensiveness during the sensual experience, a philosophic want, which summoned forms and colors and with subtle touch (spröder Hand) enthralled them to his soul, only in so far as they permitted the secret tremors of the optical, and more than optical, the world experience, to be fashioned and to be imparted through the senses."[37] In painting Dauthendey found another means of portraying the festive spirit of his universe.[38]

It is significant that Dauthendey became intensely interested in the ancient Greeks when thoughts of world festivity first began to occupy him. A temporary attraction to Aeschylus and other Greek dramatists whose works he valued far above those of Ibsen and other moderns,[39] soon led him to the discovery of the festive verse of Homer's *Odyssey* and *Iliad*, to which he refers again and again in his letters at the time of the turn of the century. While in Mexico City, he studied the language of the ancient Greeks and found the reading of Homer a solace in the Spanish-American republic, for the understanding of which he lacked the necessary spiritual affinity. When his trip to Greece in search of an idyllic home for his muse, like the Mexican venture, proved unsuccessful, it was, as Elisabeth Darge points out, a practical failure and not a spiritual one.[40] His exuberant interest in the Greeks was of a temporary nature, but was, nevertheless, influential in the gradual development of the conviction that life is indeed festive.

[36] In Mrs. Dauthendey's diaries there occurs the following reference under date of April 22, 1909: ". . . hat Frankfurter Firma Rütten und Loening Weltreise Aquarelle angeboten. Die verlangt einen Text dafür." This suggested the Novellen to him.
[37] *Frankfurter Zeitung und Handelsblatt, Abendblatt,* January 31, 1927, LXXI, p. 80.
[38] Numerous reproductions are available in various magazines. For a listing see pp. 166 ff. *infra.*
[39] *Gedankengut aus meinen Wanderjahren, Gesammelte Werke,* I, p. 728.
[40] *Op. cit.,* p. 197.

Sumatra, 1914.

To the casual reader of Dauthendey's works it seems that after the first struggle in the nineties, his life was a fairly comfortable one, spent mainly in traveling in comparative luxury. The story of his life, however, gives a different picture. He was too much a dreamer to engage in any remunerative pursuits. Poetry was his profession. He often complained that the state provided for its teachers and ministers but that its poets were left to shift for themselves, and proposed a system of stipends which would enable poets to move from place to place, lingering as long as they deemed necessary, and not bound by any shackles.[41] He tried to realize this ideal at the expense of continual financial embarrassment. When reading Adolf Paul's biography of Strindberg, he wrote to his wife from his Java exile: "My life was so similar. Always financial anxiety. Always, even if peace returns. Even if we see each other again,—until death comes, financial anxiety will always be with me. Isn't that desperate! It embitters one completely. I shall never be able to breathe freely, as long as I breathe. Not until the end of my life shall I breathe freely. That is my lot as a poet."[42]

> Nenne nichts auf Erden mein
> Von dem großen Heimatsgrunde,
> Als den Regen nur allein
> Und den Nebel in der Runde.[43]

[41] *Gedankengut aus meinen Wanderjahren, Gesammelte Werke*, I, pp. 410, 600-606. *Mich ruft dein Bild*, p. 287.

[42] Letter of September 19, 1915, *Mich ruft dein Bild*, pp. 350, 351. *Cp.* also letter of November 27, 1912 to Richard Dehmel, *Ein Herz im Lärm der Welt*, p. 174. "... oft hieß es," says Oscar A. H. Schmitz, *Dämon Welt*, p. 322, "hätten sie nichts zu essen gehabt. Trotzdem überkam einen bei ihnen das Gefühl, daß um sie immer Sonntag sei." In a letter to Annie and Korfiz Holm of July 7, 1909 (unpublished), Dauthendey's dejection is poignantly brought out: "So schändlich ist unsere Stimmung, daß wir gestern Kubin, der sich durch ein Telegramm anmeldete, daß er auf der Durchreise einen Tag hier sei, nicht die Tür aufmachen konnten." As late as January 5, 1910, when many thought him a prosperous playwright, he wrote to his wife: "Jetzt lieh sie (*i.e.*, his sister Elisabeth) mir zehn Mark, so daß ich heute wieder essen kann gehen. Ich habe nämlich immer noch nichts seit vorgestern gegessen." This passage is omitted from the printed version of that letter, *Mich ruft dein Bild*, pp. 187, 188. The diaries of Mrs. Dauthendey, who, by the way through her own initiative often succeeded in tiding the poet and herself over the roughest financial difficulties, again and again refer to their material want.

[43] *Der weiße Schlaf, Gesammelte Werke*, IV, p. 425, poem entitled: "Graues Heimatnebelland." *Cp.* also "Die Sorgen ackern," *op. cit.*, p. 441, the two poems "Ich sah am Himmel meine Sorge als Komet" and "Kein Regen meine dürren Sorgen stillt," *Lusamgärtlein, Gesammelte Werke*, IV, p. 276, and "Die Sorge," *Des großen Krieges Not, Gesammelte Werke*, IV, p. 497.

Although the poet found solace in the beauty of nature,—"Wie wenig Welt tut schon den Augen gut!"—his philosophy of world festivity was put to a severe test by the spectre of poverty and hunger. How was this to be reconciled with a festive universe? He was here confronted with a problem which has to be answered in any eudemonical system, just as it had to be answered in order to buttress Leibniz' best of all possible worlds. The solution came to Dauthendey as early as 1891, when, as preliminary studies for his "new" religion, he wrote in an unpublished notebook: "Life moves only between joy and sorrow," and as if to reconcile himself to this, the additional thought that "man does not suffer alone, everything about him suffers and rejoices."[44]

This is tersely expressed in the poem, *Phallus*:

> Leben ist Herzlust, Leben ist Herzleid,
> Sekunden der Freude, Sekunden des Schmerzes,
> Alle vereint sind unendlich ein Leben.[45]

Good and evil are necessary to produce manifestations and variations.[46] This change is essential if world processes are not to become futile: "If in the peripheral life, the life of the proximal world, the life of the phenomenal world, there were to arise eternal day, eternal good, eternal joy without pain, eternal peace, it would mean the arrest of the feast, which we love so much, and whose cessation is quite impossible, since our eternal creative force is eternally at work."[47] With constantly renewed vigor he calls attention to this persistent problem. Although his solution came to him rather early in his thinking,[48] it presented itself with exceptional force during the years of his Java exile, when despair often taxed the festive aspect of his philosophy to the limit, so that by sheer repetition he sought to drive it home—to himself quite as much as to his readers:

> Mein Fest ist nicht auf lachend Glück nur eingestellt,
> Mein Fest ist auch im Leid und in dem Gram der Welt,
> Wenn Du das Unglück grüßt, es Dich nicht lange quält,
> Wer liebt da Lebensernst, ehrt auch die Lebensqual,

---

[44] "Das Leben bewegt sich zwischen Freud und Leid." "Der Mensch leidet nicht allein, alles um ihn leidet und freut sich."
[45] *Gesammelte Werke*, IV, p. 551.
[46] *Gedankengut aus meinen Wanderjahren, Gesammelte Werke*, I, p. 336.
[47] *Op. cit.*, p. 337.
[48] It is introduced in *Verdensaltet*, pp. 63, 64.

Qual

Wie Berge einsam bin ich. Möchte klagen.
Muss täglich, stündlich, in die Leere fragen.
Reisvöglein hat es gut dort im Geäst,
Das ab und zu fliegt zu der Brut im Nest.

Der Leute Schritte in der Bäume Schatten,
Die vor dem Haus hinwandern ohn Ermatten,
Sie wissen still und stät ihr täglich Ziel;
Doch Ungewissheit treibt mit mir ihr Spiel.

Die Hahnenschreie, die vom Zaum herschallen,
Hell heimatlich im Ohr mir wiederhallen,
Ein Rechen vor der Tür scharrt hin und her,
Einfachste Laute voll Erinn'rung schwer.

Doch Krieg verhüllt mit grauer Luft die Ferne,
Vergeblich such' ich nach der Heimat Sterne,
Kein Frieden zieht mehr in die bange Brust,
Nie hat mein Blut von solcher Qual gewusst.

Garvel 1915
Max Dauthendey

Manuscript of "Qual", *Gesammelte Werke*, V, pp. 479, 480. (Reduced)

Die Welle nicht allein besteht aus Berg und Tal,
Jed' Lebensfest, es malt sich feurig und fahl.[49]

The same use of analogous situations, a method lending itself particularly to panpsychistic systems, it found in *Das Lied der Weltfestlichkeit*:

Denn kannst
du ein Bildwerk denken, wo die satten Farben
nicht gehoben sind durch Schatten?

Kannst du dir Geschichten denken, die nur
Gutes und nichts Böses auch berichten, um
die Spannung zu verdichten?[50]

"Joy and sorrow have in the world-wanderings, each its festive time"[51] we are told, and the poet counsels us to view the universal feast as a spiritual work of art, where light cannot exist without shade.[52] Sorrow and evil are necessary to joy and happiness:

Denn dem Geist ist selbst die Untat wert,
die Wohltat ihn mehr schätzen lehrt.[53]

In a similar vein he wrote to his wife: "Our present sorrow is insignificant compared with the universal joy which will later spring from it when the spirit of world festivity is able to enter everywhere."[54]

Dauthendey was able to vindicate his belief in the festive character of the universe when the resources of his festive philosophy began to fail: "I have hungered and suffered want. I have fought and have been reduced to tears. I have felt powerless, humiliated, dragged through the mire, abandoned and lost, but I should have to call myself *dishonest, deaf, blind, and obtuse, if in retrospect and anticipation I were not bound to consider life a feast at every moment.*"[55]

The close relationship of joy and sorrow and the sudden transformation from one to the other forms the subject of the one-act

---

[49] From an unpublished poem entitled: "Die letzte Küstenfahrt," written August, 1917.
[50] *Gesammelte Werke*, V, p. 615.
[51] *Op. cit.*, p. 597.
[52] *Op. cit.*, p. 646.
[53] *Op. cit.*, p. 614.
[54] Letter of May 17, 1915, *Mich ruft dein Bild*, p. 287.
[55] *Gedankengut aus meinen Wanderjahren, Gesammelte Werke*, I, p. 338, italics render spaced type of first edition, p. 73.

play, *Lachen und Sterben,* and of the historical poem, "Die Untergangsstunde der 'Titanic'," as well as of the novellettes, "Der Knabe auf dem Kopf des Elefanten" and "Likse und Panulla."

It was this festive accent of Dauthendey's Weltanschauung which constantly buoyed him up, which made life possible when the odds seemed insurmountable. Removal to the core of the world seemed the best solution in this dilemma:

> Mußt tauchen in die Welt
> Ins Unglück und ins Glück,
> Bis Dir Dein Ich entfällt;
> Kehrst festlich dann zurück.[56]

With Dauthendey's reconversion to the idea of a personal God, the theodicy problem was still ever-present and found numerous similar expressions: "Consider," he writes to his wife on August 2, 1915, two years before his complete change of belief, "God is life and death. God is not only life. He is also death. God is suffering and joy. God could impose the painful experience of birth on women and the painful experience of war[57] on men. And both of his works are as holy as life itself."[58]

When Dauthendeys' belief in a personal God had become an unshakable conviction, he could explain the existence of good and evil as rationally as he had while still believing in the "eternal mass." In a fervent prayer he addresses the God of the body and of the spirit, author of sorrow as well as joy:

. . . .
> Gott im Leibe, Gott im Geist,
> Hast die Lust und hast den Schmerz gegeben,
> Geist vom ewigen heiligen Leben.[59]

---

[56] Unpublished poem of March 10, 1917, entitled "Mein neuer Sinn." *Cp.* also *Das Lied der Weltfestlichkeit, Gesammelte Werke,* V, p. 645: "Dann kehr' zum Lebensstreit, zur Lebenslust zurück,/ Festlich zum Unglück, festlich zu dem Glück."

[57] This vindication of war Dauthendey expressed also in numerous other instances: *e.g.,* "Die letzte Küstenfahrt" (unpublished poem): "Nicht Frieden nur, auch Krieg bringt's Leben von dem Fleck" and "Das Leben ist ein Fest im Frieden und im Krieg/ Schön ist der Kampf ums Leben, mit und ohne Sieg. / Dem Mitleid sang ich Krieg, das heuchelnd sich verstieg." Such references are undoubtedly due to war psychosis as were many of the lesser and quite unimportant "patriotic" poems of the Batavia edition of *Des großen Krieges Not.* Dauthendey was anything but a soldier. *Cp.* also p. 28 *supra.*

[58] *Mich ruft dein Bild,* p. 312.

[59] Unpublished poem, written April 21, 1917, at Tosari.

IX

DAUTHENDEY AND THE ORIENT

It was Kipling, another great interpreter of the East, who said that "East is East and West is West, and never the twain shall meet." Many indeed have been the attempts to interpret Oriental thought to the Western mind. It has been doubted that a true understanding of the East is possible to the Western mind.[1] Of the interpreters of the Far East, the French, as Willy Seidel, himself an adept in the portraiture of the Oriental psyche, points out,[2] seem to excel in outward description of the Oriental scene. The Germans on the other hand, avoiding the usual Occidental modes of thought and employing empathy excel in really understanding the Oriental psyche: "How does the German make his exotic characters live? Indeed,—the German has too much respect not only for all his neighbors but also for the colored peoples to simply let them dance as they appear to his eye. No, he desires to infuse real life into them as God did into the lump of clay. Thus they do not become puppets, but rather become our brothers (no matter how great the difference), and that is to say, real human beings. And with this intuition, this psychic adaptive urge towards strange things, the German succeeds. His political error, his inordinate caution and his acknowledgment of strange modes of thought, his fanatical urge to objectivate while excluding nationalistic scruples, is a positive quantity in matters of art and as such an unconditional advantage."[3]

Dauthendey has often been celebrated for his unique empathy into the Oriental mental and psychical recesses. Mahrholz, *e.g.*, says of him: "With him there begins the inclination of German writers to delve deeply into the soul of the East, to invoke exotic

[1] *E.g.*, by Friedrich Gundolf, *George*. Berlin, 1920: Georg Bondi, pp. 38, 39.

[2] "Exotismus in deutscher Literatur," *Der Kunstwart*, XLI, 9, June, 1928, pp. 148-153 (Reprinted also in *Die Himmel der Farbigen*, Munich, 1930: Georg Müller, pp. 140-148. Frank Thieß ("Vom Abenteuerroman," *Die Neue Rundschan*, 1927, p. 3, quoted by Erich Seyfarth, *Friedrich Gerstäcker. Ein Beitrag zur Geschichte des exotischen Romans in Deutschland*, 1930, p. 1) in a like vein says "Der Amerikaner hat seine Urwälder und mächtigen Territorien als Ventil seiner Energie, der Engländer die großen Meere, der Franzose den Ozean und die Überseekolonien, der Russe das geheimnisvolle Asien, der Deutsche aber hat seine Seele. Er mußte, da es ihm nicht vergönnt war, nach außen zu projizieren, die Projektion nach innen schlagen."

[3] *Op. cit.*, p. 152.

forms, to fare forth in order to observe, to listen, to philosophize, and to conjure up strange peoples and souls."[4] Dauthendey, himself, was quite convinced of his ability in this direction and has given us a key to it:

> Geistiger Besitz ist dir die Menschheit, sind dir alle
> Völker aller Zeit. Kehrst du bei den Völkern ein,
> soll Bescheidenheit in dem Geist und Gefühl dort
> dein stiller Führer sein. Tust du anders, bist du
> nicht in ein Volk gereist, wenn du nicht der
> Sitte eines Landes und dem Geist deine Ehr-
> erbietung tief erweist. Anders dringst du
> nie in ihre Mitte.[5]

He derived his peculiar empathy from the fact that at bottom his guiding tenet of festive interdependence serves also as a basis for the philosophies of the Orient. While in his first literary endeavors he had sought to fathom the psychic life of animals and plants and even of "lifeless" objects, now the same philosophy of universal equivalence helped to unseal the Oriental mind.

As a child Dauthendey surprised his father by wishing a book about Java for Christmas. For a while the boy contemplated joining a Dutch colonial regiment in Java. In 1891 he read Multatuli-Dekker's *Max Havelaar*.[6] The works of Pierre Loti must also have been known to him at that time since he urged a friend to read *Japonneries d'Automne*. The Musée Guimet,[7] that treasure house of Far Eastern culture, in 1898 sowed the seeds of his later uncontrollable longing for the Far East, an interest which never faded. His apartment at 23 Sanderring, Würzburg, was filled with Oriental mementos. As late as 1918, only a few months before his death, he read Borel's book on China until four o'clock in the morning because he "could read and listen to conversation about China for years," listen to the wisdom of the early ancestors without ever becoming sated.[8]

Dauthendey's seven months' world trip of 1905, 1906 brought him in contact with the natives of Egypt, of India, China, and

---
[4] *Deutsche Dichtung der Gegenwart. Probleme, Ergebnisse, Gestalten.* Berlin 1926: Volksverband der Bücherfreunde, p. 335. *Cf.* also Gebhardt, *op. cit.*, pp. 65, 66, 67.
[5] *Das Lied der Weltfestlichkeit, Gesammelte Werke*, V, p. 595.
[6] Letter of June 22, 1891, *Ein Herz im Lärm der Welt*, p. 28.
[7] *Gedankengut aus meinen Wanderjahren. Gesammelte Werke*, I, p. 672.
[8] Letter of March 4, 1918, to Mrs. Dauthendey, *Gesammelte Werke*, II, p. 646.

Japan, and everywhere he found evidences of a kinship in the view of life of these peoples with his own: "The whole secret of my coming close to Asia lies in that cosmic comprehension contained in the sentence: *We are the possessors of all and are in turn possessed by all, and above us there is no other possessor.* This sentence, which stands at the beginning of my philosophy, makes every man the natural possessor of all life processes which the earth and heaven produce."[9]

Other pertinent resemblances with Oriental thought Dauthendey noted in the unpublished essay, "Plastische Bühne nach dem Vorbild asiatischer Theaterhäuser," where we are told: "With the present-day Asiatics we are united by a vividly awakened and detailed sense of nature, a sense which was never developed in such a detailed manner among the Greeks. Likewise we are united with the Asiatics by detailed psychic impressions of the universe, a loving self-surrender to the most subtle movements throughout the universe, a manner of perception that was far removed from the lordly grand manner of the Greeks, a love of sympathy, which is an achievement of modern times, and which the Buddhistic Asiatic also shares with us, and finally a vivacity free from pathos which was remote from the art of the solemn Greek."[10]

There was even a physical resemblance between Dauthendey and the Orientals. A photograph of young Dauthendey bears almost strikingly Javanese features.[11] In India moreover, it seemed to him that he met his mother in every woman he passed on the street.[12] He admired the reserve and industry of the East Indians, their ingenuousness, which was such a pleasant antidote to the stolid business-like ways of the Westerners: "The Indian sailors who clean the deck are very amusing," he writes while bound for

[9] *Gedankengut aus meinen Wanderjahren, Gesammelte Werke,* I, pp. 326, 327.

[10] Unpublished manuscript: "Mit dem heutigen Asiaten vereinigt uns lebhaft erwachter und detaillierter Natursinn, ein Sinn, der bei den Griechen nie so detailliert entwickelt war, ebenso verbinden uns mit den Asiaten eine Detaillierung seelischer Alltagseindrücke, ein liebevolles Sichversenken in die zartesten Weltallregungen, eine Betrachtungsart, die dem herrisch großzügigen Griechen fern lag, eine Mitleidsliebe, welche erst die Errungenschaft unserer Neuzeit ist, und die auch der buddhistische Asiate mit uns teilt, und endlich eine pathoslose Lebhaftigkeit, die dem feierlichen Griechen in der Kunst fern war."

[11] Julius Maria Becker in discussing the mature Dauthendey says of him: "So sah kein deutscher Dichter aus. Eher ein indischer Prinz, ein Maharadscha." "Begegnung mit Max Dauthendey" *Bavaria, Wochenschrift für bayerische Kulturpolitik.* 1. Jg., Heft 8, May 17, 1930, p. 6.

[12] *Der Geist meines Vaters, Gesammelte Werke,* I, p. 275.

India, "they are charming, quiet, industrious, and they all smile at me, while they fear the English. They are for the most part smaller than I and are very graceful. Among them are the brown faces of princes. My one consolation is that I shall see only countries where such dear little people dwell and that I do not have to go to England."[13]

He admired "the great childlike sensuousness of the Mohammedans" who squatted on all streets "as if the sun were a fireplace, where one passes his life chatting, working, dreaming and slumbering in great and small reveries."[14] Dauthendey himself enjoyed the same kind of reveries, as he tells in a letter of January 13, 1916.[15]

In the presence of the Indians Dauthendey felt plebeian, as a mere European.[16] All Indians seemed to him but variants of Bulram and Talora.[17] Although these two characters in "Der Garten ohne Jahreszeiten" particularly embody Dauthendey's great love for his Eastern brethren, all his characterizations of Easterners reflect his sympathetic understanding of these peoples.

At first the Chinese proved a disappointment. Although Dauthendey did not actually dislike them, he did not feel the same close bond that drew him to the East Indians. "A Chinese always looks through one and through everything which dwells behind one's innermost thoughts. An Indian sees nothing, he only shows the most beautiful eyes as does a picture and admires you through feeling, not through seeing. He considers any direct glance an insult."[18] Actual contact, however, with seething Canton, with evidences of the Chinese ancestor worship on all sides, soon broke down his reserve: "A land so full of people," he writes on April 9, 1906, "creates the impression that one is well taken care of there. Particularly since all parents love their children and all children love their parents as they love gods. I shall never lose the impression that I live in a land of gigantic pierrots, the streets are so full of full moon faces and white, blue, and black pierrot shirts."[19] Where but in his beloved Würzburg could he feel as

---

[13] *Mich ruft dein Bild*, p. 79.
[14] *Op. cit.*, p. 80.
[15] *Op. cit.*, p. 388.
[16] *Op. cit.*, p. 89.
[17] *Op. cit.*, p. 229.
[18] *Op. cit.*, p. 129, letter of April 6, 1906.
[19] *Op. cit.*, p. 132.

much at ease as in China? "The unshakable quiet in which the Chinese leave their opium dreams and carry on their business, amiably obese and carefree, is a heaven such as we do not possess in Europe, with the possible exception of Würzburg."[20]

Gebhardt has aptly pointed out[21] the importance of travel in Dauthendey's structural pattern. Irresistibly he was drawn to traveling as his most characteristic activity. It was a drug to him from whose influence he could not free himself, do what he might. Why did he of all people, poor as he was, squander his mite on costly tours? As a matter of fact, the goal of all his journeys was his idyllic Franconian birthplace. Every trip brought it nearer and the heartrending four Java years brought Würzburg perhaps closer to him than all the years he had spent in its confines. In spite of his craving for travel, he always found traveling "dirty and disgusting"; it always was an effort for him.[22]

We have a good description of Dauthendey the globe-trotter in the hero Rennewart of the novel *Raubmenschen,* "poet, scientist, traveler," just as the astronomer of that novel typifies Dauthendey's longing to be firmly rooted. "Weltnähe" and "Weltferne" we find here also in a less metaphysical sense. To him traveling was a realization of his philosophic tenet, that all the world is akin:

> Das Wandern ist ein Liebeshang und Wissensdrang.
> —Ein Liebeshang, ein Einstimmen beim Weltgesang.
> Ein Wissensdrang, ein Suchen nach dem Lebensgang.[23]

Such a conviction made Dauthendey feel at home in the strangest climes and among the strangest peoples. Only the Mexico of 1897 remained foreign to him. There, however, at a critical time in his life, he met with "Raubmenschen," with ugly, intimidating adventurers. He had no quarrel with the original Indian inhabitants of that country.

---

[20] *Op. cit.,* p. 136.
[21] *Op. cit.,* p. 58.
[22] Letter of April 17, 1906, *Mich ruft dein Bild,* p. 139. Referring to a projected trip to Abyssinia, Dauthendey wrote to Annie Holm, October 4, 1910, *Ein Herz im Lärm der Welt,* p. 166: "Du kannst mir's glauben, es ist absolut keine mutwillige Freude bei der ganzen Reise dabei. Ich leide mehr als vor der Reise um die Erde, da ich weiß, welch schrecklichem Alleinsein ich mich dort aussetze, von Annie getrennt, unterwegs von Menschen umgeben, die Literatur nur aus der Ferne und vom Hörensagen kennen, denen ich auf der Reise ganz unnütz erscheine, so wie ich es auf der Weltreise stündlich erlebte."
[23] "Die letzte Küstenfahrt," unpublished poem.

For Dauthendey a long sojourn in one place would have been intolerable anywhere, even in the paradise of Java where he was "in captivity"[24] for four years. In "Die Ablehnung des Paradieses"[25] inspired by a view of the majestic Javanese landscape, Adam, readmitted to Paradise, prays for a second expulsion, for without Eve there would be no Paradise and with her there, there would still be no work, the second great comforter.

Oriental poems depend a great deal for their effects, on what to our minds may seem mere mechanical devices, such as the so-called "pillow words" of Japanese poetry. To the severely critical, Dauthendey's use of Binnenreim may be such a restraining device.[26] He had early realized that conventional poetic forms were unsuited to his philosophy, that the characteristic nature of each land in its landscape, latitude, and language suggests a definite verse measure.[27] Internal rhyme seemed to afford this flexibility. Dauthendey's use of internal rhyme carries the idea to its logical conclusion. In Dauthendey's poems any two words at all of a poem may rhyme. A word may rhyme with the next following one, or the rhyme word may appear anywhere with the next few lines and may be repeated. The nature of Dauthendey's use of internal rhyme becomes clear from a typically complex pattern:

> Am nächsten Morgen, als es kaum getagt, stoppte
>   mein Schnellzug unter Schn*aufen,*
> So wie ein Pferd im *Zaum.* Im Bahnhof von
>   Ahmeda*bad* ölte man ihm das heiß*gelaufene Rad.*
> Da *sprangen* Affen an den Zug vom nächsten *Baum,*
> Auch Affenmütter *schwangen* sich, voll Selbstver*traun,*
>   mit ihren jungen Affen*rangen* an den Brüsten,
> Und ohne umzu*schau'n,* über den Bahnhof*zaun.*
> Sie kamen an den *Zug* mit ihren *langen* Armen,
> Um Mandeln oder Trauben *klug* zu *fangen.*
> Sie hockten *schwatzend* und die Jungen *atzend* im *Kreise,*
> Lebendig wie ein ganz klein Menschenvolk, und rannten zierlich übers Bahng*eleise.*

[24] The unpublished manuscript of *Der unsichtbare Weg, Lieder der Beschaulichkeit aus Tosari,* bears the legend "Auf Java geschrieben in der Gefangenschaft." Dauthendey objected to the term "Exil" employed in the magazine *Jugend.* "Would not 'Verbannung' be a better term?" he asked.

[25] *Berliner Tageblatt, Abendblatt,* June 12, 1928.

[26] *Cp., e.g.,* Carl Mumm, *op. cit., passim.*

[27] *Gedankengut aus meinen Wanderjahren, Gesammelte Werke,* I, p. 410.

Sie *blinkten* mit den Augen eine *Lichter*sprache.
Und ihre kleinen negerschwarzen Ge*sichter winkten*
 den Reisenden aufmunternd *zu:*
Du großer *Affe, du, raffe* dich auf und gib dem
 kleinen noch eine Nuß da*zu.*[28]

Far from being a limiting element, Binnenreim was for Dauthendey an intuitive rhythmic phenomenon as natural to him as his vivid color sense and his striking figures of speech, which are also characteristics of Oriental poetry.[29]

Dauthendey's understanding of the Orient was facilitated by his *a priori* love for Eastern races which pervades all his works dealing with them.[30] We have here, not an objective evaluation by a stranger within the gates, but the paeans of an admirer who felt himself one with the Orientals.[31] It was among them that he found refuge from the stilted hollowness of European life, and in his Oriental tales he draws a critical picture of the western world.

That it is not easy for the average person to understand Oriental ways of thought Dauthendey illustrates in "Den Abendschnee am Hirayama sehen," where Irene, the German wife of

---

[28] "Die Affen von Ahmedabad," *Die geflügelte Erde, Gesammelte Werke*, V, p. 88.

[29] Concerning the use of metaphors in Chinese poetry, Witter Bynner and Kiang Kang-Hu (*The Jade Mountain. A Chinese Anthology. Being Three Hundred Poems of the T'ang Dynasty*. N.Y.: Alfred A. Knopf, 1930, p. xvii) say: "If a metaphor is used, it is a metaphor directly relating to the theme, not something borrowed from the ends of the earth. The metaphor must be concurrent with the action or flow of the poem; not merely superinduced, but an integral part of both the scene and the emotion."

[30] Dauthendey's evaluation of America and Americans is based on a distaste that is similarly *a priori*. His impressions gained during a brief stay in the United States were based almost exclusively on knowledge of the well-beaten tourist lanes and of a well-thumbed Baedeker, and could only be superficial and erroneous. Thus America was for him a land where as Frau Raufenbarth (in the drama of that name, "Bürgerliche Tragödie in drei Akten," Leipzig, E. Rowohlt, p. 28) says, with glib repetition of a stereotyped phrase, "money is the heart of the world." The Americans in "Die Segelboote von Yabase im Abend heimkehren sehen," *Frau Raufenbarth,* and in the seventh adventure of *Die Ammenballade* ("Acht Liebesabenteuer gedichtet von acht Ammen am Sarge des Herrn Heinz," Munich, 1907: E. W. Bonsels and Company) are likewise drawn by one to whom America was the "Schattenseite" of his beloved Orient (*Mich ruft dein Bild*, p. 121).

[31] The other members of the Cook party seem to have had little sympathy for Dauthendey's views. Cf. *Mich ruft dein Bild*, pp. 89, 90: "The members of the Cook party naturally have no inkling of such feelings, and the German gentlemen are happy that in Delhi everything is British again. In Jeypur they grumbled hourly about the non-English character of the native city."

the Japanese actor Okuro, goes to her death from fear of the lurking, mysterious forces of his mind. Gertrude Horseshoe in "Eingeschlossene Tiere," on the other hand, with a child's intuition finds the way to Todor's love easy and natural. Only when removed from the safe pale of the European quarter of Bombay does she really see the abyss between her and the Hindu servant, and then she becomes hysterical.

In the Japanese tales we have eight novelettes deftly woven into a bouquet by the eight symbolic sights of Lake Biva, well-known in Japanese literature. Most of Dauthendey's Oriental novelettes were suggested by aquarelles painted on his trips.[32] They draw on themes one generally associates with the East, the inferiority of women in comparison with men, filial piety, and other characteristic social aspects of the Orient. Dauthendey had been reared in an atmosphere of ancestor worship. He once said of his native city:

> Auf alten Wegen, bei jedem Schritt,
> Da wandern auch alle Tote mit.[33]

He, therefore, found it easy to understand ancestor worship and filial piety, basic concepts of Chinese ethics. These ideas have perhaps nowhere found a more crystallized expression than in the twenty-four stories of the Chinese *Book of Filial Duty*.[34] The eighth story of this famous collection tells how Tung Yung sold himself so as to be able to bury his father.[35] A similar problem is touched in Dauthendey's "Der unbeerdigte Vater," where the three sons, each trying in vain to escape the ignominy of leaving their father unburied while the elaborate coffins demanded by "face" are still unpaid, are put to shame by their sister whom they have belittled but who through her faithfulness is able to preserve the family dignity.

Dauthendey's Oriental tales of his world trip (1905, 1906) represent the East suffused with ancient lore and with an emphasis on the psychic elements intuitively perceived by Dauthen-

---

[32] *Vide* appendix, pp. 166, 167.
[33] *Der Geist meines Vaters, Gesammelte Werke*, I, p. 13.
[34] Ivan Chên, translator. *The Book of Filial Duty*. Translated from the Chinese of the Hsiao Ching, with the twenty-four examples from the Chinese. London: John Murray, 1920. A less prudish translation appeared in *Chinese Repository*, VI, Canton, 1838, pp. 130-142, "Urhsheih-sze Heaou, or Twenty-four Examples of Filial Duty."
[35] *Op. cit.*, pp. 42, 43 (*Chinese Repository, loc. cit.*, p. 134).

dey as corollaries of his basic thought of "Weltallzusammengehörigkeit." In this he was aided by the reading of a few European translations of masterpieces of Oriental literature, among which he was most attracted by Paul Enderling's "Japanische Novellen und Gedichte."[36] Such reading accounts no doubt for the delicate description of characters and their actions, which remind one of Japanese prints translated into words:

"Die Farbe der Japanerin ist so diskret, nur aus dem Ärmel blitzt etwas Farbe hervor und von dem Kissen der Schärpe im Rücken, sonst ist jedes Püppchen aschgrau, stahlgrau, mäuseblau und mixpicklegrün."[37] Vain Ozuma in "Die Auferstehung allen Fleisches" rouges himself so that he has "rote, sehr rote Wangen und rote, sehr rote Lippen."[38] "Als die Schar der Fragen sich wie eine Dornenhecke um Hanake aufbaute, suchte die Singende Seemuschel nach einem rettenden Gedanken, um iher Herrin zu helfen."[39] "Bulram ging in das Haus, drückte das Mädchen an sich und schloß dabei die Augen, wie es alle Orientalen tun, wenn sie ernstlich glücklich sind."[40] "Der Wirt und die Wirtin kicherten, wie Mäuse, die über ein Stück Speck hüpfen."[41]

Dauthendey's knowledge of the Orient is all the more remarkable when one considers that all his observations as expressed in *Die geflügelte Erde, Lingam, Die acht Gesichter am Biwasee* and *Geschichten aus den vier Winden* were made during the brief space of a single Cook's Tour, not exceeding seven months, only part of which was spent in the Far East. His stay in Japan, *e.g.*, was only of four week's duration and during this time he was harassed by financial worries. However, he was able to let the Oriental scene register on his mind with his natural photographic accuracy. His frequent visits to the Japanese theatres are but one instance of his intense application, an industry he himself com-

---

[36] "Sammlung Reclam," Nr. 4747. I owe this information to Mrs. Annie Dauthendey. *Cp.* also *Gedankengut aus meinen Wanderjahren, Gesammelte Werke,* I, p. 326: "Ich muß aber immer wieder und diesmal öffentlich erklären, ich kenne nichts von japanischen oder chinesischen Urtexten. Nur ein weniges, was in Übersetzungen zu uns kam, und das jene Herren (*i.e.*, professors of literature) viel aufmerksamer studiert haben werden als ich, kenne ich."

[37] Letter of April 26, 1906, to Elisabeth Dauthendey, *Jugend,* 1919, 5, p. 87.

[38] *Lingam, Gesammelte Werke,* III, p. 94.

[39] "Die Segelboote von Yabase im Abend heimkehren sehen," *Die acht Gesichter am Biwasee, Gesammelte Werke,* III, p. 115.

[40] "Der Garten ohne Jahreszeiten," *Lingam, Gesammelte Werke,* III, p. 64.

[41] "Die Auferstehung allen Fleisches," *loc. cit., Gesammelte Werke,* III, p. 94.

pared to the bee's quest for honey.[42] He sent innumerable postcards to his wife from the points of interest visited and later consulted them to reconjure before his mind the details of this trip. It is thus that he was able to write years after the trip with a vividness apparently registered on the spot. Dauthendey was so surcharged with this spirit that he was able to write the stories at an astonishing speed, *e.g.*, *Lingam* in six days and *Die acht Gesichter am Biwasee* in two weeks.

When Dauthendey's intense longing to revisit his beloved Orient unexpectedly led to his prolonged war-time stay in Java, it was his remarkable empathy into the Oriental mind that buttressed his tenet of world-festivity, at a time when this was weakened by consuming longings of love and patriotism. This is reflected in a letter to his wife which epitomizes his manner of approach toward all strange peoples: "It is the supreme art of life to be able to *understand* all idiosyncrasies and to *value* them. I learn this very thoroughly here in this wide world among utter strangers. I try hard to be able to enjoy them all. And it is becoming easier and easier to do this with the help of humor, good will and a little self-control, the more one associates with the world and does not try to make light of the world in critical fashion.—From this standpoint one enjoys creation in a festive spirit as it should be enjoyed; that is my old motto."[43]

[42] *Mich ruft dein Bild*, p. 102.
[43] Letter of February 18, 1915, *op. cit.*, pp. 260, 261.

X
LOVE

Dauthendey's early philosophy as codified in *Verdensaltet* made no provision for the "sixth sense"[1] of love other than a general love for the "eternal mass." This does not, however, mean that he had not thought about this problem. Indeed such thoughts had occupied a good deal of his time and he later rationalized them in *Gedankengut aus meinen Wanderjahren*: "And love? Will your new world-view evaluate love properly? It seemed to me as if a distant voice were saying it from that starry point in the sky. At that time[2] I knew nothing of love and could not answer myself at once."[3] He later characterized *Ultra Violett* as having been written by a young man who had not yet embraced love.[4] Partly for this reason be was wont to look down upon his youthful works, calling them mere "Tastversuche."[5] He considered all poems prior to *Die ewige Hochzeit* and *Der brennende Kalender* as belonging to his literary adolescence,[6] believing that "the first genuine rhyme, the first genuine rhythm, a genuine song can be successfully written by a man born to be a poet only when his heart loves and glows, and only then."[7] He continues: "Today I know that I am so constituted that I should never have written a song of love, if there were no passion and longing, that I can produce a song only when my heart is stirred by tremors which may be described as neither painful nor pleasant, tremors under which my heart writhes now in the transports of blissful love fancies, and now in the melancholy of love doubts, yet intoxicated with longing."[8]

Dauthendey's literary productions after 1897 are concerned mainly with love in all its manifestations, from the very basest to the most exalted. *Phallus*,[9] as its very name implies, is a paean

[1] Letter to Mrs. Dauthendey, August 30, 1916. *Gesammelte Werke*, II, p. 404.
[2] *I.e.*, 1893.
[3] *Gesammelte Werke*, I, p. 314.
[4] *Der Geist meines Vaters, Gesammelte Werke*, I, p. 194.
[5] *Gedankengut aus meinen Wanderjahren, Gesammelte Werke*, I, p. 553.
[6] *Op. cit.*, p. 801.
[7] *Der Geist meines Vaters, Gesammelte Werke*, I, p. 254.
[8] *Loc. cit.*
[9] 1896, 1897. The point of departure of August Ewald's study of love in the works of Max Dauthendey. *Idee und Liebe, Studien in Dichtung und Kunst*. Potsdam, 1932: Müller and I. Kiepenheuer, pp. 82-91.

Cover of *Die Ammenballade.*

to the mating instinct, love in its purely physical form. It was written shortly after his marriage and in mystical language describes the efforts of the giant, Phallus, to convert humanity to a true evaluation of the mating instinct. The books of verse which followed, *Reliquien,* (1894-1896) and *Die ewige Hochzeit* (1899-1900), while transitional, are distinctly colored by Dauthendey's awakening to the omnipotence of love:

> Verwundert seh' ich die zagenden Menschen
> Noch Fragezeichen zum Nachthimmel tragen;
> Ich leg' meinen Kopf in den Schoß der Geliebten,
> Und gelöst sind für Himmel und Erde die Fragen.[10]

It was then that he interpreted the fragrance of flowers as their songs of love:

> ..... und heute weiß ich,
> Daß alle Düfte über Feld und Gärten
> Die Liebeslieder all der Blumen sind.[11]

Love became a perfect instance of the innate equality of all beings and manifestations:

> Verliebt sein ist das Himmelreich
> Da sind sich Mensch, Tier, Pflanze gleich.[12]

However, man does occupy a unique position in the universal love life:

> Endlos nur der Mensch verliebt sein kann.[13]

The next two books of verse, *Singsangbuch* (1902-1905) and *Der brennende Kalender* (1902-1905), continue to be concerned with the wonders of love. The lover constantly discovers new beauties in his mistress. Their mutual love pervades and affects all of nature. There is no hint of any but unalloyed bliss. In the mature books of verse, *Lusamgärtlein* (1907), *Insichversunkene Lieder im Laub* (1907), *Der weiße Schlaf* (1907), and *Weltspuk* (1909), each devoted to one of the seasons, the poet appears to see everything through the eyes of his beloved. Few indeed are

---

[10] "Gern höre ich die Vögel mit runden Kehlen," *Der brennende Kalender, Gesammelte Werke,* IV, p. 212; *cp.* also "Das Wissen der Menschen," *Insichversunkene Lieder im Laub, Gesammelte Werke,* IV, p. 296.

[11] "Das Geisterhaus," *Reliquien, Gesammelte Werke,* IV, p. 131.

[12] *Bänkelsang vom Balzer auf der Balz, Gesammelte Werke,* IV, p. 697.

[13] *Lusamgärtlein, Gesammelte Werke,* IV, p. 263.

the poems collected there which do not in some manner refer to his beloved wife.[14] The intense yearning during the comparatively long separation caused by the world tour appears retrospectively with all its overwhelming force in Dauthendey's apotheosis of his love for his wife in *Die geflügelte Erde,* to which he gave the characteristic subtitle: "Das Lied der Liebe und der Wunder um sieben Meere":

> So wie ein Herz geht und eilt
> Und doch weilt und immer auf einer Stelle steht,
> So wanderte ich wohl früh und spät;
> Und als einzige Helle, die in die Herzzelle fällt,
> Sah ich im dunklen Getriebe,
> Als Anfang und Ausgang in dieser Welt,
> Der Geliebten Liebe.[15]

[14] While in Sweden, for the second time, Dauthendey met Anna Johanson, daughter of the Stockholm merchant, Carl Emil Johanson. He liked her from the first. If he was a typical Southerner, she was the exact opposite, a typical representative of the North ("Sie ist ein echtes nordisches 'Rassenweib,' Barbarenweib nenne ich sie immer"—unpublished letter to Richard Dehmel from the Isle of Jersey, undated). She had been engaged to the Norwegian poet, Obstfelder, who described her as Naomi in his novelette, "Liv." This engagement had been of short duration and she had then plighted her troth to Dauthendey's friend, Uddgren. While he was pondering one day in Madame Charlotte's restaurant, Annie Johanson appeared, her engagement to Uddgren having been broken. Dauthendey renewed his wooing and before the statue of Venus de Milo in the Louvre won her consent to marry. A few days later they went to St. Hélier, on the Isle of Jersey and were married on May 6, 1896. The letters of this period are full of phrases of the beauty and wisdom of his Nordic wife. *Festliches Jahrbuch, Neunter Gesang,* is a paean to her, "die vorbestimmt und nun zum ewigen Leben zu mir kam" (*Gesammelte Werke,* IV, p. 570). Soon their money was gone. They returned to Paris and were reduced to utter indigence. Their parents were offended at not having been consulted and withheld financial aid. Although at the engagement Dauthendey had solemnly promised to take care of his beautiful wife, so as to give her courage to abide with him through life (I am quoting here directly from an unpublished letter by Mrs. Dauthendey), he had to admit several weeks later that it was impossible for him to act as the provider. It seemed natural to her that this should be so, and that she should henceforth attend to financial matters. Her untiring efforts made most of Dauthendey's trips possible ("Du hast einen anstrengenden Lebensplatz bekommen als Lyrikersgattin," letter to Mrs. Dauthendey of December 17, 1905, *Mich ruft dein Bild,* p. 78). She became the inspiration of most of his poems, so that Dauthendey wrote in his Java diary under date of November 28, 1917, an entry which gives a detailed account of the Johanson family, "I do not believe that any single woman in the world with the exception of Dante's Beatrice has been so richly surrounded with poetry by her lover as my Annie, who, however, has deserved many more songs than I shall be able to give during my life." (*Gesammelte Werke,* II, p. 605.)

[15] *Gesammelte Werke,* V, p. 7.

In *Gedankengut aus meinen Wanderjahren* (1910), Dauthendey's second accounting of his philosophy, love attains the central position in his Weltanschauung. "Than Love, there is no higher bliss in the entire universe. For each creature, love represents the highest point of life. For all creatures, it is the only goal of life, the highest life festivity which the universe knows."[16]

Thus Ata Mono, the sage, reads in the bark of the ancient Cryptomeria tree: "Know, O man, and pay heed to me, who am growing old as the surface of the earth! To me and all who become as old on the earth, love is exalted over immortality."[17]

Many of the best poems of Dauthendey's Java period gather again the thread of longing which had wound through *Die geflügelte Erde* and more immediately through the letters of the world tour:

> Diese Liebe ist der rote Faden im Labyrinth der
> sieben Meere, der niemals abreißt.[18]

Although the events of the World War quite normally produced a somewhat exaggerated patriotism in Dauthendey, he did not exalt it above love, the cardinal principle of his mature philosophy: "Only love touches the very substance of man. Patriotism is the glorification of the workaday, but it is not the sweet blissful tranquilization and exhilaration of body and heart, and knows no such fervor as love for woman."[19]

"There is nothing transitory about us," Dauthendey writes to his wife on May 7, 1915, "since we have realized that love of man for woman is all that holds the universe together and that it is the aim of all universal lives."[20]

Let us now examine briefly the problems of love treated in Dauthendey's works. The question of unfaithfulness finds repeated expression. In his own life the affair with "Mohrle," is candidly portrayed in *Bänkelsang vom Balzer auf der Balz*, but is not mentioned in any other of his published works. While the poet in Rennewart of *Raubmenschen* gave an idealized picture of himself as a typical lady's man, he was monogamously constituted

---

[16] *Gesammelte Werke*, I, p. 356.
[17] "Die Abendglocke vom Mijderatempel hören," *Die acht Gesichter am Biwasee, Gesammelte Werke*, III, p. 155.
[18] *Die geflügelte Erde, Gesammelte Werke*, V, p. 430.
[19] *Gesammelte Werke*, II, p. 466.
[20] *Mich ruft dein Bild*, p. 287.

as the "Ich" of "Auf dem Weg zu den Eulenkäfigen" explains.[21] Korfiz Holm, whose Philipp Ladurner in *Herz ist Trumpf* as a whole is an exaggerated caricature of Dauthendey, in this instance corroborates the poet's own statement. The flirtations of the lyric poet, Philipp Ladurner, are of a very innocent nature. Monogamy was Dauthendey's ideal, and in a work written as early as 1894 Bete tells Sun, champion of cosmic love:

> Lieben ist, wenn das Herz
> Nur an e i n e m Herzen zerspringt.[22]

The infidelity of Lolongku of "Im blauen Licht von Penang" is confined entirely to her dreams. The husband in the novelette, "Zur Stunde der Maus," occupies himself during most of his waking moments with thoughts of his beautiful relative, for whose sake he elaborately furnishes his apartment. There is never actual infidelity, however, and the final reconciliation between husband and wife is complete when the object of his desire dies. A morbid form of infidelity is the collection mania of Hermann Schrot in *Madame Null*, which is cured only when the loss of his wife's affections seems imminent. In "Der Garten ohne Jahreszeiten" there is a variant of this theme, found also in "Zur Stunde der Maus," and in Hasenauge's second story in "Vom Ishiyama den Herbstmond aufgehen sehen." In each case the theme is the abiding faith of the slighted wife. While in "Der Garten ohne Jahreszeiten" it is the theme of a husband's discovering that his deserted wife is the greatest love-giver, in Hausenauge's second story it is remorse and change of heart, and in "Zur Stunde der Maus" it is the realization of the wife's innocence and fidelity by the husband which brings about a reconciliation.

In three other instances the infidelity is further complicated by the birth of a love child. Dalar, in the novelette "Dalar rächt sich," on seeing his supposed son daily coming to resemble the village tailor more and more, revenges himself by leaving his wife and entering a monastery for the Jains, whose members deny the existence of intellect in women. A similar predicament in "Sonniger Himmel und Brise von Awazu"[23] where Omiya's son bears

---

[21] *Geschichten aus den vier Winden, Gesammelte Werke*, III, p. 313.
[22] *Sun, Gesammelte Werke*, VI, p. 16.
[23] Of *Die acht Gesichter am Biwasee, Gesammelte Werke*, III, where the spelling is Amazu. Dauthendey similarly uses the form "Mijderatempel," where Mijdera itself means Mij temple.

a remarkable resemblance to his friend, the teacher Amagata, leads to murder and insanity. The problem of the birth of an illegitimate child also complicates the theme of the three-act drama, *Ein Schatten fiel über den Tisch*. However, Jäger's love for his transgressing wife is so great that he not only forgives her but adopts the child as his own. The power of love here is too great to allow any retribution.

The mental suffering of a faithful wife irresistibly attracted to her wayward husband Dauthendey has set forth in "Auf dem Weg zu den Eulenkäfigen." Love, the belief in the beloved, can exist without being reciprocal. It is here that the festive side of sorrow is most poignantly depicted.

Another problem which occupied Dauthendey is the intermarriage of individuals of different races. He, himself, as we have seen, was typically Southern, Latin, while his wife by race and character was just as typically Northern, Scandinavian. He often called attention to this difference[24] which seemed to cement their love the closer. The Mohrle-interlude Mrs. Dauthendey in a letter to Dr. Schottlaender[25] explains as a manifestation of his sporadic desire for the Southern type. Dauthendey pictured his married life as a most happy one, in spite of the racial difference. In his works, however, such a union frequently leads to difficulties. Thus Rennewart's wooing of the beautiful Mexican Orla involves him in a complex situation almost costing his life. Esther, the English girl of "Eingeschlossene Tiere," awakens impossible thoughts of love in Todor's Indian mind, and the boy sets out on a trip to England where he hopes to be reunited with her. The fullest treatment of this problem we find in the novelette "Den Abendschnee am Hirayama sehen" of *Die acht Gesichter am Biwasee,* where Ilse, the German girl, is married to Okuro, a Japanese actor who has studied in Germany. The bridge to a full understanding is too long, however, and we are led to believe that Ilse's tragic death averts certain marital unhappiness.

Love at its basest, when man is completely at the mercy of instinct, Dauthendey has portrayed in *Die Ammenballade,*

---

[24] *Vide* footnote 14. Korfiz Holm in *Herz ist Trumpf*, p. 29, has his poet-egotist Philipp Ladurner exploit this difference at the expense of his Swedish wife Brita.

[25] Unpublished, copies of which were furnished by Dr. Schottlaender and Mrs. Dauthendey.

Acht Liebesabenteuer gedichtet von acht Ammen am Sarge des Herrn Heinz and in the unsuccessful farce in Wedekind's manner entitled *Menagerie Krummholz*. Here human passions are allowed unrestrained sway. What would happen if our social restraints were to be lifted completely, Dauthendey vividly pictured in the second part of *Venusinenreim*, where the passengers of the St. Gotthard-Milan express are suddenly changed into dogs, and disport themselves in truly canine fashine. Sexus, not Eros, rules here.

Dauthendey found his ideal of love most closely realized in the Far East, where it occupied a niche far above that provided for it by European civilization. He would often drift quite naturally into an elaboration of this idea, of which Arthur Kahane has noted a typical conversation: "Let man and woman not forget," Dauthendey said while discussing the Oriental concept of love, "that they have come into the world for a genuine sensuous union, for men are forgetful and unknowing and everything must be taught them again, even love."[26]

However, Dauthendey did not find his ideal of love fully realized even in his cherished East. Kutsuma, friend of Ilse's Japanese husband, has to admit: "Since I have been among you (Europeans) I realize that the world of the future will recognize the passion of love as pivotal for the world. It is not world calm, not the Nirvana, as we always believed in Asia. Neither is it cosmic sorrow and cosmic sympathy, as your expiring Christianity always believed. The passion of love is for each who lives his life seriously his God, who gives him life and death."[27]

Countless references in Dauthendey's works extol marital love. The best example is perhaps that of Jäger when he says: "Since I have become older, there is for me only *one* religion, only *one* belief, and that is *the belief in the person whom one loves*. Where my *heart* has once loved, I can never grow cold,—the one whom I love may become a murderer, liar, anything—I love. I simply must love him. And in this great fact, that one does not know why one loves, but that one must love indomitably,—in this one great fact, that love is inexplicably omnipotent, a power above all

---

[26] *Tagebuch des Dramaturgen*, p. 196.
[27] "Den Abendschnee am Hirayama sehen," *Die acht Gesichter am Biwasee, Gesammelte Werke*, III, p. 230.

powers, in this fact lies, I firmly believe, the foundation of a new religion of the future. The most exalted love between man and wife will be the ideal of the new religion, for the love experience hallows and gives man infinite powers, infinite courage, infinite endurance, and an infinite sense of duty. Everything which the state up to now has tried to force from man with the present-day religion of compassion, discipline, greatness, charity,—all that love attains not through force, but without effort, when it is considered as the highest ideal. No nation, no individual until now has completely understood the omnipotence of love between man and wife. Only when art, poetry, and the state raise not simply compassion, but love between man and wife to be the world religion, will the golden era of the world begin. Then humanity will have worn out its childhood shoes, and all the peoples of the earth can then unite in one ideal. No proud man will accept the compassion of Christianity. Compassion is intellectual, the coolest and most humiliating thing in life. Only love from husband to wife spurs on the vital power. In love between husband and wife there culminates the mightiest joy of life."[28]

It was this realization, that the completest embodiment of love is only possible in belief in the beloved, in the only mate, that made bearable the long separation on Java. When temptations were frequent and friends, fearing for the poet's sanity, tried to convince him of the folly of his faithfulness, he steadfastly refused to betray the confidence of his wife, rebuffing with Spartan rigidity even the slightest advances. The result of his struggles is to be found in rich profusion in the diary excerpts and last letters of *Letzte Reise* and *Mich ruft dein Bild*. After the war it was the fashion for a while of Germans who had returned from Java to whisper of Dauthendey's supposed immoral life while there. The evidence of close friends of that period, however, stamps this gossip as false, while autobiographic works of that period overwhelmingly disprove it. It is indeed difficult to perceive how any openminded person in examining the evidence particularly of the Java works can fail to be convinced that the poet

---

[28] *Ein Schatten fiel über den Tisch, Gesammelte Werke*, III, pp. 311, 312. Dauthendey's dramas lend themselves particularly to a study of the gradually developing omnipotence of love in his philosophy. This phase has been treated by Wilhelm Annecke in his dissertation: *Max Dauthendey als Dramatiker*, Würzburg Aumühle, 1934: Verlag Konrad Triltsch.

succeeded in living up to his cardinal principle of the omnipotence of love for one woman.[29]

Love had assumed the central position in Dauthendey's philosophy:

> Liebe im Mittelpunkt dasteht,
> Die ganze Welt sich darum dreht.[30]

Blindly and emotionally he fought for it[31] constantly,[32] and even in Java where it was put to the severest test he celebrated the festival of love yearning,[33] for even after death there was for him no heaven more splendid than love.[34] This heaven of love—the "Himmel der Gattenliebe" of *Das Lied der Weltfestlichkeit*[35]— differed to be sure from the blasphemous one of *Der Venusinenreim*, where the love-poet Dauthendey sat beside Venus at the last judgment:

> Er, der schon sein Lebtag
> Um die Venus freite.[36]

It was rather a heaven of a love refined through four years of intense suffering:

> Zusammen Schmerzen tragen, das vereint.
> Zwei weinen weniger als einer weint.[37]

. . . .

---

[29] Fritz Reck-Malleczewen fittingly answered this idle gossip in an article entitled "Für Max Dauthendey," *Berliner Tageblatt, Abend-Ausgabe*, July 25, 1925 (i.e., almost seven years after Dauthendey's death!): "Tot ist der Mann, der Mann ist wehrlos. Mit den schwachen, den überwundenen Bataillonen zu reiten aber ist für mein Gefühl eine Standesprärogative, die ich für meine alten Tage mir nicht nehmen zu lassen gedenke: Vor die Flinte soll, wer je in Zukunft den Besiegten mir schändet."

[30] *Bänkelsang vom Balzer auf der Balz, Gesammelte Werke*, IV, p. 697.

[31] *Das Lied der Weltfestlichkeit, Gesammelte Werke*, V, p. 589:
Für die Minne kämpfe blind-
lings mit Gefühl.

[32] "Lieb' kennt keine Jahreszeit," *Singsangbuch, Liebeslieder, Gesammelte Werke*, IV, p. 154.

[33] Letter of July 13, 1915, *Letzte Reise, Gesammelte Werke*, II, p. 317.

[34] *Das Lied der Weltfestlichkeit, Gesammelte Werke*, V, p. 586: "Hinterm Tode ist kein Himmel herrlicher als Liebe ist."

[35] *Gesammelte Werke*, V, p. 582.

[36] *Der Venusinenreim. Auszug der Frau Venusine aus dem Hörselberg und Venusinens Abenteuer, eine schalkhaft, heroische Liebesmär in zwölf Reimen*. Leipzig, 1911: E. Rowohlt, p. 124.

[37] "Das Lied vom Herdbau der Weltfestlichkeit," *Das Lied der Weltfestlichkeit, Gesammelte Werke*, V, p. 634.

Dieses, Menschheit, ist dein festlich Leben,
—vor dem innern Auge sichtbar wahr,—
das dir hinter Zeit und Raum gegeben,
auf dem Erdenstern und im
Weltall nah und fern, als der
ewige Kern: Liebesgeist in Unendlichkeit.[38]

[38] "Das Lied vom innern Auge," *Das Lied der Weltfestlichkeit, Gesammelte Werke,* V, p. 555

XI
DAUTHENDEY'S SEARCH FOR GOD

Dauthendey's religious development naturally is intimately linked with his view of life. As the son of a liberally inclined Protestant, he nevertheless was constantly exposed to the rigid adherence to dogma as practised in his native Catholic Würzburg. His father believed in a non-anthropomorphic God whom at times he called the "Weltgeist."[1] He often said that God was not endowed with human attributes, that He did not sit on a cloud in the sky and simply watch over humanity, but that the whole world was God.[2] Max Dauthendey in his birth-day toast of 1887 celebrates the fervid belief of his father as follows:

> Sein treuer Engel "Gottesglaube" wacht'
> Und machte seine Seele stark und groß.[3]

Although the elder Dauthendey insisted on his son's attending church regularly on Sunday mornings during his school years,[4] the pessimistic nature of the sermons was distasteful to the boy. Occasionally, however, he was permitted to accompany his father on his Sunday walks. The irate Sunday school teacher was then told that worship in nature was at least as good as in the confines of a church.[5] Like Bryant, Dauthendey's father seems to have believed that "the groves were God's first temples." When Dauthendey left for Leipzig in 1886 to become an apprentice in a lithographic studio, his father wrote the following verses of advice:

> In Not und Gefahr, wachse Dein Mut,
> Gegen Verführung Dein männlicher Wille!
> Kämpfe für Wahrheit in heiliger Glut,
> Und wenn Du betest, so bet' in der Stille![6]

As a youth Dauthendey was deeply religious as his early poems testify:

---

[1] *Der Geist meines Vaters, Gesammelte Werke*, I, p. 191.
[2] *Loc. cit.*
[3] *Meine ersten Gehversuche auf der steilen Dichterlaufbahn*, vide p. 136 *infra*.
[4] *Gedankengut aus meinen Wanderjahren, Gesammelte Werke*, I, p. 502.
[5] *Der Geist meines Vaters, Gesammelte Werke*, I, p. 107.
[6] From an unpublished volume of manuscripts in the possession of Mrs. Dauthendey.

> Wem soll mein Glück ich danken?
> Horch! Morgenglocke klingt!
> s' ist Gottes Himmelsstimme,
> Die mir zur Seele dringt.[7]

His uncritical acceptance of tradional belief was drastically challenged by his philosopher friend, Villinger. His emotional reaction almost upset his mental balance. He has vividly depicted his wrestling with the traditional idea of a personal God in a passage from "Sündflut":

> Du offenbarst dich nicht?!! . . .
> Herr, Gott, wer sagt mir,
> Daß Du bist und warst![8]

His utter bewilderment at this period has found expression in a poem written to his sister Marie Detto in 1890: "Wahrheiten wollte ich suchen . . ." which ends on the note of doubt:

> Nur e i n e Wahrheit fand ehernen Grund:
> "N i c h t s   i s t   w a h r".—[9]

Josa Gerth, in the novel of that name, is really a composite of Dauthendey and his sister, Marie, and retraces the steps of his own religious development. This novel strikingly resembles Jacobsen's *Nils Lyhne*. Dauthendey's admiration for Jens Peter Jacobsen amounted almost to idolatry.[10] He read and reread *Nils Lyhne* until he had absorbed its content and form. In *Josa Gerth* there is a resemblance not only to the style of *Nils Lyhne* but also to its religious views. Jens Peter Jacobsen's atheism was of a very mild sort. André Bellessort indeed goes so far as to call *Nils Lyhne* "la condemnation de l'athéisme par un athée."[11] Thus Dr. Wick-

---

[7] "Am Geburtstagsmorgen," *Meine ersten Gehversuche auf der steilen Dichterlaufbahn*, vide p. 140 *infra*. *Cp*. also "Osterglocken," p. 129, "Weihnachten im Walde," p. 135, "In meiner alten Bibel," p. 140, and "Bewahre dir im Herzen," p. 142.

[8] *Ultra Violett*, Gesammelte Werke, IV, p. 91.

[9] *Kaßler Allgemeine Zeitung*, XXXVII, 269, October 5, 1921, p. 5.

[10] *Vide* p. 33 *supra*. Dauthendey dedicated *Josa Gerth* to "Einem Toten," meaning thereby Jacobsen. He identifies his character, Wicking, with Jacobsen. The pen picture of Wicking is based on a photograph of his prototype. Like his *alter ego*, Wicking is a botanist, author of the study, *The Desmidiaceae*, and is of very frail health.

[11] *Madame Marie Grubbe*. (Tr. into French by Mlle T. Hammar with a preface by André Bellessort). "Bibliothèque scandinave. Collection de traductions d'auteurs scandinaves," III. Paris, 1920: Éditions Ernest Leroux, p. xiii). Hanna Astrup Larsen in her translation of *Maria Grubbe, A Lady of the Seventeenth Century*

ing, the atheist of the story, is not at all a militant one and makes no attempt to proselyte. When in the cemetery during All Souls' Day, he uncovers his head and stands in silent contemplation.[12] Again he scolds a boy who had thrown his prayer book by the way-side while playing.[13] To him it was essential that one pass through the teachings of Christianity before one could become a good atheist. Children he would have encouraged to study biblical lore, especially that of the New Testament, with its insistence on love for one's fellow man. When Josa completes her tract on atheism, Wicking counsels her to destroy it, once she has relieved herself of the revolutionary ideas it contained.

After seeing Goethe's *Faust,* Josa timidly asks Dr. Wicking about his beliefs, declaring that she had heard he did not believe in anything. He replies, "O, indeed, I do believe."[14] Although he does not believe in God, he does believe in himself.

Although Dauthendey's "new" philosophy apparently obviated the necessity of a godhead, an idea which found expression in the couplet:

> Was braucht ein Volk noch Religionen,
> Wenn Mann und Weib im Himmel wohnen?[15]

and although in *Gedankengut aus meinen Wanderjahren* traditional piety is rather looked down upon, it is only in *Der Venusinenreim* that the poet actually is blasphemous.[16] This attitude does

---

("Scandinavian Classics," VII, New York, 1917, p. ix) speaks of "the atheism that is a dreary side of Jacobsen's rich and brilliant personality. . . . In *Nils Lyhne* he emphasized again and again the bitter theory that no one even added an inch to his height by dreams, or changed the consequences of good and evil by wishes and aspirations. Nils tries to instill into himself and his wife the courage to face life as it is, without taking refuge from realities in a world of dreams. Further than this, Jacobsen attacked no sincere faith."

[12] *Gesammelte Werke,* III, p. 505.
[13] *Op. cit.,* III, p. 521.
[14] *Op. cit.,* III, p. 499.
[15] *Bänkelsang vom Balzer auf der Balz, Gesammelte Werke,* IV, p. 582.
[16] *Op. cit.,* a work published in a subscription edition of only 600 copies, Dauthendey's principal publishing firm, Albert Langen Verlag, Munich, having raised doubts as to the expediency of publishing the work in Catholic Munich. It was written at intervals between November 1905 and February 1907. For a while Dauthendey feared prosecution, as appears from a letter of October 22, 1910 to his wife, published in *Mich ruft dein Bild,* p. 210, where the following significant part is, however, deleted: "Die Götter selber waren von jeher vergänglich, warum denkt denn die Polizei, daß die katholische Religion allein eine Ausnahme macht und unvergänglich ist? So rede ich jetzt, wenn ich das arme verschämte Venusinenmanuskript betrachte. Ach es ist traurig, wenn ein Volk mehr den Pfaffen als

not, however, represent his innermost convictions. The vague idea of a godhead was so firmly rooted in him that the thought seldom left him. "I should like to cry," he tells his friend, Loewenthal, in a letter of November 12, 1894, "when I arise in the morning and do not know to whom I should pray."[17]

Dauthendey's letters to his wife show that he was not entirely divorced from the idea of a personal god even when he was proclaiming in his works that so far from having a supreme being over them, men, animals, and so-called inanimate life were themselves creators of the eternal, festive, mutable life. The Java letters particularly show a belief in the efficacy of prayer apparently addressed to an undefined deity. While drawing strength from the idea of God during moments of weakness,[18] he could yet chide his wife for her great piety and for constantly urging him to read the Bible: "You write so little about my Sumatra book of verse (*i.e., Des großen Krieges Not*) and about my poems and you again write so much about the Bible. Do consider that I am an artist, a poet, who stands in life and should vibrate with his times, and that I cannot draw edification from the Bible as is women's wont, since I consider too much biblical philosophy harmful to me from an artistic standpoint and harmful also as regards my use of German, if in addition to being in Asia, I have to read Hebraic-Asiatic literature."[19] However, in December of the same year he voices his approval of his wife's refuge in the Bible in the following terms: "Hold on to the good old true Bible words, until I can hold you again in my arms.... You did well to seek refuge

---

den großen Dichtern glaubt. Ich meine groß, im Sinne von weitblickend und weltharmonisch und das sind wirkliche Dichter doch, und nicht die Pfaffen, die nicht lieben dürfen und die Frau als überflüssig ansehen und der Frau keinen Ehrensitz im Vatikan einräumen. Aber der Venusinenreim wird trotzdem doch den Vatikan überleben." Dauthendey's youthful attitude toward Catholicism is portrayed in *Josa Gerth,* where it is mildly skeptical. A later reference in "Das Giftfläschchen" (of *Geschichten aus den vier Winden*), written on February 14, 1911, is ironical. As a character in this story, Dauthendey delivers a bottle of poison which a Swedish sea captain has for decades vainly tried to dispose of and which he has finally presented to Dauthendey, into the hands of the pope for safekeeping. "If only that doesn't cause a great misfortune!" his wife suggests. (*Gesammelte Werke,* III, p. 260). The Vatican trouble with modernists' oaths is then blamed on the fact that the pope has only cardinals as advisors and no wife. "Die Liebe einer Frau ratet besser als alle Kardinäle."

[17] *Ein Herz im Lärm der Welt,* p. 128.
[18] Letter of August 2, 1915, *Mich ruft dein Bild,* p. 312.
[19] Letter of July 13, 1915, *Gesammelte Werke,* II, pp. 316, 317.

Max Dauthendey

Tosari. (Ost-Java. Tengger Gebirge.)
Samstag
30. Juni
1917. (Fünf Monate bin ich nun hier 6000 Fuss hoch.)

Heute Morgen, als ich die 50. u. die 60. den "Psalmen David's" gelesen hatte, geschah mir eine Erkenntniss. Ich erkannte, dass es einen persönlichen Gott gibt. Drei Wochen vor meinem fünfzigsten Geburtstag wurde mir diese Offenbarung, an der ich seit meinem 20. Lebensjahr, also 30 Jahre lang, nachgegrübelt und gezweifelt und ergründet und durchgerungen habe. Welche herrliche Zielsicherheit ist heute in mein Herz, in meinen Geist, in meinen Körper eingezogen! — Gott lebt mit so persönlich, wie Alles durch ihn lebt. —

Page from Max Dauthendey's Bible. (Reduced)

in the Bible. May God bless you, so that it may strengthen you and benefit you, the good old Bible."[20] He now constantly read the Bible, a copy of which he had bought in September.[21] It was at this time that Dauthendey wrote several prayers and daily recited the Lord's prayer.[22]

Throughout his final summation of his philosophy, *Das Lied der Weltfestlichkeit,* written in 1917, there are vague hints of his groping towards a new theistic belief. After all, what did it matter whether one calls the governing principle will, world-force, the eternal life of the world-mass, spirit or God, is it not all the same in the last analysis?

> Ob ihr nun großer Gott sagt oder Weltfestgeist,
> Das eine wie das andre Gleiches heißt.[23]

The transition to a universal spirit is indeed an easy one:

> So wie du ein Ich dir weißt im Leib, das
> dich aus dem Unbewußten reißt,
> deinem Leib die Wege weist—ist ein
> Ich im Weltall, das dein Mund die
> Gottheit heißt.
>
> . . . .
>
> Dieser Gott ist nicht nur blind erdacht. Dieser Gott ist die Summe
> aller Liebesmacht.[24]

However, it was still possible to merge with God, the universal ego:

> Jedes Leben kann sich aus dem eigenen
> Ich zu dem Weltall-Ich erheben. Da
> Gefühl und Geist in Unendlichkeit und
> Unsterblichkeit jedem Lebens-Ich eingegeben.[25]

Three months later on June 30, 1917, the belief in a personal God came to Dauthendey in a flash and with overwhelming force: "A great miracle has happened to me; I wrote about it on the last page of my Bible.[26] This morning I realized that there is a

---

[20] *Mich ruft dein Bild,* p. 370.
[21] *Op. cit.,* p. 339.
[22] *Gesammelte Werke,* II, p. 475.
[23] *Gesammelte Werke,* V, p. 645.
[24] *Op. cit., Gesammelte Werke,* V, p. 621.
[25] *Op. cit., Gesammelte Werke,* V, p. 622.
[26] *Vide* illustration, p. 121.

personal God. This realization came to me after repeated reading of the psalms during the past few days. This morning I read the fiftieth and the sixtieth psalms in my Bible. All of a sudden the realization of a personal God came to me strong and tangible. Some thirty years I have considered, pondered, observed nature and myself, wishing to divine the personal God. But I could not believe in Him. How miraculously convinced I am now! In a few weeks I shall be fifty years old. This is my most beautiful birthday present, that I have recognized and understood the personality of God not only in everything that lives, but also in itself, as a living personality. All of life is a festive procession assembled by God and at its head there marches God, Himself, as a personality. The world which is infinite, eternal, and spiritual, formed by the spirit we call God, this world also has its own ego, and the ego of the world is God. For everything which lives, good and evil, strong and weak, everything is divine in the infinite universe. This universe must have an ego-feeling, a personal ego-feeling, a uniform, personal feeling of existence, and since it is divine, its ego can only be called God. This master-ego of the world is God. Do you believe that this was known before? I say no, very few have known it until now.

"No one was able to prove the existence of God. . . . But my comparison furnishes an unerring conclusion for the existence of the personality of God.—This is so simple. Why was I unable to conceive it for thirty years? I felt God emotionally; intellectually, I did not prove his existence until today. I feel freed from a great battle of life. My intellect today made peace after a thirty years' struggle with the idea of God."[27]

From the moment of this realization until his death on August 29, 1918, there was no new note in Dauthendey's philosophy. The realization of the existence of a personal God was the final development of his philosophy and his dying solace.

[27] *Letzte Reise, Gesammelte Werke,* II, p. 525.

CONCLUSION

This work has been concerned with the genesis and development of Max Dauthendey's philosophy. The conclusions may be summarized as follows: Basic conditioning influences were an intense nature perception and a great predilection for, and emphasis on, color. An acquaintance with a panpsychistic atomism led to the basic axiom of the universal equivalence and interdependence of all phenomena, involving the denial of beliefs in a personal divinity. An enthusiastic striving to portray the emotional life of the universe resulted in the programmatic *Verdensaltet* and the illustrative *Ultra Violett, Sun,* and *Sehnsucht*. The experience of love showed his previous reasoning to have suffered from false emphasis. A pessimistic reaction brought about by costly failures in an effort to find a proper abode for his poetic muse gave way to a new impulse with Dauthendey's intuitive realization of the concepts of "world-detachment" and "world-proximity." These prepared the way for "world-festivity," which then became an important characteristic of his works and thought. Love assumed a pivotal position, and in the unsystematic and wordy restatement in *Gedankengut aus meinen Wanderjahren* it dominates Dauthendey's cosmic scheme. The omnipotence of love pervades all his subsequent work. A visit to the Far East, for which he had early felt a natural affinity, seemed to give him the key to the Oriental psyche. He discovered in the Oriental view of the world much in consonance with his own. The final summation of Dauthendey's philosophy in *Das Lied der Weltfestlichkeit* foreshadowed his later conviction of the existence of a personal deity. Dauthendey's philosophy thus appears as an organic growth with shifting emphasis, changing perspective, varying enthusiasm, but inherently a living unity.

Although Dauthendey's philosophy is largely one of rediscovery, there are obviously parallels in the works of predecessors and contemporaries. His elaboration of the theory of atomism which he accepted unquestioningly from Villinger is in the tradition of Bruno, Leibniz, and Fechner. The works of Schopenhauer and Nietzsche exerted only a stylistic influence. Much of Dauthendey's early philosophy was current in the works of the young poets of the nineties. Eagerly absorbing anything germane to his philosophy, Dauthendey readily adopted and developed the synaesthesia of contemporary poetry and the delicately attuned language of Jens Peter Jacobsen, Ola Hansson, Marcellus van Eeden, and Herman Gorter, to portray the interdependence and the universal language of animate and inanimate manifestations. Although concepts of Dauthendey's world view are tangent to and indeed remarkably similar to those of other poets and philosophers, the totality of his philosophy bears marks of originality which well support his claims to newness. Colorful language, rhythm and rhyme patterns, as well as striking comparisons, were the formalistic media for expressing the festive character of his works and the innate oneness of all manifestations.

The organic development of Dauthendey's philosophy is punctuated by three attempts at codification. Of these *Verdensaltet*, because basic, has been treated in a special chapter. The later restatements and elaborations in *Gedankengut aus meinen Wanderjahren* and *Das Lied der Weltfestlichkeit* have been drawn upon throughout the present work for concepts that Dauthendey gradually introduced into his metaphysical edifice. These concepts are sometimes developments and regroupings rather than innovations. Whether he defines his categories as three "adorations,"—love, cosmic patriotism, and ancestor worship—, whether he juxtaposes them as three principal joys,—activity, love, and wisdom—, or elaborates them into the twelve heavens and chambers of *Das Lied der Weltfestlichkeit,* they remain the same underlying categories here studied.

I hope to have shown the inadvisability of approaching the work of Max Dauthendey while ignoring the metaphysical basis he himself held up as its distinguishing characteristic. May this modest investigation lead to a better understanding of the poet and his philosophy, which was born of a life of trials, and of sincere delving into the miracles of nature. Paraphrasing his own poem, we may say of Dauthendey:

Sein ganzes Leben war aus Inbrunst ein Gedicht.[1]

[1] *Der Geist meines Vaters, Gesammelte Werke,* I, p. 284.

APPENDIX A

The following lyrics with the exception of the last one[1] and "Am Geburtstagsmorgen,"[2] represent an unpublished manuscript by Max Dauthendey in the possession of Mrs. Dauthendey, and include his earliest attempts in the writing of poetry. From a formalistic standpoint they reveal clearly the influence of the folk-song and of the German family classics, particularly Goethe and Heine. They are published here in their entirety, because they are of some importance for an understanding of the poet's early thought. Reference to them has been made in the present volume.

[1] *Mich ruft dein Bild*, p. 5.
[2] *Würzburg in der Dichtung Max Dauthendeys*, p. 7.

MEINE ERSTEN GEHVERSUCHE AUF DER STEILEN DICHTERLAUFBAHN

FRÜHLINGSLIED

Frühling kam über Nacht
Hat die Erd' erwecket,
Hat ihr neues Leben 'bracht
Sie mit Blüten 'decket.

Frühling, komm' auch du zu mir,
Komme in mein Herz,
Vertreib' für immer du von hier
Des Winters herben Schmerz.

(Mai 1885)

MEIN ERSTER TOAST

Wohllöblich ist's und alter hergebrachter Brauch,
Daß man oft Reden hält bei einem Feste.
Doch reden kann ich nicht, drum denk ich, tut es auch
Ein kurzes Wort, womit ich wünsch' das Beste.
Gelinge dir im neuen Lebensjahr
Dein größtes Werk, der vielen Müh' zum Lohn,
Wonach du strebtest schon so lang' und immerdar,
Gelingen möge dir die beste, dauerhafteste—
            E m u l s i o n !—

(gesprochen zum 1. November 1885)

EIN MORGEN AUF MEINEN HEIMATSBERGEN

Wie ein Feuerball am Horizonte
Steigt die Sonne auf aus Purpurflut;
Tief errötend flammt das Himmelantlitz
Unter ihres Kusses heißer Glut.

Auf der Berge waldgekrönten Höh'n
Zittert schon des Morgens gold'ner Strahl,
Während unter grauen Nebelschichten
Noch verschleiert ruht die Stadt im Tal.

Leise aus dem taubenetzten Grase
Hebt sich neugestärkt der Morgenwind,
Flüstert einen Gruß dem neuen Tage,
Streicht liebkosend durch das Laub gelind.

Und sich wiegend sanft in grünen Zweigen
Wecket leise er Waldvögelein,
Das im weichen Neste friedlich schlummert
Träumend neuer Lieder Melodei'n.

Schwingt, nachdem er alle schnell ermuntert
Von der Höh' ins Tal sich leicht hinab,
Ziehet der schlaftrunknen Stadt dort unten
Keck die duftgewobne Decke ab.

Nun in Nichts der blaue Dunst zerflossen,
Ragen spitze Türm und Giebel auf,
Mit dem Strahlenauge blinzelt leise
In dem Licht des Kirchturms gold'ner Knauf.

Und der Morgenglocken weiche Klänge
Schwingen sich am Sonnenstrahl hinan,
Kündend weit hinaus des Schöpfers Güte,
Der den jungen Tag ließ brechen an.
(April 1886)

OSTERGLOCKEN

Kaum scheint durch die grünen Zweige
Ostermorgen licht und hell,
Regt sich's schon im Waldesdunkel,
Eilt durch's Strauchwerk flink und schnell.

Heimlich raschelnd in dem Laube
Schlüpft es hin durch Strauch und Busch,
Hurtig über dürre Äste
Hüpfend, polternd: husch, husch, husch.

Kleine, bärt'ge Wichtelmännlein
Trippeln ohne Unterlaß
Mit den kurzen, krummen Beinen
Durch das frisch betaute Gras.

Aus den düst'ren Erdenhöhlen
Krabbeln kichernd sie heraus,
Rennen dann mit wicht'ger Miene
Allesammt zum Wald hinaus.

Draußen vor dem Rand des Holzes
Halten sie im Laufe inn',
Horchen mit gespitzten Ohren
Nach dem nahen Dorfe hin.

Leise wagen sie sich endlich
Auf die Wiese vor den Wald,
Wo die zarten Osterblumen
Still erblüh'n auf grüner Hald'.

Und ein jedes altes Männlein
Schlingt ein feines Spinnenseil
Um den Stil der Blumenkelche
Emsig schnell in hast'ger Eil'.

Alsdann zieh'n sie unaufhörlich
An den blauen Osterglocken
Deren dunkelfarbnen Kelchen
Süße Töne sie entlocken.

Und so läuten sie geschäftig
Unverdrossen fort und fort,
Bis die Kund' vom Osterfeste
Jubelnd zieht von Ort zu Ort.

Sieh, da lugen durch die Zweige
Reh' und Häschen scheu und sacht
Und den Glockenstimmen lauschend
Halten sie hier Waldandacht.

Und wenn dann die letzte Glocke
Ausgeklungen sanft ihr Lied,
Leise durch die Waldesstille
Heil'ger Osterfriede zieht.

(April 1886)

DAS KREUZ IM SEE

Feuchte Nebelschleier lagern
Träumend über düster'm Moor,
Scheues Vöglein klaget leise,
Leise seufzt das schwanke Rohr.

Auf dem Schilf im Abendwinde
Wiegt sich sinnend die Libell'.
An die zarte Wasserrose
Schmieget kosend Well' an Well'.

Graue Dämm'rung spinnet dichter
Ihre Fäden über'm See,
Kleines Vöglein klaget schüchtern
Gott dem Herrn sein Leid und Weh.

Tiefe Nacht verschlingt die Klagen;
Keine Antwort hallt zurück,
Nur die lauen Lüfte flüstern,
Plaudern leis' von künft'gem Glück.

Plötzlich gleitet's leuchtend nieder,
Durch zerrissene Wolkenschleier,
Matter Schimmer bebet leise,
Spiegelt zitternd tief im Weiher.

Und von bleichem Schein umlichtet
Hebt sich's aus der Flut empor,
Wie von schimmernd Erz gegossen
Ragt ein mächtig Kreuz empor.

WALDMÄRCHENS LIED

In grüner Dämmrung im Walde
Flüstert's gar wunderbar,
Da ruhet unter Zweigen
Eine Maid im goldenen Haar.

Blüten nicken vom Haupte,
Kosend im Abendwind;
Was will zur späten Stunde
Im dunkeln Wald das Kind?

Jetzt tönt aus seinem Munde;
Horch, kannst du es verstehen?
Die alte traute Weise,
„vom Werden und Vergehen."

„Waldmärchen" ist's, das singet
Dies Lied so hell, so rein;
Der Wald hat's ihn gelehret,
Er rauscht's jahraus, jahrein.

(1887 im Sommer)

DAS ZERPFLÜCKTE RÖSLEIN

Ich wanderte im Freien,
Hatt' noch kein Ziel im Sinn,
Und kam zum Erlengrunde
Zur alten Mühle hin.

Das Mühlenrad stand stille,
Und friedlich war's umher,
Nur Waldbächlein sprang munter,
Leis plätschernd übers Wehr.

Und an der Gartenmauer
Lehnt' einsam und allein
Des alten, grauen Müllers
Liebliches Töchterlein.

Sie blicket gar so traurig
Stumm klagend vor sich hin.
Was für Gedanken mögen
Durch ihre Seele zieh'n?

Und dort in dunkler Laube
Auf jenem morschen Tisch
Liegt ein zerpflücktes Röslein,
So jung und blütenfrisch.

In Mutwill war's gebrochen
Zum Zeitvertreib und Scherz,
Nun welkt's dem Tod entgegen,
Das zarte Blütenherz.

DIE ELBJUNGFRAUEN

Im Elbwasser, im rauschenden Strom
Da hausen die Elbjungfrauen,
Beim Mondenglanz, im wilden Tanz
Kannst du sie heimlich schauen.
Wenn dumpf vom hohen Turm die Mitternacht erschallt
Und dann der zwölfte Schlag im Tale leis verhallt,

Lebet das Schilf, schauert das Rohr,
Und angstvoll scheu sie lauschen,
Wenn in der Luft, aus Nebelduft,
Gewänder unheimlich rauschen.
Wenn bleiche Gestalten in schwindelndem Reigen
Den düsteren Fluten der Elbe entsteigen.

Es flüstern die Erlen, es spiegelt das Licht
Des Mondes im Wasser sich wieder,
Es schweben leise die Jungfrau'n im Kreise

Zum feuchten Ufergras nieder.
Sie ruhen ermattet vom lustigen Tanze
Und winden Schilfblüten zu zierlichem Kranze.

Es zittert durchs Rohr, es hallet dumpf
Der klagende Ton ihrer Lieder.
Der düstere Sang, so traurig, so bang,
Die Wellen flüstern ihn wieder;
Sie erzählen von längst vergessenen Zeiten,
Von entschwundenem Glück und vergänglichen Freuden.

Der Mond verblaßt, das Lied ist verstummt,
Und Hahnenrufe laut erschallen.
Es grauet im Tal der Morgen so fahl,
Auf dem Strom die Nebel wallen.

OSTERKLÄNGE

Ostermorgen . . . ohne Sorgen,
Hell und licht . . . jed' Gesicht;
Ostersonne . . . süße Wonne,
Blaue Luft . . . Veilchenduft;
Osterhase . . . in dem Grase,
Eierstecken . . . in den Hecken,
Osterkuchen . . . gern versuchen
Kleine Leute . . . große Freude,
Osterklänge . . . Jubelsänge,
In der Brust . . . wonn'ge Lust,
Osterlieder . . . hallen wieder,
Frühlingswehen . . . Auferstehen,
Osterglocken . . . laut Frohlocken,
Hocherfreut . . . fromm Geläut',
Osterfrieden . . . zieht hienieden
In die Herzen . . . lindert Schmerzen;
Ostergrüße . . . tausend Küsse
Glück und Segen . . . allerwegen.

FRÜHLINGSZAUBER

Die lauen Lüfte kosen
Und flattern über'n Rain,
Und wecken aus dem Schlafe
Viel Blüten groß und klein.

Den zarten Blütenzelten
Entschweben Elfen hold,
Sie steigen auf zur Sonne
Und naschen von dem Gold.

Mit ihren kleinen Fingern
Betupfen sie das Grün
Der Wiese, wo dann leise
Goldblumen rasch erblüh'n.

Flink huschen sie zum Bächlein;
Dort schöpfen sie gewandt
Das Wasser silberhelle
In ihrer hohlen Hand.

Sie träufeln's auf die Gräser
Und auf die Halme all';
Die Tropfen in dem Lichte
Erglänzen wie Kristall.

Dann lassen sie sich nieder,
Die Elfen rings im Kreis,
Und weben emsig schnelle
Gespinnste strahlend weiß.

Vom bleichen Duft des Nebels,
Von Sonnenfäden auch,
Bereiten sie Gewebe
Durchsichtig wie ein Hauch.

Den feinen Silberschleier
Wirft dann im Flug geschwind
Über die graue Weide
Der neck'sche Morgenwind.

Und an die Dornenhecken
Heftet der Elfen Schar
Schimmernde Blütensterne
Aus zartem Feenhaar.

Dann fliegen sie zum Himmel
Und von dem reinen Blau
Streuen sie kleine Stücke
Auf Wiese und auf Au.

Dann blüh'n dort lauter Veilchen
Und strömen warmen Duft
Hinauf zur Himmelshöhe
Hinauf zur blauen Luft.

Da nun die fleiß'gen Elfen
Geschmückt so Wies' und Hald',
Entschweben sie und eilen
Zum traumversunknen Wald.

Hier schwingen sie den Reigen
In trauter Waldesnacht,
Wo Maienblumen schüchtern
Erblüh'n in stiller Pracht.

Sanft beben all' die Glöcklein,
Hell klinget ihr Geläut,
Und leise zieht der Frühling
In die Waldeinsamkeit.
(Mai 1886)

WEIHNACHTEN IM WALDE

Spät in der heil'gen Weihnachtsnacht,
Wenn hell der Glocken Stimme schallt,
Wenn bei der Silbersternenpracht
Der Gläub'ge fromm zur Mette wallt:
Dann gehet leise nach seiner Weise
Der Sohn des Himmels durch den Wald.

Waldmärchen mit dem goldnen Haar
Anbetend nahet es sogleich
Und bringt den Weihnachtsgruß ihm dar
Von Groß und Klein im Waldbereich.
Leis auf dem Schnee huschen die Rehe
Und schauen Christus durchs Gezweig.

Da, wo sein Fuß gewandelt war,
Heben sich Knospen mit Gewalt;
Die Weihnachtsrosen wunderbar
Erblüh'n im tiefen Schnee alsbald.
Sie flüstern leise, ringsum im Kreise:
„Der Gottessohn geht durch den Wald."

DIE EICHE

Der weite Wald lag traurig, öd und kahl,
Grau, feuchte Nebel wehten eis'gen Hauch,
Die Abendschleier zogen übers Tal,
Und müde sank das letzte Blatt vom Strauch.

Da grünte spät noch, wunderlieb und fein,
Als Scheidegruß der sterbenden Natur,
Ein junges Eichenreis im stillen Hain;
Das einz'ge Leben rings auf toter Flur.

Und heimlich leise durch die Dämmrung schwebt'
Ein guter Engel, der in jeder Nacht
Den zarten Keim mit neuer Kraft belebt,
Mit weicher Hand behütet und bewacht.

Und Jahre flohen ohne Aufenthalt.
Manch' trüber Winter, sonn'ger Frühlingstraum,
Manch' wilder Sturm verrauschte in dem Wald,
Bis jenes Eichenreis erstarkt zum Baum.

Um dessen rauhe Rinde zärtlich treu
Die Epheuranke ihre Arme schloß,
Und jenem trauten Bunde dann aufs neu
Ein Kranz von jungem Eichenreis entsproß.

Die Zeit verging, die Epheuranke sank,
Bleich und verwelkt glitt sie ins kühle Moos,
Und manches schwache Reis, das matt und krank
Am Stamme bebte, riß der Sturmwind los.

Und achtundsechzig Jahre trotzt' der Baum
Dem Sturm und Wind, dem Kummer und dem Gram.
Doch floh'n die Sorgen wie ein böser Traum,
Wenn tröstend dann sein guter Engel kam.

Und fragt ihr mich, wo jene Eiche rauscht,
Wer jener Engel, der ihr Schutz und Hort,
So hört', ich hab' es nach und nach erlauscht
Am treuen Herzen meines Vaters dort:

Er ist's, der einst in rauher Herbstesnacht
Als Eichenreis dem Harzgebirg entsproß.
Sein treuer Engel „Gottesglaube" wacht'
Und machte seine Seele stark und groß.

Wir alle, die uns jene Eiche schützt,
Die Kindesliebe eng um sie geschart,
Wir bitten jenen Engel der sie schützt
Daß er den Vater uns noch lang bewahrt.

Seht wie der Wein gleich flüß'gem Golde strahlt,
So hell bestrahlt uns Vaterliebe noch,
Drum hebt die Gläser, daß es jubelnd schallt
Gott schütze ihn, der Vater lebe hoch!
(Toast zum 1. November 1887)

EIN WELKER SOMMERSTRAUSZ

Kleine Blüten tief im Grase,
Habt ihr da nicht still gelauscht,
Als zwei Herzen und zwei Seelen
All' ihr Denken leis getauscht?

Welk und farblos seid ihr worden,
Grau, verblaßt und ohne Duft,
Doch aus euren fahlen Kelchen
Wehet warme Frühlingsluft.

Eure kleinen Blumengrüße
Flüstern leise, stets aufs neu
Die Erinnrung einer Stunde,
Zweier Herzen Lieb' und Treu.
(August 1887)

SINNSPRUCH

Da die Zufriedenheit der Welt verloren,
Wurde die Laune als Ersatz geboren.

AUF WIEDERSEHEN!

Es klagte ihre schönsten Lieder
Im dunklen Hain die Nachtigall,
Weil nun der wonn'ge Frühling wieder
Leis Abschied nahm von Berg und Tal.

„Du weinst?" Hört' ich die Rose fragen,
„Warum? Weil jetzt der Frühling geht?
Lebst du nicht fort? Weshalb verzagen?
Wein' ich, die mit dem Lenz verweht?

Hoffnung und Leben sind umschlungen.
Du lebst! Drum hoffe fort und fort,
Und wenn dein letztes Lied verklungen,
Sei ‚Wiedersehn!' dein Hoffnungswort."

Sie sprach's. Im abenddunklen Hage
Sah' ich die Rose sacht verweh'n,
Still, ohne Träne, ohne Klage,
Nur leise klang's „auf Wiedersehn!"
(in ein Album, Sommer 1888)

WAHRHEIT

Die Wahrheit ist es, die Natur
Als Urkraft uns gegeben.
Sie gipfelt nicht im höchsten Schwur,
Sie wurzelt tief im Leben.

Zwar bietet sie oft schroff und rauh
Manch harte, schwere Lose.
Doch gab sie Dornen: hoff'! vertrau'!
—Aus Dornen blüht die Rose.
(in ein Album, Sommer 1888)

ES WAR DIE LAUE SOMMERNACHT

Es war die laue Sommernacht
So märchenduftig blau.
Die Blumen wiegten sich im Schlaf
Und leise sank der Tau.

Die Rebe rankte um den Berg,
Hoch oben stand ein Baum,
Und drunter wob die stille Nacht
Den schönsten Sommertraum.
(Juli 1888)

MEIN STÜBERL

Das sag' mir doch keiner,
Daß mei' Stüberl nit nett,
Als ob wohl ein and'rer
Solch 'n Stüberl noch hätt'.

Mei' Schatzkästerl is es.
Drin glänzt es gar fein;
Es streut ja die Sonne
Ihr Gold all' hinein.

Und der Himmel, der blaue,
Und der Mond, und die Stern'
Sie all' ruh'n drin nieder,
Und jedes hat's gern.

Und einsam is gar nit,
Wir versteh'n all einand'
Die Bücher, die Bleamerl,
Die Bilder an d' Wand,

Die schwätzen und plaudern,
Denn auch die hab'n ihr Sprach',
Und red'n am laut'sten
Von vergangene Tag'.

S'is nit immer lustig
Doch gemütlich's gar sehr,
Und gemütlich heißt friedlich,
Was wollt ihr denn mehr?

Drum sag' mir nur keiner
Daß mei' Stüberl nit nett,
Wär't froh wenn ihr selber
Solch 'n Prachtstüberl hätt'!
(August 1888)

AM GEBURTSTAGSMORGEN

Durchs Fenster lacht die Sonne,
Die Amsel lockt vom Baum.
Da spring' ich flink vom Lager
Und fort sind Schlaf und Traum.

Es ist Geburtstagsmorgen,
Drum strahlt's und leuchtet's so,
Drum ist's mir auch im Herzen
So sorgenfrei und froh.

Wem soll mein Glück ich danken?
Horch! Morgenglocke klingt!
's ist Gottes Himmelsstimme,
Die mir zur Seele dringt.

Ich knie leise nieder
Und bete Herr zu Dir,
Daß Du mich segnen möchtest,
Und lieben für und für.
(Juli 1888)

IN MEINER ALTEN BIBEL

In meiner alten Bibel
Da liegt ein Epheublatt,
Das mir vor langen Zeiten
So viel versprochen hat.

Doch wenn ich's jetzt beschaue
Wird weh Erinnern wach,
Hat nichts von dem gehalten
Was es mir einst versprach.

In meiner alten Bibel
Liegt ein Vergißmeinnicht;
Wie kann ich es vergessen,
Dein liebes Angesicht.

Wie kann ich es vergessen
Wenn ich das Blümlein seh',
Die Hand die's mir gegeben,
Sie schlug mir tiefstes Weh.

In meiner alten Bibel
Da steht ein frommer Spruch:
„O, segne die dich kränken!"
So spricht das heil'ge Buch.

Wo sollte ich da segnen,
Wo nichts zu segnen ist.
Die Liebe selber segnet,
Die liebend nie vergißt!
(Juli 1888)

ZU SPÄT

Ein bleicher stiller Knabe
Der sang dort unterm Strauch
Und schaute in die Ferne
Mit sehnsuchtsheißem Aug'.

Dicht neben ihm ein Veilchen
Das stand im Gras versteckt,
Das hatten seine Lieder
Aus tiefem Schlaf erweckt.

Es duftete gar lieblich,
Als ob's ihm freundlich grüßt.
Der Knabe beugt sich nieder
Und hat es still geküßt.

Er flüstert zärtlich, leise,
Das Veilchen lauscht beglückt.
Er fragt: „Darf ich dich nehmen?"
Da hat es stumm genickt!

Laut jubelnd will er's pflücken,
Da denkt er an sein Wort,
Und denket an die Rose,
Springt auf und eilet fort.

Das Veilchen blieb und weinte
Und grämt sich gar so sehr.
Da kam ein wilder Bursche
Im Sturm des Weg's daher.

Der sah es unterm Strauche
Blauleuchtend tief im Laub,
Er pflückt's des Duftes wegen
Wirft's achtlos dann zum Staub.

Und als der Knab' im Garten
Am Rosenbusche stand,
Da war sein Lieb verschwunden,
Gepflückt von fremder Hand.

Er kehrte langsam wieder
Zum wilden Strauch zurück

Und wollt' zum Veilchen sprechen,
Sei du mein einzig Glück.

Doch sucht er es vergebens
Im Gras am Wiesenrand,
Bis er's am Weg im Staube
Verwelkt zertreten fand.

Die Abendwinde kamen
Mit feuchtem kalten Hauch,
Die sah'n den bleichen Knaben
Noch bleicher unterm Strauch.

Die Drossel schlug im Hage,
Das klang so traurig schwer,
Sie wollt dem Knaben singen,
Doch er hört's nimmermehr.

IN EIN ALBUM

Bewahre Dir im Herzen
Ein kindlich rein Gemüt,
Dann wohnt ein Engel drinnen,
Der Dich vor Sünd' behüt'.

———

Um „glücklich zu sein", mußt du
„glücklich machen".

———

Achtung, Liebe,
Die uns Edle gütig zollen,
Treiben mächt'ge Geistestriebe,
Seelenkraft und festes Wollen.

Achtung und Liebe,
Die der Starke Schwachen schenket,
Sind wie fruchtbeladne Zweige,
Die der Baum zum Kinde senket.

———

Des Menschen Antlitz ist ein Buch;
Die Augen halten die Vorrede,
Die Züge erzählen den Inhalt,
Und der Mund sorgt für die nötigen Druckfehler.

———

Schweige, zersprich nicht dein Glück.

Mustere nicht lange
Deine Spuren im Schnee.
Du sinkst ein,
Weh dann deinem Fortgang.

Ich habe mich oft
Im Schweigen gesucht und bespiegelt.
Aber es thront ein Dunkel in mir,
Keine Brücke führt, wo meine Seele wohnt.
Nie hab' ich mich selber entsiegelt.

(Jersey, Mai 1896)

APPENDIX B

CHRONOLOGY OF MAX DAUTHENDEY'S LIFE[1]

1867	born in Würzburg, July 25
1867–1884	Würzburg
1873	death of mother, Neue Welt, Würzburg
1884	September, Munich, art exhibition
1885	Würzburg, Nürnberg (trip)
1886	Würzburg (May-July), trip to Dresden, Sächsische Schweiz, Berlin, Wittstock, Magdeburg, Dessau, Lobitz, Weimar, Eisenach (Wartburg); Leipzig (September-December)
1887	Würzburg, Munich (art exhibition), Herren Chiemsee (September)
1888	Würzburg, Bayreuth (August, Parsifal)
1889	Würzburg, Geneva (April-June), Berlin, Thuringia (July), St. Petersburg (July-December)
1890	Würzburg, Neue Welt (summer), Wörishofen (September, October)
1891	Würzburg, Neue Welt (summer), Bad Brückenau (August), Berlin (December)
1892	Breslau, Berlin (February), Wittstock (February), Munich (April), Venice, Partenkirchen (August), Aachensee, Berlin, Breslau, Vienna, Freiburg, Berlin (November-)
1893	Berlin (January-March), Quille (March-June), Gjepperup (July, August), Copenhagen (August, September), Stockholm (October-November), Würzburg (December), Stockholm (Christmas)
1894	Quille (January-March), London (March 17-June), Berlin (July), Munich (August), Stockholm (August), Lindersvik (August), Dalaroe (October), Stockholm (November 12-June, 1895)
1895	Stockholm (to June), Munich, Schliersee (July, August), Würzburg (August), Stockholm (September-January, 1896)

[1] This list is based on an autobiographical fragment entitled "Im Spiegel" (*Das literarische Echo*, X, 24, September 15, 1908, columns 1698-1700), on a list of dates from 1884-1899 in Dauthendey's own handwriting in a diary in the possession of Mrs. Annie Dauthendey, on data in Mrs. Dauthendey's own diaries, on unpublished letters, and on the published work.

Appendix B

1896   Stockholm (January), Copenhagen, Hamburg, Copenhagen, Würzburg (April), Paris (April-May 1), Isle of Jersey (May 1-June), Paris (June), St. Petersburg (June 6, 7, 8), Paris (Rue Boissonade, June 15-September 5), Würzburg (-September 20), Karlsruhe, Taormina (September, October), Naples (-end of October), Paris (October-December)

1897   Paris (-April), Würzburg (April), Paris (April-May), Würzburg (May), Pouldu-Bretagne (May-June 10), St. Malo, Southampton, New York, Philadelphia, Havana, Vera Cruz, Mexico, Cuautla, Amecameca, Mexico City (July-December 14), Vera Cruz, Tampico (December 25)

1898   New Orleans, Havre (February 5), Paris (February-March 2), Marseilles, Genoa (March 21), Piraeus, Athens (March 27-April 2), Delphi (April 3), Olympia (April 7), Kalamata (April 10), Tripolitza, Epidaurus, Athens, Patras, Trieste (end of April), Würzburg (Neue Welt, end of April to November), Berlin (November-)

1899   Berlin (-February 1), Paris (-May 25), Stockholm, Wisby (June 2-October), Würzburg (Neue Welt, October), Munich (October)

1900   Munich (-April), Würzburg (Neue Welt, May-September), Munich (September-)

1901   Munich, Florence, Munich (-May), Würzburg (Neue Welt, summer), Bernried am Starnberger See, Munich (-December), Paris

1902   Paris (-February), Munich (-July), Wartenberg, Munich, Paris (October-December)

1903   Paris (January-end of June), Södertelje (Sweden, -August 15), Wisby, Dröback (Norway, August-September), Oslo (-end of November), Paris

1904   Paris (January-July), Barbizon (until end of September), Paris (October)

1905   Paris (-February 20), Würzburg (February-November), Rome (November), Würzburg (December), Paris (December), Marseilles

1906   Cairo (January 4-8), Port Said (January 9), Bombay (January 19, 20), Delhi (January 28, 29), Cownpore (February 4), Lucknow (February 5), Benares (February 9), Darjeeling (February 12, 13, 14), Calcutta (February 16, 17, 18), Rangoon (February 21-24), Mandalay (February 25, 26), Madras (March 5), Colombo (March 11-15), Kandy (March 16-19), Colombo (March 23-25), Penang (March 29), Hongkong (April

146   APPENDIX B

6-16), Canton, Nagasaki (April 23), Kobe (April 25, 26), Kioto (April 27-29), Kodzu (May 6-9), Nikko (May 12), Yokohama (May 18-20), Honolulu (May 31), San Francisco (June 8), Los Angeles (June 11), El Tovar (June 15), Denver (June 18), Manitou (June 22), Chicago (June 23), Niagara Falls (June 28), New York (June 29), London (July 8, 9), Würzburg (August-September), Schloß Mainberg, Schweinfurth (-October), Munich

1907 Munich (-May), Würzburg (-September), Schloß Schwanenberg (September), Würzburg (October-)

1908 Würzburg (-June), Berlin (one week in June), Würzburg (Neue Welt, July-September)

1909 Würzburg (-December), Berlin

1910 Berlin (-end of February), Munich (-April), Mannheim, Frankfurt, Munich, Würzburg (-July 11), Koster (-August 17), Limone, Garda (September-October), Munich (October), Rome (November), Würzburg

1911 Würzburg (-May 11), Munich, Würzburg (May-June), Koster (-end of August), Berlin (September), Munich (October 5-13), Hamburg (October 18-22), Cologne (October 29-November 5), Munich (November), Würzburg

1912 Würzburg

1913 Würzburg (-end of August), Venice, Liparian Isles, Rome (November), Berlin, Munich, Berlin

1914 Berlin (-April 14), Bremen, Antwerp, Algiers (April 26), Genoa (April 30), Naples, Messina (May 2), Port Said (May 4), Aden (May 10), Singapore (May 22, 23), Batavia (May 23), Weltevreden (May 24-June), Amboina (August 19), Sumatra (September-)

1915 Sumatra (-end of February), Garoet, Java (Solo, October 23-November 1)

1916 Garoet (-end of February), Soerabaja (March-July), Malang (-December), Soerabaja

1917 Soerabaja (-February), Mt. Smeroe (May 5-10), Tosari

1918 Tosari (-August), Songgoriti (August), Malang, died August 29, 1918, Malang

APPENDIX C
CHRONOLOGICAL LIST OF WORKS[1]
Arranged in the sequence of writing

	WRITTEN	FIRST PUBLISHED
Meine ersten Gehversuche auf der steilen Dichterlaufbahn	1885-1888 (Würzburg)	1936
Der Eindringling (translation of Maurice Maeterlinck's *L'intruse*)	June 1891 (Würzburg)	unpublished
Die Blinden (translation of Maurice Maeterlinck's *Les aveugles*)	1891 (Würzburg)	unpublished
Vom Kampfplatz	1891 (Würzburg)	unpublished
Philosophie eines Dienstmannes	1891 (?) (Würzburg)	unpublished
Ein Park	1891 (?) (Würzburg)	unpublished
Siebzig Jahre	1891 (Würzburg)	1891
Barmherzige Schwestern	1891 (Würzburg)	1891
Aus langer Weile!	1891 (Würzburg)	1891
Todwund	1891 (Würzburg)	unpublished
Josa Gerth. Roman	June-December 1891 (Würzburg)	1893
Das Kind. Drama in zwei Teilen	Summer of 1892 (Munich)	1895
Teufelstriller	December 21, 1892 (Berlin)	unpublished
Ultra Violett. Einsame Poesien	1892, 1893 (Berlin and Quille)	1893

[1] This list is based chiefly on information from the diaries of Mrs. Annie Dauthendey.

Appendix C

	WRITTEN	FIRST PUBLISHED
Die Kunst des Intimen	1893	(published in Danish translation: *Verdensaltet*)
Die Kunst des Erhabenen	(Berlin)	
Glück. Drama in vier Szenen	Autumn of 1894 (Sweden)	1895
Die schwarze Sonne	1893-1896 (Isefjord, Stockholm, London, Schliersee)	1897
Sehnsucht	December 1892- March 1894 (Quille)	1895
Sun	June 1894 (Berlin)	1895
Reliquien	1894-1896 (principally autumn of 1894, Dalarö, Stockholm)	1897
Phallus	Summer 1896 and 1897 (Paris)	1897
König Proß. König Eng. König Gier	1897 (Mexico)	unpublished
Festliches Jahrbuch. Erster Gesang	August 1898 (Würzburg)	1898
Die Frau von Thule	March 1899 (Paris)	1902
Das Unabwendbare. Szene aus der Einführung des Zölibats	August, September 1899 (Würzburg)	1900
Die ewige Hochzeit. Liebeslieder	1899, 1900 (Würzburg)	1905
Festliches Jahrbuch. Neunter Gesang	May 9, 1899 (Würzburg)	1899
Das Tagebuch des Verführers (translation of Sören Kierkegaard's *Forförerens Dagbog*)	May-July, 1903 (Paris)	1903

Appendix C

	WRITTEN	FIRST PUBLISHED
Bänkelsang vom Balzer auf der Balz	November 1903, February 1904 (Paris)	1905
Die Ammenballade	1904 (Paris and Barbizon)	1907
Neun Pariser Moritaten	1904 (Paris)	1907
Singsangbuch. Liebeslieder	1902-1905 (Paris and Barbizon)	1907
Der Waldklaus	Spring of 1904 (Barbizon)	unpublished
Der brennende Kalender. Liebeslieder	1902-1905 (Munich and Paris)	1905
Frau Raufenbarth. Bürgerliche Tragödie in drei Akten	February 1905 (Würzburg)	1911
Menagerie Krummholz. Jahrmarktskomödie in drei Akten	Act I: June 26, 1905 Act II: June 29, 1905 Act III: June 30, 1905 (Munich)	1911
Der Drache Grauli. Drama in drei Akten	Act I: March 5, 1907, 4 P.M.—3 A.M. Act II: March 8, 1907, 1 P.M.—10 P.M. Act III: March 9, 1907, 12 M.—9 P.M. (Munich)	1911
Fünfuhrtee. Tragischer Akt	March 11, 1907 2 P.M.—11 P.M. (Munich)	1911
Humoristische Reisebeschreibung um die Erde	March 1907 (Munich)	unpublished
Lusamgärtlein, Frühlingslieder aus Franken	Spring of 1907 (Munich, greater part in Würzburg)	1909

APPENDIX C

	WRITTEN	FIRST PUBLISHED
Ein Schatten fiel über den Tisch. Schauspiel in drei Akten	Act I: August 21, 1907, 5:30 P.M.—10:30 P.M. Act II: August 22, 1907, 3:30 P.M.—9:30 P.M. Act III: August 24, 1907, 4:00 P.M.—8:00 P.M. (Munich)	1911
Chronik der Ereignisse Würzburgs	June 1907 (Würzburg)	unpublished
Lachen und Sterben. Tragischer Akt	June 15-18, 1907 (Würzburg)	1911
Madame Null. Schwank in drei Akten	1905-1907 (Würzburg)	1911
Insichversunkene Lieder im Laub	Summer 1907 (Würzburg)	1908
Der weiße Schlaf. Lieder der langen Nächte	October-November 1907 (Würzburg)	1908
Plastische Bühne nach dem Vorbild asiatischer Theaterhäuser. Essay	August 1907	unpublished
Der Venusinenreim	November 1905-February 1907 (Würzburg and Munich)	1911
Messina im Mörser. Episches Gedicht	January 1908 (Würzburg)	1909
Die Spielereien einer Kaiserin. Drama in vier Akten, einem Vorspiel und einem Epilog	Conceived November 1907 Act V: July 25, 1908 Act IV: July 28, 1908 Act III: July 31, 1908 Epilogue: August 3, 1908	1910

APPENDIX C

	WRITTEN	FIRST PUBLISHED
	Acts I and II: August 5-7, 1908 (Würzburg)	
Weltspuk. Lieder der Vergänglichkeit	Autumn 1909 (Würzburg)	1910
Lingam. Zwölf asiatische Novellen	End of April-May 1909 (Nine Novellen in six days) (Würzburg)	1909
Die geflügelte Erde. Ein Lied der Liebe und der Wunder um sieben Meere	July 14, 1907-September 21, 1909	1910
Maja. Skandinavische Bohême. Komödie in drei Akten	September 18-25, 1909 (Würzburg)	1911
Die acht Gesichter am Biwasee. Japanische Liebesgeschichten[2]	February 24-March 15, 1910 (Munich)	1911
Raubmenschen. Einer von Rennewarts Romanen	Conceived April 1910, written, December 1910-February 1911 (Würzburg)	1911
Der Geist meines Vaters. Aufzeichnungen aus einem begrabenen Jahrhundert	Conceived March 1911, written December 1911, February 9-March 23, 1912 (Würzburg)	1912
Die Heidin Geilane. Die Kilianstragödie	Conceived 1907 Written April	1912

[2] "Die Segelboote von Yabase im Abend heimkehren sehen", February 24, 1910, completed March 22, 1910. "Den Nachtregen regnen hören in Karasaki", February 15, 1910, 10 A. M.—7 P. M. "Die Abendglocke vom Mijderatempel hören", February 27, 1910. "Sonniger Himmel und Brise von Awazu", March 1, 1910. "Der Wildgänse Flug in Katata nachschauen", March 2, 1910. "Von Ishiyama den Herbstmond aufgehen sehen", Hasenauge's first story, March 6, 1910; Hasenauge's second story, March 7, 1910; Hasenauge's third story, March 8, 1910. "Das Abendrot zu Seta", March 9, 10, 1910. "Den Abendschnee am Hirayama sehen", March 11-15, 1910. "Einführung", March 18, 1910.

Appendix C

	WRITTEN	FIRST PUBLISHED
	17-26, 1912 (Würzburg)	
Die Untergangsstunde der „Titanic"	December 26, 1912 (Würzburg)	1913
Gedankengut aus meinen Wanderjahren	January-March 1913	1913
Geschichten aus den vier Winden[3]	1910, 1911 February, March 1914 (Würzburg, Berlin)	1915
Das Erz von Mataram. Javanische Ballade	November 25, 1915 (Garoet, Java)	December 1915
Des großen Krieges Not. Lieder	August 1914-1915 (Sumatra and Java)	1915
Die Hochzeit des „Nagels der Erde"	October-November 1915 (Garoet)	1921
Das Märchenbriefbuch der heiligen Nächte im Javanerlande	January, February, 1916 (Garoet)	1921
Ohnmächtige Schiffe	May 1916 (Soerabaja)	1925
Ablehnung des Paradieses	February 17, 1917 (Tosari)	June 1928
Der unsichtbare Weg. Lieder der Beschaulichkeit aus Tosari	Spring 1917 (Tosari, Java)	unpublished
Meine Smeroe-Besteigung	May 1917 (Tosari, Java)	1925
Das Lied der Weltfestlichkeit	March 19-30, 1917 (Tosari, Java)	1917
Die letzte Küstenfahrt	August 1917 (Tosari)	unpublished
Letzte Reise. Aus Tagebüchern, Briefen und Aufzeichnungen	May 1914-July 1918 (Java)	1925

[3] "Das Iguanodon", October 8, 1910, Limone. "Das Giftfläschchen", February 14, 1911. "Himalayafinsternis", November 27-30, 1911.

BIBLIOGRAPHY

1. COLLECTED WORKS

Gesammelte Werke. Munich, 1925: A. Langen. 6 volumes. (Volumes I, III and IV appeared also separately in 1930.) Contents: I. „Autobiographisches": *Der Geist meines Vaters. Gedankengut aus meinen Wanderjahren.* II. „Aus fernen Ländern": *Erlebnisse auf Java. Letzte Reise. Das Märchenbriefbuch.* III. „Novellen und Romane": *Lingam. Die acht Gesichter am Biwasee. Geschichten aus den vier Winden. Josa Gerth. Raubmenschen.* IV. „Lyrik und kleinere Versdichtungen": *Ultra Violett. Reliquien. Singsangbuch. Die ewige Hochzeit. Der brennende Kalender. Lusamgärtlein. Insichversunkene Lieder im Laub. Weltspuk. Der weiße Schlaf. Des großen Krieges Not. Die schwarze Sonne. Phallus. Festliches Jahrbuch: Achter Gesang, Neunter Gesang. Bänkelsang vom Balzer auf der Balz. Messina im Mörser. Die Untergangsstunde der Titanic.* V. „Die großen Versdichtungen": *Die geflügelte Erde. Das Lied der Weltfestlichkeit.* VI. „Dramen": *Sun. Sehnsucht. Das Kind. Glück. Das Unabwendbare. Fünfuhrtee. Lachen und Sterben. Ein Schatten fiel über den Tisch. Maja. Der Drache Grauli. Die Spielereien einer Kaiserin. Die Heidin Geilane.*[1]

---

[1] The following books are not included in the collected works: *Das Tagebuch des Verführers* (translation of Kierkegaard's *Forførerens Dagbog*), *Der Venusinenreim, Die Ammenballade* (including also *Neun Pariser Moritaten*), *Frau Raufenbarth, Madame Null, Menagerie Krummholz, Mich ruft dein Bild, Verdensaltet* (in collaboration with G. Uddgren). Omitted also are three short stories: „Aus langer Weile!", „Barmherzige Schwestern", and „Siebzig Jahre", and numerous letters and poems listed in this bibliography. Publications in book form are listed below. Works which are reprinted in *Gesammelte Werke*, having appeared before only in serial publications, are as follows:

Festliches Jahrbuch, Achter Gesang, appeared first in *Pan,* IV, 4, 1898, pp. 215-219 („Erster Gesang aus ‚Festliches Jahrbuch' ". Buch in 12 Gesängen, regiert von den 12 Sternbildern). The change from first to eighth appears to have been arbitrarily made by the editors of the collected works.

Festliches Jahrbuch, Neunter Gesang, appeared first in *Blätter für die Kunst,* series 4, IV, 1897-1899, pp. 104-106.

Das Unabwendbare. Szene aus der Zeit der Einführung des Zölibats appeared first in *Die Insel,* I, July-September, 1900, pp. 21-38.

Messina im Mörser appeared first in *Pro Italia.* „Eine deutsche Kunstspende". Munich, 1909, 1920: Georg Müller Verlag, pp. 312-320, then as an appendix to *Weltspuk.*

2. LIST OF POEMS NOT INCLUDED IN COLLECTED WORKS[2]

„Achtung, Liebe", *vide*, p. 142.

„Als Adam wohl fünfhundert Jahre war", *Berliner Tageblatt, Abendblatt*, June 12, 1928 (title: „Ablehnung des Paradieses").

„Auf dem Acker draußen", *Velhagen und Klasings Monatshefte*, XXVI, 1911/1912, p. 637, (title: „Der Sämann").

„Bewahre Dir im Herzen", *vide*, p. 142.

„Da draußen in der Nacht", *Velhagen und Klasings Monatshefte*, XXVII, 1912/1913, p. 153.

„Das sag' mir doch keiner", *vide*, p. 138.

„Dein Blut wird mein Blut, wenn der Abend funkelt", *Die neue Rundschau*, 1912, p. 1740.

„Der Fluß kommt grün dahergezogen", *Velhagen und Klasings Almanach*, V, 1913, p. 194, (title: „Verjüngung").

„Der glatte Mond, er weckt dich leis", *Die neue Rundschau*, 1912, p. 1739.

„Der stille Weg", *Pan*, III, 1897, p. 253.

„Der Vollmond, der alte Schatzgräber", *Jugend*, 1902, no. 50, p. 844.

„Der Weg war hart gefroren", *Simplicissimus*, XVII, 47 (February 17, 1913), p. 780, (title: „Der leere Wald").

„Der weite Wald lag traurig, öd und kahl", (title: „Die Eiche"), *vide* p. 136.

[2] A number of poems are found scattered through the prose volumes. A list of those not also included in a volume of poetry is appended herewith.

The following poems appear only in *Der Geist meines Vaters, Gesammelte Werke*, I: „Der immer dunkle Efeu, der sich klammernd rankt", p. 11; „Der Vater sprach vom Feuerschlund", pp. 192, 193; „Wo ist Wirklichkeit", p. 279.

The following poems appear only in *Letzte Reise, Gesammelte Werke*, II: „Abschiednehmend im fallenden Tag", p. 482; „Auf breiter, weißer Treppe im nächlichen Garten", p. 588; „Bergnebel, von Sonnenlicht erfüllt", p. 590; „Da draußen regnet es weit und breit", pp. 588, 589; „Da draußen schwebt ein feierlicher Berg", p. 699; „Die Frühsonne hängt ihr Licht an die Spitzen vom hohen Rosenstrauch", p. 583; „Die langen Nadeln der Tannenzweige", p. 573; „Die Lüfte sind heut nicht mehr stumm", p. 573; „Die Wolken lagern unter mir im Abendraum", p. 609; „Du bringst zum Leben mit", p. 717; „Du Schwalbe, Vogel der Seele", p. 538; „Du sollst nicht nur Mensch mit Menschen sein", p. 676; „Dunkel liegt die Nacht noch vor den Türen", p. 575; „Eine Grille singt wie ein leiser Wille", p. 590; „Einwiegend ist die Luft heute hier", p. 716; „Es rührt mich im Abend an", p. 424; „Fern steht heut die Welt im Sonnenschein", p. 571; „Ich lebe nicht mein Leben", p. 217; „Ich schleiche im Abend, du bist mir im Sinn", p. 534; „Ihr dürft mich nicht verlachen", p. 577; „Im Morgenäther hängt des Mondes", p. 640; „Im Nachbarhaus steht oft ein Fenster offen", pp. 409, 410; „Möchte so gern es singen, wie mir's ums Herz bestellt", p. 341; „Nun blühen rot die Feuerbäume zum fünftenmal!", p. 717; „Sage mir, wie wohl das tut—plumm, plumm", p. 693; „Still, in Nebel eingesargt und stumpf", p. 597; „Was ist das Herz ein derbes Ding", p. 598; „Wenn dein Haar fern leuchtet im Mittaglicht", p. 676; „Will mir denn keine Erlösung werden", p. 591.

The following poems are to be found only in the volume of letters entitled: *Mich*

„Der Wind wühlt in dem Lindenbaum", *Velhagen und Klasings Monatshefte*, XXVI, 1911/1912, p. 304.
„Des Menschen Antlitz ist ein Buch", *vide* p. 143.
„Die Bäume waren stille", *Pan*, III, 1897, p. 253.
„Die lauen Lüfte kosen", (title: „Frühlingszauber"); *vide* p. 133.
„Die Sonne wurde breit und sank", *Jugend*, 1912, no. 46, p. 1369 (title: „Das Wasser glänzt noch weit und blank").
„Die Wahrheit ist es, die Natur", (title: „Wahrheit"), *vide* p. 138.
„Die Welt voll blühender Gärten stand", *Velhagen und Klasings Almanach*, VI, 1914, p. 27.
„Dort steht auf der Höh' ein einäugig Haus", *Velhagen und Klasings Almanach*, VII, 1915, p. 188, (title: „Das einäugige Haus").
„Draußen steht das große Volk der Sterne", *Jugend*, 1916, no. 13, p. 266.
„Durchs Fenster lacht die Sonne", (title: „Am Geburtstagsmorgen"), *vide* p. 139.
„Ein bleicher stiller Knabe", (title: „Zu spät"), *vide* p. 141.
„Eine goldgebräunte Wange war der Abendhimmel", *Licht und Schatten*, I, 1910/1911, no. 17, (title: „Läuft noch eine in den Garten").
„Es ging der Mond im Ährenfelde mit", *Licht und Schatten*, I, 1910/1911, no. 11.
„Es grübelt der Abend unterm Brückenbogen", *Simplicissimus*, XVIII, 41 (January 5, 1914), p. 694, (title: „Am Brückengeländer").

---

ruft dein Bild: „Das Heimweh macht mich genesen", pp. 413, 414; „Das Schiff, von den Wellen begleitet", p. 175; „Friedliche Bäche rauschen", p. 287; „Ich habe mich oft im Schweigen gesucht und bespiegelt", p. 5; „Liebe Mulde, höre zu", pp. 61-63; „O März, du blasser Monat du", p. 72; „Wenn ich morgens an dem tauig frischen Wege stehe", p. 365; „Wir küßten mit Zagen und Bangen", p. 74.

The following poems of the Batavia edition of *Des großen Krieges Not* are omitted from the collected works: „Auch Du, Italien! Blaues Land!", p. 86; „Aus der steinernen Halle durch offene Bogen", p. 93; „Den Tod er tags ins Leben rief", p. 67 (Munich, 1915 edition, p. 47); „Der Hindenburg, der hat's geschafft", p. 61; „Der Trommelwirbel rauh zum Ansturm trieb", p. 35 (also in Medan edition, 1914); „Die Deutschen sind da", p. 21 (Munich, p. 32, also Medan); „Die Hilfsbereiten, sie wurden ein Heer", p. 28 (Munich, p. 32, also Medan); „Die Nebel schwinden im Morgenlicht", p. 76; „Es mußt' der Mann zum Töten ziehn", p. 25 (Munich, p. 30, also Medan); „Granaten heulen voller Wucht", p. 112; „Hochwasserflut bedeckt das Land", p. 105; „Ich hörte eine rührende wahre Geschichte erzählen", p. 116; „Ich sehe im Kalender nach", p. 103; „Im Acker lag er todeswund", p. 66 (Munich, p. 48); „Im Vogesenwald schrillt ein blitzartig Pfeifen", p. 55 (Munich, p. 63; *Deutsche Wacht*, I, 8, August, 1915, p. 515); „Muß heut' ein Lied dem Kaiser singen", p. 51 (*Deutsche Wacht*, loc. cit., pp. 513, 514); „Nachts wir sie Schulter bei Schulter hart fühlen", p. 59 (Munich, p. 50); „Oft muß ich an die Verstümmelten denken", p. 23 (Munich, p. 28, also Medan); „Sie schrieben sich ein", p. 26 (Munich, p. 31, also Medan); „Sie waren ausgesandt, zu spähen", p. 88 (Munich, p. 51); „Vom Kriegsmut sprechen auch die Kleinen", p. 30 (Munich, p. 33, also Medan).

The following poem appeared only in the Munich edition of *Des großen Krieges Not*, 1915: „So muß ich nun sitzen und warten", p. 70.

„Es ist ein roter Frühling angebrochen", *Deutsche Wacht*, IV, 7 (July, 1918), pp. 567, 568, (title: „Der rote Frühling 1918").
„Es klagte ihre schönsten Lieder", (title: „Auf Wiedersehen"), vide p. 137.
„Es war die laue Sommernacht", vide p. 138.
„Es war vor Belfort. Glatt stieg im Flug", *Deutsche Wacht*, I, 12 (December, 1915), pp. 895, 896, (title: „Sieg im Flug").
„Feuchte Nebelschleier lagern", (title: „Das Kreuz im See"), vide p. 130.
„Frühling kam über Nacht", (title: „Frühlingslied"), vide p. 128.
„Hängt heut die letzten Tore aus", *Jugend*, 1912, no. 40, p. 1162, (title: „Heut drängt sich tätig Meer zu Meer").
„Hinter Fenstern heben Funken an zu brennen", *Bayerische Landeszeitung*, Würzburg, XXVI, no. 369 (December 24, 1910), (title: „Weihnachtskerzen").
„Ich und ein Stern wir sind im dunklen Zimmer", *Pan*, II, 7 (January 4, 1912), p. 211, (title: „Sterngespräch").
„Ich wanderte im Freien", (title „Das zerpflückte Röslein"), vide p. 131.
„Ich will euch heute führen in eine Kaiserstadt", *Deutsche Wacht*, I, 12 (December, 1915), pp. 889-894, (title: „Das Erz von Mataram").
„Im Elbwasser, im rauschenden Strom", (title: „Die Elbjungfrauen"), vide p. 132.
„Im Winter, wenn verflogen auf der Flur", *Die neue Rundschau*, 1912, p. 1739, (title: „Versteinerungen").
„In meiner alten Bibel", vide p. 140.
„In einer jungen Pappel wohnt", *Simplicissimus*, XIX, 4 (April 27, 1914), p. 55, (title: „Der Blick der Frühlingsnacht").
„In grüner Dämmerung im Walde", (title: „Waldmärchens Lied"), vide p. 131.
„Kaum scheint durch die grünen Zweige", (title: „Osterglocken"), vide p. 129.
„Klein werden die Worte, die großen wie Mäuse", *Simplicissimus*, XVII, 37 (December 9, 1912), p. 607, (title: „Das große Wort Krieg, das kleine Wort Sieg").
„Kleine Blüten tief im Grase", (title: "Ein welker Sommerstrauß"), vide p. 137.
„Liebe Mutter, heilige Frau", *Simplicissimus*, November 23, 1915, p. 406, (title: „Heimweh").
„Mein Herz allein lebt in dem Abendraum", *Simplicissimus*, XVI, 30, October 23, 1911, p. 508, (title: „Windstille am Meer").
„Meine Hände sind so heiß", *Pan*, III, 1897, p. 253.
„Möchte heute ohne Ende", *Simplicissimus*, October 26, 1915, p. 350, (title: „In der Fremde").

„Mond, Duzfreund du verliebter Toren", *Simplicissimus,* XVI, January 8, 1912, p. 724, (title: „Grüß mir die Stundenschar im Raum").
„Mustere nicht lange", *vide* p. 143.
„Nur kleine rote Sommerbeeren", *Jugend,* 1911, 48, p. 1300, (title: „Im Winterrauch").
„Ostermorgen ... ohne Sorgen", (title: „Osterklänge), *vide* p. 133.
„Rot, gelb und lila sind jetzt die Hügel", *Simplicissimus,* XVII, 26, September 23, 1912, p. 408, (title: „Fort fliegt der Sommer").
„Sah drei Kinder heut am Wege kauern", *Velhagen und Klasings Monatshefte,* XXVII, 1912/1913, p. 74, (title: „Veilchensuchend knieten sie im Grase").
„Schnitter, die das hohe Korn abmähen", *Pan,* I, 21, September 1, 1911, p. 693, (title: „Riesenspielzeug").
„Schwer an Blut und Liebe ist Thule", *Die Insel,* III, no. 7/8, April-May, 1902, pp. 165-167, (title: „Die Frau von Thule").
„Sind sie glücklich, die schönen Frauen", *Simplicissimus,* XVII, 1912, *Badenummer,* p. 3, (title: „Spiegelscherzo"). (Reprinted in modified form as „Der Spiegel", *Gesammelte Werke,* IV, p. 139).
„Spät in der heil'gen Weihnachtsnacht", (title: „Weihnachten im Walde"), *vide* p. 135.
„Unter schwarzen röchelnden Algen", *Moderner Musenalmanach auf das Jahr 1894,* Munich, p. 205. (Appeared also in Hans Benzmann: *Moderne deutsche Lyrik, Leipzig,* 1903: Philipp Reclam, jun., p. 139).
„Wahrheiten wollte ich suchen", *Kaßler Allgemeine Zeitung,* XXXVII, 269, October 5, 1921, p. 5.
„Weithin, so weit wir sehen", *Velhagen und Klasings Monatshefte,* XXVI, 1911/1912, 3. Band, p. 69, (title: „Frühlingserde").
„Wie dunkle Tücher liegen die Schatten unter den Sommerbäumen", *Licht und Schatten,* I, 39, 1910/1911, (title: „Ich schau' den Schmetterlingen nach").
„Wie ein Feuerball am Horizonte", (title: „Ein Morgen auf meinen Heimatbergen"); *vide* p. 128.
„Wie sind die Wege so traurig nur", *Simplicissimus,* XXVI, 5, April 27, 1921, p. 54, (title: „Tosari-Abend").
„Wir ließen uns vom Tag vergessen", *Simplicissimus,* XVI, 39, December 25, 1911, p. 687, (title: „Wir alle zusammen").
„Wir wußten kaum mehr noch, was Helden waren", *Deutsche Wacht,* III, 2, February, 1917, pp. 169-172, (title: „Gedicht zur Enthüllung der Gedenktafel im Deutschen Verein").
„Wohllöblich ist's und alter hergebrachter Brauch", (title: „Mein erster Toast"); *vide* p. 128.
„Zwei Lampen leuchten", *Pan,* III, 1897, p. 253.

3. COLLECTED POEMS

Ultra Violett. Einsame Poesien.[3] Berlin, 1893: Max Haase (*Gesammelte Werke*, IV, pp. 7-92).

Reliquien.[4] Mexico, 1897: Hijas de J. F. Jens (*Gesammelte Werke*, IV, pp. 93-132).

―――*Second edition:* Minden i. W., 1900: J. C. C. Bruns' Verlag.

―――*Third edition:* Leipzig, 1913: K. Wolff.

Schwarze Sonne. Phallus.[5] Mexico, 1897: Hijas de J. F. Jens (*Gesammelte Werke*, IV, 93-132).

―――*Second edition:* Leipzig, 1910: E. Rowohlt.

Bänkelsang vom Balzer auf der Balz. Stuttgart, 1905: Axel Juncker (*Gesammelte Werke*, IV, 573-698).

Die ewige Hochzeit.[6] *Der brennende Kalender.*[7] *Liebeslieder.* Stuttgart, 1905: Axel Juncker. „Axel Junckers Sammlung moderner deutscher Lyrik . . . Band I." (*Gesammelte Werke*, IV, pp. 175-199, *Hochzeit;* IV, pp. 201-226, *Kalender*).

―――*Second edition:* Munich, 1911: Albert Langen.

Die Ammenballade. Acht Liebesabenteuer gedichtet von acht Ammen am Sarge des Herrn Heinz. Munich, 1907: E. W. Bonsels and Company. *Neun Pariser Moritaten.*

―――*Second edition:* Leipzig, 1913: K. Wolff.

Singsangbuch; Liebeslieder. Munich, 1913: E. W. Bonsels and Company. (*Gesammelte Werke*, IV, pp. 133-173).

―――*Second edition:* Leipzig, 1912: E. Rowohlt.

Insichversunkene Lieder im Laub. Stuttgart, 1908: Axel Junckers Verlag. (*Gesammelte Werke*, IV, pp. 291-343).

―――*Second edition:* Munich, 1911: A. Langen.

---

[3] Many poems appeared first in periodicals. Since important changes were often made in the book editions, it was deemed desirable to list first printings of the poems in footnotes. „Abend", (IV, p. 51,) *Blätter für die Kunst*, second series, 1894/5, p. 16. „Amselsang", (IV, p. 52,) *ibid.* „Auferstehung", (IV, pp. 18, 19,) *Moderner Musenalmanach auf das Jahr 1893*, Munich, pp. 261-263. „Gesänge der Düfte" („Regenduft", „Jasmin", „Morgenduft", „Rosen") (IV, pp. 52-54,) *Moderner Musenalmanach 1894*, Munich, pp. 205, 206. „Schmerzstimmung", (IV, pp. 19, 20,) *Blätter für die Kunst*, III, March, 1893, pp. 79, 80. „Vision", (IV, p. 44,) *ibid.*, pp. 81, 82. For translations of these and the following see pp. 164 ff.

[4] „Auf deinem Haupt schmolz eine goldenrote Krone", (IV, p. 97,) *Pan*, II, 3, 1896, p. 192. „Und jede Pore, die einst für dich brannte", (IV, p. 111,) *ibid.* „Unsere Augen so leer", (IV, p. 114,) *ibid.*

[5] *Phallus* appeared also in *Die Insel*, III, 7/8, April-May, 1902, pp. 3-22.

[6] This book of verse appeared first under the title of "Herzlied" in *Die Insel*, II, January, 1901, no. 4, pp. 23-27; June, 1901, no. 9, pp. 259-263; III, 7, 8, April, May 1902, pp. 73-78; no. 11, 12, August, September, 1902, pp. 253-255.

[7] „ Die Nebel kommen zaudernd zum Haus", IV, 219, *Simplicissimus*, VII, 1902, p. 267. „Hinfällig wie die Erinnerungen", IV, 217, *ibid.* „Wissen die Amseln von Sehnsucht etwas?" IV, 218, *ibid.*

Der weiße Schlaf; Lieder der langen Nächte. Berlin, 1908: Axel Junckers Verlag. (*Gesammelte Werke*, IV, pp. 411-450).
Lusamgärtlein; Frühlingslieder aus Franken. Berlin, 1909: Axel Junckers Verlag. (*Gesammelte Werke*, IV, pp. 227-290).
Weltspuk, Lieder der Vergänglichkeit. Munich, 1910: A. Langen. (*Gesammelte Werke*, IV, pp. 345-409).[8]
Die geflügelte Erde, ein Lied der Liebe und der Wunder um sieben Meere. Munich, 1910: A. Langen. (*Gesammelte Werke*, V, pp. 5-543).[9]
Der Venusinenreim. Auszug der Frau Venusine aus dem Hörselberg und Venusinens Abenteuer, eine schalkhaft heroische Liebesmär in zwölf Reimen. Leipzig: E. Rowohlt. 1911.
Die Untergangsstunde der „Titanic". (Zum Jahrestag, 16. April, 1913). Berlin-Wilmersdorf, 1913: A. R. Meyer. (*Gesammelte Werke*, IV, pp. 715-727).
Des großen Krieges Not.[10] Medan, 1914.
———Batavia: Deutscher Bund. 1915.
———Munich: A. Langen. 1915.
Das Lied der Weltfestlichkeit. Tosari. 1918. (*Gesammelte Werke*, V, pp. 545-647).

[8] „Atemloser August", (IV, p. 361,) *Pro Italia. Eine deutsche Kunstspende.* Munich, 1909, 1920², pp. 169, 170. „Die Mondscheinrune", (IV, p. 357,) *Hyperion*, 1908, Heft 2, pp. 105-107. „Die Stunde stirbt wie in dem Wind die Frucht", (IV, p. 353,) *Pro Italia, op. cit.*, p. 169. „Ich kann die Nacht zum Reden zwingen", (IV, p. 381,) *loc. cit.*, pp. 170, 171. „Jeder kommt einmal zu der Erde Rand", (IV, p. 347,) *Simplicissimus*, XV, 7, May 16, 1910, p. 108. „Mitten hin durch der Urstoffe eiserne Schwere", (IV, p. 379,) *Pro Italia*, p. 171. „Muß bald wirklich, bald unwirklich sein", (IV, p. 376,) *loc. cit.*, p. 170. „Sieben Gespenster und die Zeit", (IV, pp. 350, 351,) *Hyperion*, 1908, Heft 6, pp. 117, 118. „Messina im Mörser", *Pro Italia*, pp. 312-320.
[9] „Indische Reise", *Jugend*, 1909, nos. 31, 33, 43, 51: I. „Hundertdreizehn Schritte", (V, p. 137), p. 722. II. „Auf der Gangesbrücke", (V, p. 145), p. 722. III. „Agras Teppichblumen", (V, p. 133), p. 722. IV. „Kobra und Mango", (V, p. 163), p. 770. V. „Die Asketen", (V, p. 163), p. 1010. VI. „Einige Regentropfen", (V, p. 169), p. 1010. VII. „Buddhas alter Wohnort Sarnath", (V, p. 172), p. 1234. VIII. „Von Silleguri nach Darjeeling", (V, p. 178), p. 1234.
„Die Pyramiden, ein Gedichtszyklus". *März*, IV, no. 19, 1910: „Unter den Pyramiden", (V, p. 21), p. 33. „Alltag um die Pyramiden", (V, p. 22), pp. 33, 34. „Der Begriff von oben und unten", (V, p. 22), p. 34. „In der Cheopspyramide", (V, p. 23), p. 35. „Der Klang der Totenkammer", (V, p. 24), pp. 35, 36. „Die Königskammern", (V, p. 24), p. 36. „Es ist gleich, wohin du mich trägst", (V, p. 25), pp. 36, 37. „Der Sphinxleib", (V, p. 25), pp. 37, 38. „Durch Japans Inlandsee", (V, p. 354), *Jugend*, 1910, no. 47, p. 1125.
„Glocke und Schildkrötenteich im Tennoyitempel in Osaka", (V, p. 371), *Jugend*, 1910, no. 47, p. 1127.
[10] „Kriegsgedichte" (*Gesammelte Werke*, IV, pp. 451-486); „Alle großen Berge wurden klein" (IV, p. 461), *Simplicissimus*, XX, 16, July 20, 1915, p. 182. „Der Mond zieht hinterm Schiff einher" (IV, p. 458), *Jugend*, 1915, no. 41, p. 786. „Die Äcker platzen dürr" (IV, p. 513), *Simplicissimus*, XXVI, 17, July 20, 1921, p. 214.

4. DRAMATIC WRITINGS

Sun. Drama. Sehnsucht. Drama. Berlin, 1895: Max Haase (*Sun*, VI, pp. 5-37; *Sehnsucht*, VI, pp. 39-50).

Das Kind. Drama in zwei Teilen. Glück. Drama in 4 Szenen. Berlin, 1895: Max Haase. (*Das Kind*, VI, pp. 51-139; *Das Glück*, VI, pp. 141-173).

Das Unabwendbare. Szene aus der Zeit der Einführung des Zölibats. Die Insel, I, no. 10, July, 1900, pp. 21-38; (VI, pp. 175-189).

Die Spielereien einer Kaiserin;[11] *Drama in vier Akten, einem Vorspiel und einem Epilog.* Munich, 1910: A. Langen. (VI, pp. 583-759).

Madame Null, Schwank in drei Akten. Leipzig, 1911: E. Rowohlt.

Menagerie Krummholz; Jahrmarktskomödie in drei Akten. Leipzig, 1911: E. Rowohlt.

Frau Raufenbarth; bürgerliche Tragödie in drei Akten. Leipzig, 1911: E. Rowohlt.

Lachen und Sterben; Fünfuhrtee, zwei tragische Akte. Leipzig, 1911: E. Rowohlt. (*Lachen und Sterben*, VI, pp. 215-246; *Fünfuhrtee*, VI, pp. 191-213).

Ein Schatten fiel über den Tisch, Schauspiel in drei Akten. Leipzig, 1911: E. Rowohlt (pp. 247-322).

Maja; skandinavische Bohêmekomödie in drei Akten. Leipzig, 1911: E. Rowohlt (VI, pp. 323-465).

Der Drache Grauli, Drama in drei Akten. Munich, 1911: A. Langen (VI, pp. 467-581).

Die Heiden Geilane. Die Kilianstragödie. Munich, 1912: A. Langen (VI, pp. 761-896).

5. PROSE

Imaginative

„Aus langer Weile!" *Moderne Rundschau*, Halbmonatsschrift herausgegeben von Dr. Joachim und E. M. Kafka, III, 5, 6, columns 231-237, Vienna, June 1891.

„Es springen Ziegen am Straßenrand" (IV, p. 473), *Deutsche Wacht*, I, 8, August 1915, p. 515, also *Jugend*, XX, 24, September 14, 1915, p. 286. „Immer gurren eingesperrte Tauben" (IV, p. 470), *Simplicissimus*, XXII, 21, August 21, 1917, p. 262. „Indiens Tannen aufrecht in der Nacht" (IV, p. 460), *Jugend*, 1915, no. 41, p. 786. „War doch, so lang die Erde steht" (IV, pp. 474, 475), *Deutsche Wacht*, I, 8, 1915, p. 516.

„Lieder der Trennung" (*Gesammelte Werke*, IV, pp. 487-527), „Die Wolken warten ohne Flucht" (IV, p. 525), *Simplicissimus*, XXVI, 12, June 15, 1921, p. 142. „Gerne möchte ich die Hände falten" (IV, pp. 493, 494), *Simplicissimus*, XX, 8, May 25, 1915, p. 87. „Ich ging und ließ die Sonne versinken" (IV, pp. 495, 496), *Jugend*, 1915, no. 41, p. 786. „Mit Sehnsucht schau ich nach Westen gewandt", (IV, pp. 502, 503), *Jugend*, 1916, p. 266.

[11] Act III, „Das Taschentuch"; ein Bild aus den „Spielereien der Kaiserin", appeared in *Hyperion*, 1909, 9, 10, pp. 1-18.

„Siebzig Jahre". *Moderne Rundschau*, III, 9, August 1, 1891, pp. 321-327.

„Barmherzige Schwestern." *Die Gesellschaft*, 1891, pp. 1591-1596.

Josa Gerth. Roman. Dresden und Leipzig, 1893: E. Pierson's Verlag. (III, pp. 429-569).

Lingam[12]; *zwölf asiatische Novellen.* Munich, 1909: A. Langen. Contents: Dalar rächt sich. Der Zauberer Walai. Unter den Totentürmen. Der Knabe auf dem Kopf des Elefanten. Eingeschlossene Tiere. Der Kuli Kimgun. Der Garten ohne Jahreszeiten. Im blauen Licht von Penang. Likse und Panulla. Der unbeerdigte Vater. Im Mandarinenklub. Die Auferstehung allen Fleisches. (III, p. 7-96).

Die acht Gesichter am Biwasee;[13] *japanische Liebesgeschichten.* Munich, 1911: A. Langen. Contents: Die Segelboote von Yabase im Abend heimkehren sehen. Den Nachtregen regnen hören in Karasaki. Die Abendglocke vom Mijderatempel hören. Sonniger Himmel und Brise von Awazu. Der Wildgänse Flug in Katata nachschauen. Vom Ishiyama den Herbstmond aufgehen sehen. Das Abendrot zu Seta. Den Abendschnee am Hirayama sehen. (III, pp. 97-239).

Raubmenschen. Einer von Rennewarts Romanen. Munich, 1911: A. Langen (III, pp. 571-950).

―――――Reprint by *Deutsche Buch-Gemeinschaft.* Berlin, 1927. Volume 180.

Geschichten aus den vier Winden.[14] Munich, A. Langen, 1915. Contents: Das Giftfläschchen. Himalayafinsternis. Hecksel und die Bergwerkflöhe. Zwei Reiter am Meer. Auf dem Weg zu den Eulenkäfigen. Nächtliche Schaufenster. An eine Sechzehnjährige. Zur Stunde der Maus. Die Kurzsichtige und der Komet. Das Iguanodon. (III, pp. 241-426).

Das Märchenbriefbuch der heiligen Nächte im Javanerlande. Munich, 1921: A. Langen. (III, pp. 727-861).

―――――Reprint by *Deutsche Buch-Gemeinschaft.* Berlin, 1930. Volume 346.

[12] The following novelettes of *Lingam* appeared also before publication in book form: „Dalar rächt sich", *Simplicissimus*, XIV, 33, November 15, 1909, pp. 550, 554. „Der Garten ohne Jahreszeiten", *März*, III, 17, 1909, pp. 387-397.

[13] The following stories appeared also before publication in book form as follows: „Die Segelboote von Yabase im Abend heimkehren sehen." *Die neue Rundschau,* XXII, i, 1911, pp. 51-66. „Den Nachtregen regnen hören in Karasaki", *März*, V, 7 (February 14, 1911), pp. 314-325; 8 (February 21, 1911), pp. 354-363. „Die Abendglocke vom Mijderatempel hören", *Deutsche Monatshefte*, 1911, pp. 57-60. „Sonniger Himmel und Brise von Awazu", *Licht und Schatten*, I, 19, 1910/11. „Von Ishiyama den Herbstmond aufgehen sehen", *Simplicissimus*, XV, 5, 1910, pp. 72-74, 79.

[14] The following stories appeared in magazines before publication in book form: „Das Giftfläschchen", *Pan*, I, 12, April 16, 1911, pp. 405-413; 13, May 1, 1911, pp. 446-451. „Himalayafinsternis", *Die weißen Blätter*, I, 1913, 1914, pp. 1209-1225. „An eine Sechzehnjährige", *Jugend*, I, 19, 1915, pp. 346-348. „Das Iguanodon", *Die neue Rundschau*, XXV, ii, 1914, pp. 927-958.

Descriptive and autobiographic

„Im Spiegel. Autobiographische Skizze." *Das Literarische Echo.* X, no. 24, September 15, 1908, columns 1698-1700. Reprinted in *Die Frankenwarte*, VI, no. 40, Würzburg, October 6, 1918.

Der Geist meines Vaters, Aufzeichnungen aus einem begrabenen Jahrhundert. Munich, 1912: A. Langen. (I, 5-284).

Gedankengut aus meinen Wanderjahren. 2 volumes. Munich, 1913: A. Langen. (I, pp. 287-816).

Erlebnisse auf Java, aus Tagebüchern von Max Dauthendey. Munich, 1924: A. Langen. Contents: Die Hochzeit des „Nagels der Erde".[15] Meine Smeroe-Besteigung.

Letzte Reise; aus Tagebüchern, Briefen und Aufzeichnungen. Munich, 1925: A. Langen. (II, 147-726).

6. AESTHETICS

Uddgren, C. (*sic*) G. and Max Dauthendey: *Verdensaltet. Det nye sublime i kunsten.* Oversættelse. Kjøbenhavn, 1893: A. Christiansen's Kunstforlag.

7. TRANSLATIONS BY MAX DAUTHENDEY

„Gedichte von Herman Gorter aus dem Holländischen übersetzt." *Pan*, III, iv, 1897, p. 253.

Kierkegaard, Sören: *Das Tagebuch des Verführers.* Vollständige deutsche Übertragung. Leipzig, 1903: Insel-Verlag.

——— Second edition, 1905.

8. LETTERS[16]

Letzte Reise. Cf. above.

Mich ruft dein Bild. Briefe an seine Frau. Munich, 1930: Albert Langen.

Ein Herz im Lärm der Welt. Briefe an Freunde, Munich, 1933: Albert Langen, Georg Müller.

---

[15] Previously printed in *Die neue Rundschau* as follows: „Die Hochzeit des ‚Nagels der Erde' ", XXXII, 6 (June, 1921), pp. 577-602; 7 (July, 1921), pp. 732-760. (II, pp. 7-77).

[16] The following letters have appeared only in newspapers and periodicals:

to ELISABETH DAUTHENDEY: January 20, 1906 (Bombay); March 12, 1906 (Ceylon); March 22, 1906 (Ceylon); April 13, 1906 (Macao); April 26, 1906 (Kioto); August 11, 1914 (Amboina); April 7, 1915 (Garoet); *Jugend*, Munich, 1919, no. 5, pp. 86, 87.

to ANNA FRAZIER: February 3, 1916 (Garoet); *The Germanic Review*, V, 2, April, 1930, pp. 189-190.

to OTTO GOETZE: February 9, 1892 (Berlin); *Berliner Mittag*, December, 1928. July 2, 1894 (Berlin); *Der Jungdeutsche,* July, 1928.

to JULIUS HART: October, 1911; *Der Tag*, Berlin, October 3, 1911, no. 503.

to GERTRAUD ROSTOSKY: September 7, 1915 (Garoet), *Das literarische Echo;*

BIBLIOGRAPHY

9. SELECTIONS
Poetry
Ausgewählte Lieder aus sieben Büchern. Munich, 1914: A. Langen.
Ausgewählte Lieder aus neun Büchern. Munich, 1928: A. Langen.
Zwölf Gedichte. Lithographed by Bruno Krauskopf. *Das geschriebene Buch,* III. Berlin, 1921: Fritz Gurlitt.
Winde quälen die Bäume. Woodcuts by Karl Lorenz. Malente-Gremsmühlen, Ost-Holstein, Villa Augustus, Turmpresse, 1930.

Prose
Der Garten ohne Jahreszeiten, ausgewählte asiatische Novellen. Munich, 1914: A. Langen. „Langens Mark-Bücher, eine Sammlung moderner Literatur", II. Contents: Der Garten ohne Jahreszeiten. Dalar rächt sich. Der Knabe auf dem Kopf des Elefanten. Likse und Panulla. Die Auferstehung allen Fleisches. Die Segelboote von Yabase am Abend heimkehren sehen. Der unbeerdigte Vater.
Das Schönste von Max Dauthendey, ausgewählt und eingeleitet von Walter von Molo. Munich, 1919: A. Langen. Contents: a number of poems and the following prose works: Zur Stunde der Maus. Himalayafinsternis. Der Garten ohne Jahreszeiten. Im blauen Licht von Penang. Der Wildgänse Flug in Katata nachschauen. Likse und Panulla. Das Abendrot zu Seta. Der unbeerdigte Vater. Die Abendglocke vom Mijderatempel hören. Den Abendschnee am Hirayama sehen. Eingeschlossene Tiere. Zwei Reiter am Meer.
Den Nachtregen regnen hören in Karasaki und andere Geschichten. (*i.e.,* Zur Stunde der Maus. Unter den Totentürmen). Berlin, 1928: Deutsche Buch-Gemeinschaft, no. 1005.
Fernöstliche Geschichten. 3 Novellen. Frankfurt a. M., 1930: Verlag Moritz Diesterweg, „Kranzbücherei", no. 78. Contents: Der unbeerdigte Vater. Der Knabe auf dem Kopf des Elefanten. Himalayafinsternis.
Himalayafinsternis und andere Geschichten aus Asien. (*i.e.,* Der Knabe auf dem Kopf des Elefanten. Der unbeerdigte Vater). Leipzig, 1931: Hermann Hillger Verlag, „Deutsche Jugendbücherei", no. 371.
Zur Stunde der Maus und anderes (*i.e.,* Der Wildgänse Flug in Katata nachschauen). „Deutsche Novellen des 19. und 20. Jahrhunderts", edited by Kurt Levinstein. Leipzig, 1930: Quelle und Meyer.

Vol. 23, no. 10, (February 15, 1921), columns 581-586. Excerpts from letters of March 24, April 8, 17, 19, 1914, January 18, 1916, appeared in *Der Tag,* Berlin, 1927, no. 177, (July 26). An excerpt from another letter of September 7, 1915 (Garoet), appeared in *Würzburger General-Anzeiger,* 1927, no. 167, (July 25), p. 3.

to KARL WILLY STRAUB: Summer, 1914 (Batavia); *Saarbrücker Zeitung,* 1921, no. 308. Also excerpts from letter of 1913, *Hannoverischer Anzeiger,* December 13, 1925.

Aus fremdem Land. („Tierra caliente". „Meine Smeroe-Besteigung". Gedichte. „Hirts Deutsche Sammlung". Gruppe II. „Novellen und Erzählungen", Band 44. Breslau: Ferdinand Hirt.

Reise in Griechenland (Delphi, Olympia, Tiryns, Mykene). „Bunte Bücher", Heft 210. Reutlingen: Enßlin and Laiblin.

Segeljahrt zur Leuchtturminsel im Skagerrak. „Bunte Bücher", Heft 211. Reutlingen: Enßlin and Laiblin.

Die festliche Weltreise des Dichters Dauthendey. Edited by Kurt Matthies, Munich, 1935: Albert Langen, Georg Müller. "Die kleine Bücherei," no. 51.

Würzburg in der Dichtung Max Dauthendeys. Edited by Annie Dauthendey, Würzburg-Aumühle, 1936: Verlag Konrad Triltsch.

10. TRANSLATIONS OF DAUTHENDEY'S WORKS

Danish

Uddgren, G. „En tynd, hvid slange" (IV, p. 54, "Jasmin"), *Politiken*, Copenhagen, August 3, 1893, no. 215, p. 1.

——— „Purperne er i slumrende Fjærne" (IV, p. 52, "Amselsang"), *id. loc.*

——— „Visnende Kalablomster lyser" (IV, p. 52, "Vollmond"), *id. loc.*

——— „Dobbeltliv.[17] Skitse fra Danmark" (IV, pp. 65-67, "Doppelleben"), *Politiken*, Copenhagen, August 16, 1893, no. 228, p. 1.

——— „Sort".[18] (IV, pp. 45-49, "Schwarz"), *Politiken*, Copenhagen, August 3, 1893, no. 215, p. 1.

English

Bithell, Jethro. *Contemporary German Poetry.*[19] London, 1909: Scott.

Deutsch, Babette and Avrahm Yarmolinsky. *Contemporary German Poetry.*[20] New York, 1923: Harcourt, Brace and Company.

---

[17] *Cf.* also parody „Dobbeltsyn. Skitse fra Benegalien af M. Dauthentisk". *Dannebrog,* Copenhagen, August 22, 1893, no. 357.

[18] *Cf.* also parody „Sort", *Avisen*, August 5, 1893, no. 217, p. 3.

[19] Contains: "Angels Gray", p. 21 (IV, p. 110: „Graue Engel gehen um mich"); "Winds Torment the Trees", p. 21 (IV, p. 110: „Winde quälen die Bäume"); "Past the Sweet Lilac Cloverfield", p. 21 (IV, p. 100: „Am süßen lila Kleefeld vorbei"); "As he were wounded croaks the raven", p. 22 (IV, p. 194: „Die Raben schreien wie verwundet"); "Our Eyes so Empty", p. 22 (IV, p. 114: „Unsere Augen so leer"); "On thy Visage", p. 23 (IV, p .123: „In deinem Angesicht"); "The Air as Lead", p. 23 (IV, p. 109: „Die Luft so schwer"); "I looked into the Garden", p. 23 (IV, p. 187: „Ich schaute in den Garten"); "Thy Breast with my Breast Was One", p. 24 (IV, p. 123: „Deine Brüste an meiner Brust"); "Silence Waves into the Room", p. 24 (IV, 123: „Stille weht in das Haus").

[20] Contains: "Deep in the Nosegay", p. 43 (IV, p. 318: „Drinnen im Strauss"); "The Moon is a Fiery Rose", p. 44 (IV, p. 312: „Der Mond ist wie eine feurige Ros'"); "We Walk by the Sea", p. 45 (IV, p. 181: „Wir gehen am Meer im tiefen

Drake, William A. "The Weary Day-king lays his Crown Aside", (IV, pp. 188, 189: „Der Tag legt endlich die Krone ab"). *New York Herald Tribune Books*, April 17, 1927, p. 9.

French

Guilbeaux, H. *Anthologie des lyriques allemands contemporains depuis Nietzsche*.[21] Paris, 1913: E. Figuière et Cie.

Marc, Henry. „Kimgun le Coolie" (III, pp. 42-53: „Der Kuli Kimgun"), *La Revue de France*, VII, 24 (December 15, 1927), pp. 650-661.

Italian

"Il fanciullo sulla testa dell' elefante" („Der Knabe auf dem Kopf des Elefanten"). *Il Mondo*, August 13, 1926, p. 3.

Gianturco, Elio. *Antologia della lirica tedesca contemporanea*[22] Torino, 1926.

Lettish

Die acht Gesichter am Biwasee. "Universalà Biblioteka", Nr. 95/96. St. Petersburg, 1912.

Russian

Piśmaskazki s ostrova Javy (Das Märchenbriefbuch [der heiligen Nächte im Javanerland]). Perevod s německago A. Damanskoj. Berlin, 1922: S. Efron.

Vosem' lizov ozera Biva (Die acht Gesichter am Biwasee). Japonskija

---

Sand"); "The Rain Seems Possessed", p. 46 (IV, p. 314: „Der Regen scheint besessen"); "Every Leaf Tends Earthward", p. 47 (IV, p. 334: „Ein jedes Blatt zur Erde will"); "Love's Calendar: March", p. 48 (IV, p. 203: „Nun müssen Märzwinde die Bäume reiten"); "Love's Calendar: July", p. 49 (IV, p. 214: „Als ich im Abend dich traf"); "Love's Calendar: August", p. 50 (IV, p. 216: „Wir gingen an den flinken Bach"); "Love's Calendar: November", p. 51 (IV, p. 221: „Die Raben stehlen die Monde").

[21] Contains: "Nos yeux", p. 77 (IV, p. 114: „Unsere Augen so leer"); "Sur la maison . . .", p. 78 (IV, p. 123: „Stille weht in das Haus"); "Oh! laisse-moi", p. 78 (IV, p. 99: „Laß mich in deinem stillen Auge ruhen"); "Tes Seins", p. 79 (IV, p. 123: „Deine Brüste an meiner Brust"); "La lune de mai est sur le toit", p. 79 (IV, p. 101: „Maimond über dem Dach"); "Mes yeux emplis de cendres . . .", p. 80 (IV, p. 117: „Meine Augen voll Asche"); "Juillet", p. 80 (IV, p. 213, „Juli"); "Aujourd'hui, il n'y aura pas de soir", p. 81 (IV, p. 293: „Heut es kein Abend werden will"); "Entre, entre", p. 81 (IV, p. 333: „Komm heim"); "Le soleil du soir . . .", p. 82 (IV, p. 269: „Kaum hat sich die Abendsonne über den Fluß verloren").

[22] Contains: "Rifoli di tempesta", p. 82 (IV, p. 53: „Weinrot brennen Gewitterwinde"); "Chi mi chiamo", p. 82 (IV, p. 120: „Wer rief?"); "Grigi Angeli", p. 83 (IV, p. 110; „Graue Engel gehen um mich"); "La Rada", p. 83 (IV, p. 100: „Am süßen lila Kleefeld vorbei"); "L'Ultime Sillabe", p. 84 (IV, p. 110: „Winde quälen die Bäume"); "Desolazione", p. 84 (IV, pp. 109, 110: „Die Luft so schwer"); "Pace", p. 84 (IV, p. 123: „In deinem Angesicht"); "Notte di luna", p. 85 (IV, p. 123: „Stille weht in das Haus"); "Il fascio di fiori", p. 85 (IV, p. 318: „Der Abendhimmel leuchtet wie ein Blumenstrauß"); "Tramonto", p. 86 (IV, p. 260: „In der gelben und grünlichen Abendhelle").

novelly o ljubvi. Perevod s německago Evgenija Raiča. Berlin, 1921: S. Efron.

II. LIST OF REPRODUCTIONS OF AQUARELLES

Alt-Tosari, Java. Der Türmer, XXXVI, October, 1933, p. 15.
Abstieg vom Smeroe. Cover of *Erlebnisse auf Java.* Munich: Langen. 1924.
Auf Java. Weltstimmen, Stuttgart, August 27, 1925, p. 160.
Ausblick aufs Meer. Der Schünemann-Monat, April, 1928, p. 384. Also in *Westermanns Monatshefte,* July, 1930, p. 476.
Ausbootung. Molukken-Inseln, 1914. Cover of *Die Koralle,* IV, 5, August, 1928.
Ausgestorbener Eichenhain, Griechenland 1897. Der Türmer, XXXVI, 1, October, 1933, p. 11.
Auslegeboot bei Neu-Guinea, 1914. Sport im Bild, March 16, 1928, p. 348.
Aussicht über den Ozean von Dorf Gorey auf der Insel Jersey. Der Türmer, XXXVI, 1, October, 1933, p. 10.
Bambushain (Java). *Der Schünemann-Monat,* April, 1928, p. 389. Also in *Westermanns Monatshefte,* July, 1930, p. 480.
Batakische Marktleute, Sumatra. Der Türmer, XXXVI, 1, October, 1933, p. 14.
Bucht in Friedrich-Wilhelmshafen auf Neu-Guinea. Cover of *Letzte Reise.* Munich, 1924: Langen.
Chinesischer Laden. Canton, 1906. *Westermanns Monatshefte,* July, 1930, p. 482.
Der Vulkan Tjikorai auf Java. Cover of *Das Märchenbriefbuch der heiligen Nächte im Javanerlande.* Munich, 1921: Langen.
Die acht Ammen. Cover of *Die Ammenballade. Neun Pariser Moritaten.* Munich, 1907: E. W. Bonsels.
Die Türme des Schweigens. Der Schünemann-Monat, April, 1928, p. 385.
Duck-Ducktanz. Neu Guinea. *Die Lesestunde,* IV, 12, June 15, 1927, p. 223. Also in *Sport im Bild,* March 16, 1928, p. 346.
Haus in Lima. Sumatra. *Die Lesestunde,* June 15, 1927, p. 222.
Im Hafen von Makassar. (Insel Celebes.) *Illustrirte Zeitung,* August 9, 1923, p. 105.
Japanisches Haus zur Kirschblütenzeit. Sport im Bild, March 2, 1928, p. 268.
Kanaker-Dorf bei Potsdam-Hafen. Neu Guinea, 1914. *Westermanns Monatshefte,* July, 1930, p. 481.
Kanaker-Soldat an Bord der „Manila". Neu Guinea, 1914. *Westermanns Monatshefte,* July, 1930, p. 481.
Lotosteich auf Ceylon. Der Schünemann-Monat, April, 1928, p. 388.
Maskentanz im Südsee-Archipel. Sport im Bild, March, 1928, p. 348.

Mexikanerin, Orangen verkaufend. Atlantis, 8, August 1929, p. 486.
Nacht-Tanz, Bandoeng, Java. Der Türmer, XXXVI, 1, October, 1933, p. 13.
Papandajan-Krater (Java). *Die Lesestunde*, June 15, 1927, p. 231. Also in *Sport im Bild*, March 2, 1928, p. 266.
Potsdamhafen auf Neu Guinea. 1914. *Sport im Bild*, March 2, 1928, p. 267. Also in *Die literarische Welt*, July 22, 1927, p. 1.
Reis-Stampf-Haus. Sumatra, 1914. *Westermanns Monatshefte*, July, 1930, p. 475.
Straße in Bandoeng. Java, 1918. *Westermanns Monatshefte*, July, 1930, p. 477.
Straßenbild aus Bombay. 1906. *Sport im Bild*, March 2, 1928, p. 268.
Studien in stilisierten Rosen. Dekorative Kunst, IV, 1899, p. 204. Vide also p. 61 *supra*.
Sumatra, 1914. Der Türmer, XXXVI, October, 1933, p. 16. Vide also illustration opposite page 90 *supra*.
Tropisches Idyll. Sport im Bild, March 2, 1928, p. 266.
Ufer am Irawadi in Birma. 1906. *Westermanns Monatshefte*, July, 1930, p. 478.
Villa in Penang. Der Schünemann-Monat, April, 1928, p. 381.
Weiang-Wong Puppen. Java, 1915. *Sport im Bild*, March 16, 1928, p. 347. Vide also: *Schattenpuppen, Java. Der Türmer*, XXXVI, 1, October, 1933, p. 12.
Weiang-Wong Theater. Sport im Bild, March 16, 1928, p. 347.
Wisby, 2. Oktober, 1895. Jacket of *Ein Herz im Lärm der Welt*. Also in *Die Neue Literatur*, XXXIV, March, 1933, opposite p. 126.

12. CRITICAL BIBLIOGRAPHY (SELECTED)[23]

Ade, Hans Christoph. "Dauthendeys Selbstgeschichte." *Die Flöte*, II, 5, August, 1919, pp. 65-68.
Annecke, Wilhelm. *Max Dauthendey als Dramatiker*. Würzburg Aumühle, 1934; Verlag Konrad Triltsch.
Anschütz, Georg. *Farbe-Ton-Forschungen*. I. Leipzig, 1927. Especially Chapter 4: Friedrich Mahling: „Das Problem der ‚Audition colorée' ".
Arnold, Paul Joh. "Dauthendeys epische Kleinkunst." *Hamburger Nachrichten*. „Zeitschrift für Wissenschaft, Literatur und Kunst", no. 8, February 22, 1914.
Bab, Julius. "Von den Meistern deutscher Lyrik." *Die neue Rundschau*, XX, pp. 1058-1066.
─────*Die deutsche Kriegslyrik, 1914-1918*. Stettin, 1920: Norddeutscher Verlag für Literatur und Kunst, pp. 82-84.

[23] In the case of syndicated newspaper articles, I list only the most accessible issue. German general bibliographies, of course, do not differentiate duplicates as such.

———*Die Chronik des deutschen Dramas*, III, 1911-1913. Berlin, 1922: Oesterheld and Company, pp. 9-11.
Bahr, Hermann. *Renaissance, Neue Studien zur Kritik der Moderne.* Berlin, 1897: S. Fischer. "Colour Music", pp. 59-66. Also in: *Das Hermann-Bahr-Buch.* Berlin: S. Fischer, pp. 129-135.
Banaschewski, A. "Mörikes und Dauthendeys Lyrik." *Schleswiger Nachrichten,* Schleswig, August 28, 1926.
Becker, Julius Maria. "Erinnerungen an Max Dauthendey." *Fränkischer Kurier,* Nürnberg, October 15, 1926.
———"Begegnung mit Max Dauthendey." *Bavaria,* „Wochenschrift für bayerische Kulturpolitik", I, 8, May 17, 1930, p. 5-7.
Benzmann, Hans. *Moderne deutsche Lyrik, ältere Generation* (1880-1914). 4th edition. Leipzig, 1924: Philipp Reclam jun.
Biese, Alfred. "Der Dichter des 'Als ob'." *Unterhaltungsbeilage der Täglichen Rundschau,* Berlin, December 12, XLV, no. 555, p. 2.
———*Deutsche Literaturgeschichte.* III. Munich: C. H. Becksche Verlagsbuchhandlung.
Binz, Arthur Friedrich. „Max Dauthendey und Friedrich Huch". In: *Von Aufbruch und Untergang. Aufsätze über Dichter und Dichtungen.* Heidelberg, 1927: Verlag Hermann Meister, pp. 13-22.
Blei, Franz, "Erinnerungen an Max Dauthendey." *Roland,* XXIII, no. 26, June 25, 1925, pp. 31-33.
Blochert, W. "Dem Andenken Max Dauthendeys." *Deutsche Wacht,* Batavia, IV, no. 9, September 1918, pp. 715-719.
Bonsels, Waldemar, "Max Dauthendey," *Die Zukunft,* LXXIV, no. 19, February 4, 1911, pp. 192-195.
Darge, Elizabeth, *Lebensbejahung in der deutschen Dichtung um 1900.* „Deutschkundliche Arbeiten", 1934, A., Allgemeine Reihe, Band I.
Dauthendey, Annie. "Max Dauthendey, der Heimweh-Deutsche". *Der Türmer,* XXXVI, 1, October, 1933, pp. 9-16.
Dauthendey, Elisabeth. "Max Dauthendey." *Das Bayerland,* XXX, 3rd October number, 1918, p. 65.
———"Nänie an Max Dauthendey." "In Memoriam." "Daß Max Dauthendey in Würzburg geboren wurde." . . . "Das Ahnenbild." „Literarische Beilage", *Würzburger General-Anzeiger,* May 24, 1930, no. 11.
———"In Memoriam." *Das Bayerland,* 41, 5, 1. Märzheft, 1930, pp. 149, 150.
Drews, Arthur. "Max Dauthendey." *Preußische Jahrbücher,* CLXXIV, no. 2, November 1918, pp. 263-270.
Edschmid, Kasimir. "Erzählungs-Literatur. VIII. Dauthendey." *Frankfurter Zeitung,* LXVI, no. 239, March 30, 1922, pp. 1, 2.
———"Nachfolger der Minnesänger." *Deutsche Zeitung Bohemia,* LXXXXV, no. 259, Prag, November 4, 1922, p. 3.

———Das Bücher Dekameron, Berlin, 1923; Erich Reiß Verlag, pp. 51, 53-56, 63, 113.
von Erhardt-Siebold, Erika: "Harmony of the Senses in English, German, and French Romanticism." *PMLA*, XLVII, 2 (June, 1932), pp. 577-592.
———"Synaesthesien in der englischen Dichtung des 19 Jahrhunderts." *Englische Studien*, 53 (1919), pp. 1-157.
Ewald, August. *Idee und Liebe*. Potsdam, 1932: Müller & I. Kiepenheuer. Chapter: "Phallus," pp. 82-91.
Eloesser, Arthur, "Erbgut und Gedankengut." *Die neue Rundschau*, XXV. Jahrgang der freien Bühne, 1914, pp. 566-571.
Fischer, Walther. "Max Dauthendey als Dramatiker." *Das literarische Echo*, XXII, no. 22, August 15, 1920, columns 1352-1362.
———"Max Dauthendeys letzte Grüße an die Heimat." *Das literarische Echo*, XXIII, no. 10, February 15, 1921, columns 579-581.
Frobenius, Else. "Max Dauthendey, der Dichter des Heimwehs." *Der Schatzgräber, Zeitschrift der Gesellschaft deutscher Literaturfreunde*, V, no. 8, May 1926, pp. 7-11.
Gebhardt, M. "Würzburg und die beiden Dauthendey." *Fränkischer Kurier, Würzburger Ausgabe*, 1927, no. 324.
———„Max Dauthendey", in *Lebensläufe aus Franken*, III, edited by Anton Chroust. Würzburg, 1927; Kabitzsch and Mönnich.
Gosse, Edmund. Letter to the Editor of the *London Times*, Wednesday, November 3, 1915, no. 41,002, p. 13.
Hamann, Richard. *Der Impressionismus in Leben und Kunst*. Cologne, 1907.
Hamecher, Peter. "Max Dauthendey." *Die Gegenwart*, XLI, no. 17, April 27, 1912, pp. 262-266.
———"Der Dichter kehrt heim." „Literarische Beilage", *Würzburger General-Anzeiger*, May 24, 1930, no. 11.
———"Max Dauthendey." In: *Das Märchenbriefbuch der heiligen Nächte im Javanerlande*. Berlin, 1921: Deutsche Buch-Gemeinschaft, no. 346, pp. 7-22.
Handwerker, O. "Max Dauthendey als Dichter der Heimat." *Würzburger General-Anzeiger*, no. 293, December 19, 1925.
Hitschmann, E. "Ein Dichter und sein Vater", *Imago*, IV, 6, 1916, pp. 337-345.
——— "Telepathie und Psychoanalyse", *Imago*, IX, 3, 1923, pp. 368-382.
Holitscher, Arthur. "Lyrikers Weltreise." *Die neue Rundschau*, XXII, no. 2, pp. 260-264.
Holm, Korfiz. *ich-kleingeschrieben*, Munich, 1932: Albert Langen.
Hunich, Fritz Adolf. "Dichter als Maler." *Illustrirte Zeitung*, CLXI, 4106, August 9, 1932, pp. 104, 105.

Ježower, Ignaz. *Das Buch der Träume*. Berlin, 1928: Ernst Rowohlt.
Jungnickel, Max. "Max Dauthendey." In: *Raubmenschen*. Berlin, Deutsche Buchgemeinschaft, no. 180, pp. 5-8.
Kahane, Arthur. "Begegnungen. Max Dauthendey." *Berliner Tageblatt*, LVI, no. 348, July 26, 1927, p. 2; also in *Tagebuch des Dramaturgen*. Berlin, 1928: Bruno Cassierer Verlag, pp. 193-197.
Knab, Armin. "Dehmel an und über Dauthendey." „Literarische Beilage", *Würzburger General-Anzeiger*, May 24, 1930, no. 11.
Kubin, Alfred, "Erinnerungen an Max Dauthendey." *Der Zwiebelfisch. Zeitschrift über Bücher, Kunst und Lebensstil*, XVI, no. 1, 2, Munich, 1923, pp. 15, 16.
Kühn, Julius. "Dauthendeys Gedichte." *Die Flöte, Monatsschrift für neue Dichtung*, II, no. 5, August 1919, pp. 68-72.
Loerke, Oskar. "Gedenken an Max Dauthendey." *Die neue Rundschau*, XXIX, no. 11, November 1918, pp. 1488-1491. Also in: *Zeitgenossen aus vielen Zeiten*, Berlin, 1925: S. Fischer, pp. 234-240.
Mahling, Friedrich. *Vide* Georg Anschütz.
Marholm, Laura. "Ein Abseitsgehender." *Neue Freie Presse, Morgenblatt*, January 26, 1895, no. 10929.
Matthies, Kurt. "Die tausend Gedichte des Herrn Dauthendey". *Deutsches Volkstum*, XVII, 1, January, 1935, pp. 53-58.
Merbach, Paul Alfred. "Der Dramatiker Max Dauthendey." *Zwischenakt*, „Blätter des Lessingtheaters und des deutschen Künstlertheaters", II, no. 1, pp. 2-11.
Meyer, Alfred Richard. "Dauthendey in der Karikatur". *Max Dauthendey Gemeinschaft Rundbrief*, 2, 1934, pp. 3-6.
Moeller-Bruck, Arthur. "Max Dauthendeys 'Reliquien'." *Die Gesellschaft, Halbmonatsschrift für Litteratur, Kunst und Sozialpolitik*, 1898, no. 17, pp. 338-345.
————"Max Dauthendey." In: *Die Moderne Literatur in Gruppen- und Einzeldarstellungen*, XII, „Propheten". Berlin and Leipzig, 1902; Schuster and Loeffler, pp. 12-23.
Molo, Walther von. "Max Dauthendey." In: *Das Schönste von Max Dauthendey*. Munich, 1919: Albert Langen, pp. 7-13.
————"Dauthendeys erzählende Kunst." *Die Flöte, Monatsschrift für neue Dichtung*, II, no. 5, August 1919, pp. 74-76.
————"In Memoriam Max Dauthendey." *Berliner Tageblatt, Morgenausgabe*, LVI, 294, June 24, 1927. Also in *Der Bücherwurm*, XV, 5, May, 1930, pp. 120, 121. Also in *Zwischen Tag und Traum. Gesammelte Reden und Aufsätze*. Berlin, 1930: Paul Zsolnay, pp. 281-285.
Mumm, Carl. *Max Dauthendeys Sprache und Stil*. Dissertation, Frankfurt a. M., 1925. Typewritten manuscript. Also printed „Auszug" of seven pages.

Naumann, Hans. *Die deutsche Dichtung der Gegenwart*, Stuttgart, 1927: J. B. Metzlersche Verlagsbuchhandlung, pp. 314-318.
Prévôt, R. "Dichter der Zeit. II." *Express*, Mühlhausen, XXXV, no. 267, November 16, 1911, p. 1.
Rademacher, Georg. "Vom Sterben Max Dauthendeys." *Berliner Tageblatt*, no. 341, July 21, 1927.
Rath, Willy. "Max Dauthendeys 'Singsangbuch'. Ein lyrisches Exempel." *Tägliche Rundschau, „Unterhaltungs-Beilage,"* no. 157, July 7, p. 628; no. 158, July 8, 1908, p. 631.
————"Schildernde Lyrik." *Kunstwart*, XXV, second October number, 1911, pp. 122-126.
Reck-Malleczewen. "Für Max Dauthendey." *Berliner Tageblatt*, LIV, Abend-Ausgabe, no. 349, July 25, 1925. Also in *Berliner Tageblatt*, Morgenausgabe, August 6, 1925.
Reinhart, Hans. "Max Dauthendey, zu seinem Gedächtnis." *Wissen und Leben*. Zürich, XII, no. 3, November 1, 1918, pp. 81-86.
————"Zum Gedächtnis Max Dauthendeys." *Jahrbuch der literarischen Vereinigung Winterthur:* 1922, pp. 77-87.
Rostosky, Gertrud. "Wie ich Max Dauthendey malte." In: *Das fränkische Buch*. Würzburg, 1928: Verlag der Gesellschaft für Literatur und Bühnenkunst, pp. 29-32.
Schacht, R. "Max Dauthendey." *Die Grenzboten, Zeitschrift für Politik, Literatur und Kunst*, LXXI, no. 44, October 30, 1912, pp. 226-233.
Schellenberg, A. "Max Dauthendey. Die beiden Ausgaben 'Des großen Krieges Not'." *Hellweg*, Essen, II, no. 21, May 24, 1922, pp. 401-404.
Schmitz, Oscar A. H. *Dämon Welt. Jahre der Entwicklung*. Munich, 1926: Georg Müller.
Schneider, Ferdinand Josef. "Max Dauthendey und der moderne Panpsychismus." *Zeitschrift für Ästhetik und allgemeine Kunstwissenschaft*, XXIII, 4, October, 1929, pp. 326-347.
Seidel, Willy. "Zu Dauthendeys 60. Geburtstag." *Die literarische Welt*, III, no. 29, July 22, 1927, p. 1. Reprinted in modified form as "Gruß an Dauthendey" in *Die Himmel der Farbigen*, Munich, 1920: Georg Müller, pp. 7-10.
————"Exotismus in deutscher Literatur." *Der Kunstwart*, XLI, no. 9, June 1928, pp. 148-153. Also in *Die Himmel der Farbigen, vide supra*, pp. 140-148.
Soergel, Albert. "Max Dauthendey." *Dichtung und Dichter der Zeit*. 19th edition. Leipzig, 1928: R. Voigtländers Verlag. *Passim* and pp. 655-664.
Stang, Carl. "Dauthendeys Dramen." *Die Flöte, Monatsschrift für neue Dichtung*, II, no. 5, August 1919, pp. 79-81.

Steiger, Edgar, "Gedanken um Max Dauthendey herum." *Zeit im Bild*, X, no. 48, November 19, 1912, pp. 1527, 1528.
Straub, Karl Willy. "Der Dichter Max Dauthendey als Philosoph." *Bayerische Landeszeitung*, XXIX, no. 576, Würzburg, December 11, 1913, pp. 3, 4.
————"Der Dichter Max Dauthendey als Mensch." *Bayerische Landeszeitung*, XXIX, 576, Würzburg, December 12, 1913, pp. 3, 4.
————"Der Dichter Max Dauthendey als Chroniker." *Bayerische Landeszeitung*, XXIX, no. 578, December 13, 1913, pp. 3, 4.
————"Erinnerung an Max Dauthendey," *Saarbrücker Zeitung*, 1921, no. 308.
————"Aus Max Dauthendeys letztem Lebensjahr." *Saarbrücker Zeitung*, 1922, no. 344.
————"Max Dauthendeys Ausfahrt und Heimkehr." (Poem). *Die Horen*, VI, 7, July, 1930, pp. 577-581.
Thon, Luise. *Die Sprache des deutschen Impressionismus. Ein Beitrag zur Erfassung ihrer Wesenszüge*. Munich, 1928: Max Hueber Verlag.
Uddgren, Gustaf. "Den tyske 'farve' digter M. Dauthendey." *Politiken*, Copenhagen, August 3, 1893, no. 215.
————"Forfattaren Max Dauthendey död." *Svenska Dagbladet*, Stockholm, September 11, 1918, no. 244, p. 7.
Vesper, Will. "Max Dauthendey." *Das literarische Echo*, X, no. 24, September 15, 1908, columns 1694-1698.
Villinger, Arnold. *Das Buch vom Wesen aller Dinge*. Dresden, 1896: E. Pierson.
————*Grundzüge einer Weltanschauung*. Leipzig, 1910: J. A. Barth.
Wadenklee, Hannes. "Max Dauthendey." *Fränkischer Volksfreund*, no. 170, July 27, 1927; no. 172, July 29, 1927; no. 173, July 30, 1927.
Wencker, Friedrich, "Erinnerungen an Max Dauthendey." *Fränkischer Kurier, Mittwoch-Ausgabe*, no. 287, October 15, 1924, p. 21.
Wocke, Helmut. *Neue Jugend und neue Dichter*. Chapter: "Weltfestlichkeit. Max Dauthendey." Munich, no date: Albert Langen, pp. 34-49.

INDEX[1]

Aeschylus, 90
Albert Langen Verlag, 119
Alt, Johannes, 12
ancestor worship, 21
Annecke, Wilhelm, 16, 114
aquarelles, 165, 166
audition colorée, *vide* synaesthesia

Bahr, Hermann, 71
Bartels, Adolf, 2
Baudelaire, 68
Becker, J. M., 6
Belgian poetry, influence of, 46
Bellamy, J., 38
Bellessort, André, 118
Benzmann, Hans, 2
Berendsohn, 3
Besant, A., 30, 44
Bethge, H., 51
Bible, page from Dauthendey's Bible, 121
Biese, Alfred, 12
Binnenreim, *vide* internal rhyme
Blake, 30
Blei, Franz, 5, 39
Bodmer, 59
Böcklin, 48, 53
Bölsche, W., 73
Bouissinesq, 35
Book of Filial Duty, 103
Borel, 97
Brandes, Georg, 45
Breitinger, 59
Bruno, Giardano, 30, 37, 73, 124
Bryant, 117
Buch vom Wesen aller Dinge, Das, 34, 36, 37, 38, 40
Byron, 46, 54

Cabbala, 30
Charon, 6
Coleridge, 10
color vision, *vide* synaesthesia
Conrad, M. G., 12, 25
Cook's Tour, 6, 8, 18, 145, 146

Darge, Elisabeth, 9, 13, 14, 16, 26, 28, 84, 90
Darwin, 54

Dauthendey, Annie, 3, 4, 5, 109, 112
Dauthendey, Carl Albrecht, 20, 21, 23, 117
Dauthendey, Casparus, 7, 21
Dauthendey, Elisabeth, 1, 5, 9, 18, 21, 22
Dauthendey, Karoline, 21
Dauthendey, Marie, 22, 23, 118
Dauthendey, Max
  ancestry, *vide* Casparus Dauthendey
  caricatures, 5, 68
  chronological list of works, 147-152
  chronology of life, 144-146
  coat of arms, 70
  father, *vide* Carl Albrecht Dauthendey
  knowledge of Japanese, 6
  mother, *vide* Karoline Dauthendey
  schooling, 25, 77
  search for God, 117-123
  sisters, *vide* Elisabeth and Marie Dauthendey
  Studien in stilisierten Rosen, 61
  Works:
  "Abendglocke vom Mijderatempel hören, Die," 110, 151
  "Abendrot zu Seta, Das," 151
  "Abendschnee am Hirayama sehen, Den," 8, 102, 113, 151
  "Ablehnung des Paradieses, Die," 101, 152
  acht Gesichter am Biwasee, Die, 1, 9, 11, 74, 87, 104, 105, 110, 111, 112, 113, 151
  Ammenballade, Die, 11, 102, 107, 112, 149
  "Auferstehung allen Fleisches, Die," 9, 68, 70, 104
  Aus fernen Ländern, 30
  "Aus langer Weile!" 11, 147
  Ausgewählte Lieder, 1
  Bänkelsang vom Balzer auf der Balz, 8, 27, 28, 29, 39, 108, 110, 115, 119, 149
  "Barmherzige Schwestern," 1, 147
  Blinden, Die, 147
  brennende Kalender, Der, 3, 11, 74, 85, 106, 108, 149
  Charakteristikum aller Städte der Reise, 8

[1] The bibliographies are excluded from this index.

Index

Chronik der Ereignisse Würzburgs, 150
"Dalar rächt sich," 8, 111
Drache Grauli, Der, 24, 41, 149
Eindringling, Der, 147
"Eingeschlossene Tiere," 9, 103, 112
Erlebnisse auf Java, 1
"Erz von Mataram, Das," 152
ewige Hochzeit, Die, 3, 11, 66, 106, 108, 148
festliche Jahrbuch, Das, 8, 38, 41, 84, 109, 148
Frau Raufenbarth, 11, 18, 102, 149
"Frau von Thule, Die," 148
"Fünfuhrtee," 26, 149
"Garten ohne Jahreszeiten, Der," 1, 9, 80, 104, 111
Gedankengut aus meinen Wanderjahren, 1, 3, 6, 8, 11, 12, 13, 14, 15, 28, 30, 34, 36, 37, 38, 39, 46, 56, 57, 58, 59, 70, 71, 74, 76, 77, 78, 79, 81, 82, 90, 91, 92, 94, 97, 98, 101, 106, 110, 119, 120, 124, 125, 152
geflügelte Erde, Die, 1, 8, 68, 74, 86, 87, 88, 102, 104, 109, 110, 151
Geist meines Vater, Der, 1, 6, 18, 20, 21, 22, 24, 32, 98, 106, 117, 151
Geschichten aus den vier Winden, 1, 9, 58, 82, 87, 111, 152
"Giftfläschchen, Das," 9, 24, 84, 89, 120
Glück, 148
großen Krieges Not, Des, 1, 12, 18, 91, 95, 120, 152
"Häcksel und die Bergwerksflöhe," 58
"Hasenauge's first story," 151
"Hasenauge's second story," 151
"Hasenauge's third story," 151
Heidin Geilane, Die, 1, 18, 76, 86, 151
Herz im Lärm der Welt, Ein, 9, 11, 15, 30, 32, 34, 43, 45, 46, 52, 53, 55, 59, 60, 62, 78, 97, 100, 120
"Himalayafinsternis," 9, 24
Hochzeit des "Nagels der Erde," 152
Humoristische Reisebeschreibung um die Erde, 149
"Iguanodon, Das," 9, 24
"Im Mandarinenklub," 9

"Im blauen Licht von Penang," 9, 24, 111
Insichversunkene Lieder im Laub, 11, 108, 150
Josa Gerth, 8, 18, 19, 22, 52, 60, 65, 118, 120, 147
Kind, Das, 18, 147
"Knabe auf dem Kopf des Elefanten, Der," 8, 95
"König Eng," 148
"König Gier," 148
"König Proß," 148
letzte Küstenfahrt, Die, 94, 95, 100, 152
"Kuli Kimgun, Der," 9
Kunst des Erhabenen, Die, vide Verdensaltet
Kunst des Intimen, vide Verdensaltet
Lachen und Sterben, 95, 149
Letzte Reise, 1, 9, 114, 115, 122, 152
Lied der Weltfestlichkeit, Das, 15, 22, 24, 26, 32, 33, 52, 57, 77, 94, 95, 97, 115, 116, 122, 124, 152
Lieder der Beschaulichkeit, 77
"Likse und Panulla," 95
Lingam, 1, 22, 86, 104, 151
Lusamgärtlein, 73, 85, 91, 108, 149
Madame Null, 11, 18, 111, 150
Märchenbriefbuch der heiligen Nächte im Javanerlande, Das, 1, 77, 88, 152
Maja, 1, 41, 151
Meine ersten Gehversuche auf der steilen Dichterlaufbahn, 23, 117, 120-143, 147
Meine Smeroe-Besteigung, 152
Menagerie Krummholz, 11, 113, 149
Messina im Mörser, 27, 150
Mich ruft dein Bild, 1, 6, 8, 9, 24, 32, 76, 77, 86, 87, 91, 94, 95, 99, 100, 102, 105, 109, 110, 114, 119, 120, 122
"Nachtregen regnen hören in Karasaki, Den," 2, 151
"Nächtliche Schaufenster," 85
Neun Pariser Moritaten, 149
Ohnmächtige Schiffe, 152
"Park, Ein," 147
Phallus, 92, 106, 148
"Philosophie eines Dienstmannes," 147
"Plastische Bühne nach dem Vorbild

asiatischer Theaterhäuser," 98, 150
"Qual," 93
Raubmenschen, 1, 8, 39, 100, 110, 151
Reliquien, 18, 21, 66, 68, 69, 73, 108, 148
Schatten fiel über den Tisch, Ein, 18, 112, 114, 150
schwarze Sonne, Die, 38, 148
"Segelboote von Yabase im Abend heimkehren sehen, Die," 102, 151
Sehnsucht, 48, 58, 59, 62, 66, 68, 124, 148
"Siebzig Jahre," 11, 27, 147
Singsangbuch, 18, 85, 108, 115, 149
"Sonniger Himmel und Brise von Awazu," 151
Spielereien einer Kaiserin, Die, 1, 86, 150
Sun, 58, 59, 66, 68, 71, 111, 124, 148
Tagebuch des Verführers, Das, 148
"Teufelstriller," 147
"Todwund," 147
translations by Max Dauthendey, 162
Ultra Violett, 3, 6, 18, 32, 45, 48, 106, 147
"Unabwendbare, Das," 148
"unbeerdigte Vater, Der," 9, 22, 87, 103
"unsichtbare Weg, Der," 101, 152
"Unter den Totentürmen," 8
Untergangsstunde der "Titanic," Die, 27, 58, 95, 152
Venusinenreim, Der, 1, 11, 76, 113, 115, 150
Verdensaltet, 10, 12, 15, 26, 28, 32, 34, 37, 43-59, 66, 67, 68, 71, 72, 92, 106, 124, 125, 148
"Vom Ishiyama den Herbstmond aufgehen sehen," 151
"Vom Kampfplatz," 147
Waldklaus, Der, 149
weiße Schlaf, Der, 85, 91, 150
Weltall, vide Verdensaltet
Weltspuk, 18, 25, 58, 73, 74, 75, 108, 151
"Wildgänse Flug in Katata nachschauen, Der," 74, 151
"Zauberer Walai, Der," 8
"Zur Stunde der Maus," 111
"Zwei Reiter am Meer," 81

Dekker, 27, 97
Dehmel, Ida, 4
Dehmel, Richard, 10, 30, 32, 41, 42, 46, 60, 64, 71, 91
Detto, Marie, *vide* Dauthendey, Marie
Dilthey, W., 54
Dostoyevsky, 55
Downes, Olin, 64
Downey, J. E., 63, 68
Du Bois-Reymond, 35
Dürer, 39
Durand, James and Theodosia, 24, 38

Edschmid, Kasimir, 2
Eichendorff, 67
Emerson, 26
Enderling, Paul, 104
Engel, Eduard, 2, 3
Erhardt-Siebold, E., 62
Eßwein, Hermann, 90
Ewald, August, 106

farbiges Hören, *vide* synaesthesia
Fechner, Gustav, 16, 30, 47, 73, 124
Fick, A., 33, 34
Fiedler, J. K., 47
Fischer, S., 4
Forførerens Dagbog, vide Dauthendey, Max, Works, *Das Tagebuch des Verführers*
Francis of Assisi, 30, 73
Fraser-Harris, D. F., 62
Friedrichshagen, 46
Fundamentum geographicum, 7

Garschin, 55
Gebhardt, M., 5, 6, 13, 44
Geiger, Eugen, 12
George, 32
Goethe, 5, 49, 54, 119
Goetze, Otto, 4, 5, 43
Gorter, Herman, 46, 53, 125
Greeks, Dauthendey's attitude towards the, 25, 28
Grieg, 46, 51
Großmann, Stefan, 64
Guilbeaux, Henri, 6
Gundolf, F., 96

Häckel, 40
Hamann, Richard, 62
Hamsun, Knut, 3

Hansson, Ola, 32, 46, 51, 60, 125
Hauptmann, Gerhart, 55
Hegel, 26
Heinse, 59
Hermann, Georg, 6
Hitschmann, E., 24
Holm, Annie, 4, 100
Holm, Korfiz, 4, 5, 42, 111, 112
Homer, 90
Hsiao Ching, 103

Ibsen, 55
internal rhyme, 101, 102

Jacobsen, J. P., 44, 45, 51, 60, 118, 119, 125
Jensen, Hemning, 44, 45
Ježower, Ignaz, 24
Johanson, Axel, 4
Jungnickel, Max, 2

Kahane, Arthur, 16, 113
Kant, 54
Keyserling, Eduard, 84
Kipling, 96
Kleist, Ewald, 59
Kosch, Wilhelm, 6
Koster, 5, 84
Kubin, 5, 91
Kvile, *vide* Quille

Langguth, Franz, 4
Leadbeater, W., 30
Lederer, Max, 2
Leibniz, 30, 56, 73, 92, 124
Leonardo da Vinci, 39
Leoncavallo, 46, 48, 49
Lessing, 59
Liebe, Reinhold, 30
Linde, Otto zur, 5
Löffler, Fritz, 10
Loerke, 5
Loewenthal, Siegfried, 4, 11, 26, 32, 33, 43, 44, 52, 53, 55, 60, 120
Loti, Pierre, 97
Lotze, 73
love, 106-116
Lowes, John L., 10

Mack, Hans, 28
Maeterlinck, 46, 60
Mahling, Friedrich, 63
Mahrholz, Werner, 96
Marholm, Laura, 5, 46

Mascagni, 46, 48, 49
Max Havelaar, 27, 97
metaphysical "communism"
metempsychosis, 81
Mexico, 8, 38, 39
Meyer, A. R., 70
Michelangelo, 39
"Mohrle," 8, 112
Molo, Walter von, 2
Müller-Freienfels, 14
Multatuli, *vide* Dekker
Mumm, Carl, 2, 11, 12, 66, 101
Munch, Edvard, 48, 51, 53
Muret, Maurice, 12

Nachlaß, 4, 8, 26, 27, 39, 44, 45, 65
Nadler, Josef, 67
Naumann, Hans, 3
Newton, 48
Nibelungenlied, 49
Nietzsche, 26, 28, 54, 82, 124
number symbolism, 24

Obstfelder, 109
occultism, 30, 38
Orient, 28, 96-105

Panzerbieter, Willy, 4
Paris, 6, 8
parodies, 68 ff.
Paul, Adolf, 91
polar concepts, 15
Przybyszewski, S., 60
Pushkin, 55

Quille, 6, 42

Rademacher, Georg, 4, 5, 15, 25
Raphael, 55
Reck-Malleczewen, 115
Rembrandt, 39
Robertson, J. G., 6
Rowohlt, Ernst, 4
Rostosky, Gertraud, 5, 23, 67

Schenck, Friedrich, 33
Schiller, 16
Schleichert, 6
Schmidt, 5, 91
Schmitz, 5, 91
Schneider, 16, 33, 57
Schnitzler, Arthur, 11
Schopenhauer, 26, 27, 28, 54, 58, 124

INDEX

Schottlaender, 112
Seidel, Willy, 9, 96
Seyfarth, E., 96
Silesius, Angelus, 33
Slochower, Harry, 10
Sörgel, Albert, 3
Steiger, Edgar, 2
Steinert, 68
Straub, K. W., 5
Strindberg, 55, 91
Strömstad, 5, 6
Stuck, 48
Stucken, Eduard, 64
Symonds, Arthur, 68
synaesthesia, 13, 59-72

Thieß, Frank, 96
Thomas, Calvin, 84
Thomson, 59
Tolstoi, 44
transmigration of souls, *vide* metempsychosis

Uddgren, Gustaf, 4, 28, 32, 41, 45, 53, 60, 67, 109
Uhde, 49
"universal language," 73-77
Urhsheih-sze Heaou, 103

van Eeden, F., 46, 125
Villinger, Arnold, 4, 11, 26, 30, 32, 33, 35, 36, 37, 40, 47, 53, 60, 78, 118, 124

Wadenklee, 5
Wagner, 12, 45, 46, 48, 51, 53
Walther von der Vogelweide, 1, 8
Weber's Law, 35
Welt als Wille und Vorstellung, Die, 26, 58
Weltallsprache, *vide* "universal language"
Welt-compounds, 14
Weltferne, *vide* world-detachment
Weltfestlichkeit, *vide* world-festivity
Weltnähe, *vide* world-proximity
Wencker, 5, 6
Wieland, 49
Wille, Bruno, 28, 30, 32, 73
Wocke, Helmuth, 33
world-detachment, 15, 38, 78-83, 100, 124
world-festivity, 20, 33, 38, 84-95, 124
world-proximity, 15, 39, 78-83, 100, 124
Wundt, Wilhelm, 16
Würzburg, 18, 20, 51, 99, 100, 117

Zola, 55